Stock Patterns
for
Day Trading
and
Swing Trading

Barry Rudd

1975 ~ 2000
25th Anniversary

Traders Press, Inc.®
PO Box 6206
Greenville, SC 29606

Traders Press, Inc.®

1975~2000
25th Anniversary

Traders Press, Inc.®
PO Box 6206
Greenville, SC 29606

800-927-8222 ~ 964-298-0222 ~ Fax 864-298-0221
E-mail Catalog@TradersPress.com
Website http://www.TradersPress.com

To my parents
William and Dianna Rudd
for all of their support

ACKNOWLEDGMENTS

Special thanks to Matt Rudd, my brother and fellow trader who regularly spent time in brain storming sessions with me. Whenever I slipped into mental "vapor lock" trying to put my ideas down on paper, his writing talents made all of the difference.

I also want to recognize my friend, Neal Weintraub, who taught me to keep my market analysis simple and straightforward. I carried this principle from my futures trading over into my stock trading where I finally found my home.

Thanks to Charlie Lacey for designing the book's jacket cover.

Also, my gratitude goes to Ed Dobson of Traders Press for helping make this book available to all the other traders out there who do battle with the markets daily.

Finally, I wish to thank collectively all of the other experienced SOES traders who have shared trading ideas with me. In particular I would like to acknowledge Emilio, Todd, and Duane "the wonderkid", as well as my friends whom I trade next to every day.

No one holds all of the keys to successful trading; the ideas are passed on from trader to trader as trading techniques evolve with the markets. So, in a sense, this is more than just my book, it's theirs also.

INTRODUCTION

Traders Press takes pride in making this book available to the trading public. It represents an especially worthwhile contribution to trading literature, given the virtual nonexistence of any worthwhile material, at this writing, on the subject of day trading in individual stocks. Further adding to its value is the fact that it is written by a serious trader, who teaches what DOES work in the real world (based on personal experience) instead of what SHOULD work (based on theory).

The genesis for the material came from Barry Rudd's work in codifying his own trading stategies to improve himself as a trader. The ideas came both from friends who were successful traders, as well as his own experience with SOES trading. The book relates his intraday trend trading approach for stocks, and provides a scalping approach designed around the same trade entry setups but with the intent of small, quick profits. Mr. Rudd has made a living for well over a year using the methods he describes in his book.

This book was formerly privately published by the author in two manuals, one titled *Stock Patterns for Day Trading and Swing Trading*, and the other a *Scalping Module*. Any references herein to separate manuals were in the original material. Both of the original manuals have been combined in this book.

Edward D. Dobson, President
Traders Press, Inc.
January, 1998

FOREWORD

I have not come across very many books on day trading stocks. Of the ones available, very few offer good, reliable strategies that can actually be applied in the vocation of day trading. Based on this, I have assimilated what I have learned from other successful traders, as well as what I have learned through my own experience. Since I have traded futures, stocks, and options over the past ten years, I have seen many people fall by the wayside for lack of a sound methodology and good money management. I want you to learn the techniques and strategies that will allow you to become a successful trader. Most books on day trading are long on theory and short on results. This manual bridges the gap between knowledge about the market and the ability to actually trade the market successfully. My hope is that you will use this manual to enhance your trading skills and achieve more consistent profits.

Good luck with your trading!

CONTENTS

INTRADAY TREND METHODOLOGY

This manual is your toolbox for finding high probability trades for success as you trade the stock market. The technical ideas are primarily crafted around the personality of the NASDAQ market but may also be implemented in New York trades. The theory behind what you'll be reading hinges upon stock price movement which is reflected in daily and intraday bar charts. Many approaches to trading are espoused in books and address how to find, enter, and manage your trades. However, you will not find anything in publication or in training which provides you with the experience, dollar potential, and detail behind the trading methodology that is explained in this manual.

These methods are the same ones that have provided some of the earliest electronic (computer) day traders with profits which mounted into hundreds of thousands per year. Although this trading style is sound and profitable, it also must incorporate the art and mental discipline of each person who applies it. This is why many actual chart examples are provided to give you a feel for what really works. You will learn to time your trade entries and exits from experience with the aid of some helpful tips in later chapters. Be a student of the market and learn how each individual stock moves, its personality, and how the main overall market indexes affect the stock's movement on a daily and intraday basis.

This method looks for price patterns which typically set up for an intraday trend in a stock. Entering the trade is only the first (and probably the easiest) part of trading. How do you know where to exit if the trade goes against you? When do you exit if you have an open profit? You have to manage the trade based on the principle that the stock has chosen a direction for the day, and you are on board for the ride. This means you have to be willing to give the trade the room for price pullbacks against your direction of the trade. The idea is that on a buy setup a stock will move up, then pull back some, move up to make a higher high on the day, pull back some etc. as it continues its upward movement into the end of the day. Likewise, on a sell setup, the stock will move down to make a new low, then rally some, move down to make a lower low on the day, rally some etc. as it continues its downward movement. You want to stay on board for as much of the ride as possible and not exit the trade too soon and miss out on a substantial profit. These pullbacks are known as "wiggles" and are explained under the "terms and definitions" section of this manual. Each stock usually has its own particular "wiggle" which can be determined based on the information provided later in the manual. Although there are times when a stock will reach a price where you will "cut" (or exit) the trade at a likely profit target, the key to this methodology's success is letting your winners run by giving them "wiggle" room.

Once you have evaluated a stock and taken a position in it, you have to follow your trade exit rules established using principles from this manual. Don't be too quick to take a profit. The methodology by which you chose that particular trade is sound and you should manage it that way. You've chosen that stock for a large intraday trend move. Sometimes a stock will immediately move in your direction and provide a good sized open profit. Give it wiggle room to continue for further profit. Other stocks are slower in their response. Be patient and give them the chance to make their move. The reason you chose the trade was based on high probabilities. Let the odds work for you and stick to your guns as you manage the exit. As you near the end of the trading session you may want to take profits on current open positions, especially in the last 30 minutes as you assess the stock and the overall market direction.

Money management must be an integral part of your trading. You always cut your losers and let your winners run. Although this is common sense and sounds simple, it is often hard to stick to. This is why mental discipline is so important when managing your trades during the day. On the stocks that you will be trading, an initial loss of 1/4 point (and sometimes 3/8 point) is strictly adhered to. Once a trade has moved far enough in your favor and you have an open profit, the "standard wiggle" for a stock kicks in as a trailing stop-loss. This is explained in more detail later.

The day trade setups are based purely on price action from the daily bar chart and intraday 5 minute bar chart. The only mathematical indicators used are the 50 and 200 day simple moving average lines based on the daily closes. Simplicity is your friend in this game. Get too technical and the probabilities of success begin to fade.

Since this manual is not geared toward scalping, you will only be taking the highest probability price setups which have the potential for a 1+ point move on the day. Any trade that offers less profit potential will usually be passed up. The characteristics of these setups are defined for you with textbook graphs as well as actual examples.

Which stocks will you be trading? This question will also be answered so that you will have a universe of stocks on a "ticker" screen that you follow regularly and will come to recognize the price movement personality of each one. Trade only the most "trader-friendly" stocks that provide the least downside risk along with the best profit opportunity. You will be given the criterion for these stocks so that you can easily choose which ones that you will want to follow.

The manual is divided into two main sections; day trading and swing trading. For day trading you are initially presented the intraday 5 minute bar chart trade setups. This is followed by a section on 1 to 3 daily bar chart setups as well as longer term setups for high probability day trades. Expected price support and resistance areas are then described. All descriptions will include exhaustive actual examples and how they typically play out. Since timing of entry and exit are extremely important, I've also included a section covering the market maker and time of sale screens. These components are all used together to trade the best price setups, long or short, for your day trading success in the market.

The section on "swing trading" addresses trade setups that are geared for multiple day holds (typically 2 to 5 days). These are obviously traded differently than the above described day trade setups. Finally, a worksheet is provided that gives you a template for analyzing high probability setups for both day trades and swing trades coming into the following day.

Many chart examples are included with commentary. This provides you a real world feel for how these trades set up and how they tend to play out in actual "live" trading.

NOTE: Thoroughly read through the section covering "terms and definitions" before moving on to the rest of the manual. They are key to fully understanding and applying the trading methodology.

WHY USE PRICE BAR CHARTS

Price bar charts paint a graphic picture of a stock's price movements both during the day with the 5 minute bars, and longer term with the daily bars. The picture unfolds showing short and long term supply and demand and how it has moved the stock's price. This helps pinpoint specific areas of buying or selling pressure as they develop. The bar charts alert you to this "at a glance" when the bars trade into a tight range that hugs up or down against a certain price (usually the day's current high or low). This consolidation creates a price "compression" point where pressure builds and is finally released when the price level that held the stock is penetrated. Often this penetration is a the beginning of an intraday trend. By monitoring different stock charts throughout the day, a trader can quickly identify these pattern setups. Since the trader knows which stocks are currently setting up for a potential move, he or she has the edge of catching the beginning of a good trade. The advantages of using a daily bar chart in conjunction with the 5 minute bar chart are covered throughout the manual. Using the 5 minute bar chart in particular gives you an edge over other market participants in 3 ways:

- It allows you to follow a larger number of stocks, because all it takes is a quick glance at the chart to see if a trade is setting up. With more stocks on your ticker, more trading opportunities are uncovered and therefore more potential profits are available.

- The specific price bar setups in the manual make sure you are entering the stock at the beginning of the initial move leading to a higher success rate per trade and a larger average profit per trade.

- Since these price pattern setups reflect compression built up against the day's current high or low, the breakout is a very high-odds trade. The success rate of the stock's chosen direction far exceeds the random movements ("noise") back and forth in price throughout most of the day.

Without charts you are only looking at a snapshot of price in time. So much more can be seen with charts to give you an edge. Trading without charts is like flying blind!

TERMS AND DEFINITIONS

DAY TRADE - Refers to entering and exiting a stock on the same day, typically using 1000 shares.

SWING TRADE - In this manual "swing trading" describes trades that may last from 2 to 5 days or more. You are looking for a bigger price move than you normally would in a day trade -- trying to catch a larger price "swing".

DAILY BAR CHART - A daily bar shows the open, high, low, and close of a day's trading activity for a stock.

INTRADAY BAR CHART - An intraday bar chart shows a stock's price movement during the day, usually with 5 minute bars.

SUPPORT & RESISTANCE - (also referred to as "S/R") Price support and resistance are areas on a chart that have halted past price movement. A support area tends to halt downward price action, and resistance often halts upward price movement. You can visually see these on both daily and intraday bar charts. It may help to draw a horizontal line through these areas. The significance of support and resistance is to determine if a potential trade setup has enough room to give you a reasonable profit before the stock stalls at one of these S/R areas. Also, a penetration up through a resistance area may open the door for follow-through in the stock's upward movement. Conversely, a penetration down through a support area may then enable the stock to more easily continue its downward movement.

CONSOLIDATION (daily and intraday) - Is when the stock trades in a tight, well defined price range for more than a few price bars. Consolidation can be seen on both the intraday and daily time frames simply by looking at the chart. On an intraday basis, consolidation at the high of the day or at the low of the day can be a potential setup to enter a trade on the breakout to new highs or lows. Price "congestion" is somewhat different and applies primarily to the daily chart. Usually it is best not to trade a stock while it is congested (i.e., has a lot of daily bars clustered together side by side without a well defined support or resistance area). This is characteristic of choppy price movement. Wait for the stock to break out of a congestion area and begin moving before you trade it

PRICE "CONGESTION" - This is when a stock trades in a sideways, choppy manner without a definite direction or trend. It can easily be seen on a daily chart. Avoid trading stocks while they are in this mode. Wait for the price to move out of the congestion area or until it has a good consolidation type breakout setup as described in the price setup patterns of this manual.

WIDE RANGE (W/R) BAR W/ EXTREME CLOSE - See "1 to 3 daily bar" section

REVERSAL BAR(S) - See "1 to 3 daily bar" section

BREAKOUT - Consider a stock that has consolidated against a price level for several bars (especially on the 5 minute chart). The point where it breaks beyond that price level is called the "breakout" and often is the beginning of a short to intermediate term move in the direction of the breakout.

FILL-PRICE - When you put an order out to buy or sell a stock, the actual price at which it is executed is called the "fill-price".

WIGGLE - Wiggle refers to the intraday price action of a stock. When entering a day trade you are expecting the stock to begin trending in your direction on the 5 minute bar chart. Usually price doesn't go straight up or down. If you are long, the stock will typically rally, then pull back, rally to a new intraday high, then pull back, etc. The question is: How far do you let a stock pull back against the direction of the trade before you exit? You don't want to get out too soon and leave further profits "on the table". To solve this problem, look at the past 5+ days of a stock's 5 minute bar chart. On trending days, determine how far a stock pulls back on average before continuing the trend. If the average pullback is 1/2 point then you should allow that much room for the stock to "wiggle" before it resumes its trend. Each stock tends to have its own particular wiggle amount ranging anywhere from 1/2 to 1+ points. Usually 5/8 to 3/4 points will hold the stocks that you will be trading. This does not mean that if you buy a stock at 40 that you exit at 39 3/8 for a 5/8 loss. You always use an initial stop-loss of 1/4 (sometimes 3/8) from your entry price. Once the stock moves up to 40 3/8 you would then begin trailing your exit point 5/8 behind the stock's current high as it continues to move up. This example assumes a 5/8 standard wiggle for that stock.

STANDARD WIGGLE - Each stock has its own price movement personality. What you determine as the typical wiggle for a particular stock can be referred to as that stock's "standard wiggle". Be aware that these can change over time, so they may need to be updated occasionally.

WIGGLED OUT - Once you are in a trade, you then manage it based on giving it the wiggle room to continue the anticipated intraday trend. If at some point the stock retraces back beyond its standard wiggle amount, you immediately exit the trade. You are then said to have been "wiggled out" (hopefully with a good profit).

STOP-LOSS - This is your mental exit price from a trade that you have entered. It is initially 1/4 point (sometimes 3/8 point) from your actual "fill-price" when you have taken a long or short position in a stock. If the stock moves against you, you exit the trade and are said to be "stopped out" for a loss. On the other hand, if the stock moves in your favor you convert to a trailing stop when your open profit + initial stop-loss (1/4) is equal to the wiggle for that particular stock. Therefore, if a stock's wiggle is 5/8 point then you must have an open profit of 3/8 point before you begin adjusting your exit point. You are then trailing your mental exit price in the direction of the trade to lock in profits. Strictly adhere to your initial and subsequent trailing stop-losses. It is an integral part of money management.

SCALPING - Scalping is a style of trading based on taking small, quick profits. If a stock has a momentum surge in price, the trader quickly buys or sells in the direction of the price movement. He or she then puts out a bid or offer anywhere from 1/16 to 1/4 point from the fill price before the momentum surge slows. Hopefully their bid or offer is taken and a quick profit made on their 1000 share trade. A scalp trade will typically last from just a few seconds to a minute or two. To make a decent profit scalping requires a significant number of trades and a high success rate per trade. Only one mistake can wipe out 5 or more profitable trades when you take into consideration commissions and fees.
The trade-exit strategy in this particular manual is not based on scalping, although scalping is another viable way to trade the market.

HOW THE "WIGGLE" WORKS

This will graphically show you how the wiggle works by monitoring the 5 minute bar chart after you enter a day trade. Assume a 5/8 point standard wiggle for this example. Look to the market maker screen bid/ask for timing your exit at the appropriate price.

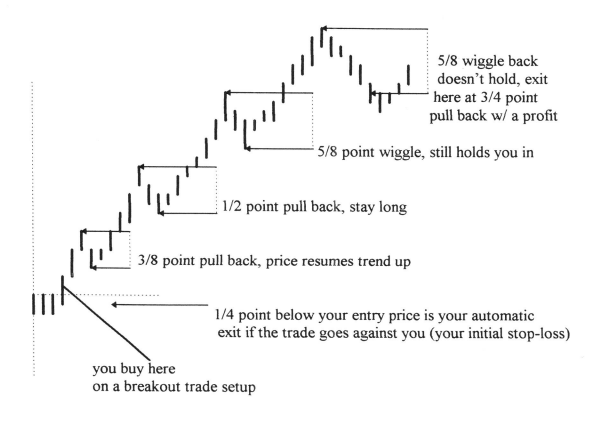

5/8 wiggle back doesn't hold, exit here at 3/4 point pull back w/ a profit

5/8 point wiggle, still holds you in

1/2 point pull back, stay long

3/8 point pull back, price resumes trend up

1/4 point below your entry price is your automatic exit if the trade goes against you (your initial stop-loss)

you buy here on a breakout trade setup

In the above diagram assume that you bought the stock at 30 1/8. This means that your initial stop-loss exit would be 29 7/8 (1/4 point below your entry). Since this stock has a 5/8 wiggle, you would not begin moving up (trailing) your exit price until the stock price has reached 30 1/2. Once the difference between the current stock price and the initial stop-loss price of 29 7/8 equals the wiggle amount of 5/8, you begin moving your exit price up to where it is 5/8 below the highest current price on the day. Never adjust the stop-loss back down. Every time the stock makes a higher high on the day, it pulls up the 5/8 wiggle's exit price to help lock in profits. This gives the stock room to move around as it continues its intraday trend up. Don't just arbitrarily take a profit. Although some likely price targets are covered later, you have to let the wiggle work for you.

DAY TRADES

INTRADAY TRADING PATTERNS

(for day trading)

INTRODUCTION:

This section covers intraday, day trade setups using 5 minute bar charts.
You will almost always be buying and selling breakouts of the current day's high or low
based primarily on bar chart pattern setups. Momentum of price movement will be the key
to timing the entry. Momentum can be seen with action on the market maker screen and
time of sale screen. Recognizing the best setup pattern is the key to entering the highest
probability trade. We will present the most consistent trade setups and where to enter
long or short with diagrams. Other secondary trades which may also be taken under
certain circumstances will be graphically analyzed and explained. Remember, although
these rules are not set in stone, they provide the foundation of a strong, high probability
methodology for choosing profitable trades. Vertical dotted lines represent the start of the
day, horizontal dotted lines show support and resistance areas as well as consolidation
boundaries.

* Most examples show buy setups. Sell setups are the same, just inverted.

HIGH PROBABILITY TRADES:

The first trade is an intraday pattern of a 5 minute bar chart that is the basic "dip and rally"
setup for a buy breakout.

1)

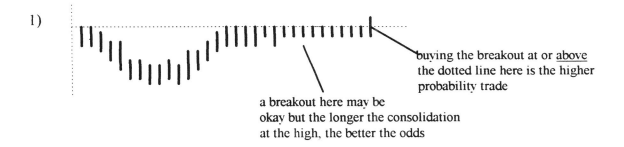

buying the breakout at or <u>above</u>
the dotted line here is the higher
probability trade

a breakout here may be
okay but the longer the consolidation
at the high, the better the odds

The <u>consolidation</u> at the high of the day is the key to the success of this setup, as it is with
other pattern variations. The longer and tighter the consolidation, the better. This is a
setup that develops through the day. Another more obvious pattern looks like this:

2)

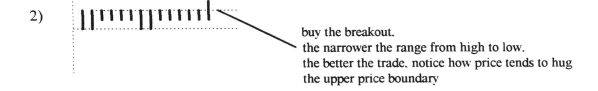

buy the breakout.
the narrower the range from high to low,
the better the trade. notice how price tends to hug
the upper price boundary

Another intraday consolidation pattern that you may see looks a bit different but it can also be a powerful setup:

3)

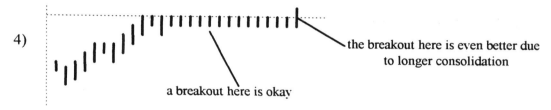

buy the breakout, especially since the price tends to hug the upper boundary, a breakout trade to the downside may also be okay if it is a tight range

In the above setup #3, an active stock can show a deceptively illiquid intraday bar chart. The key to this chart pattern is to make sure the stock averages good volume on a daily basis (i.e. 100k shares +), and that the daily bar chart shows good room for movement to the upside without nearby price resistance. You can also keep tabs on its volume in the market maker screen.

The next chart is another common example leading to consolidation and a good breakout trade:

4)

the breakout here is even better due to longer consolidation

a breakout here is okay

Early morning consolidation (similar to pattern #2) can be an integral part of entering trades at the start of the trading day (although it is best to wait 10 minutes before you enter a trade). This way you can catch the first and best breakout. If you are following a particular stock with the expectation of a good move on the day (or simply stumble across one with the following pattern), it may be a strong trade candidate. This is especially true if your market maker screen is moving and showing momentum coming into the breakout. The pattern consists of just a few bars on the morning and a range of only a 1/8 to 1/4.

5)

buy the breakout

The point here is to catch the earliest breakout and best price...otherwise pass up the trade. Never chase a stock.

Once a breakout takes place, the stock normally begins a move. If you miss the initial breakout, other consolidation opportunities may setup in the stock as the day progresses. For example:

6)

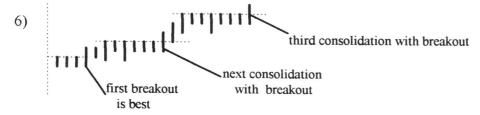

third consolidation with breakout

next consolidation
with breakout

first breakout
is best

Obviously the first breakout is the best to take. The question arises as to whether you should take the second, third, fourth, etc... breakout. If you missed the earlier breakout(s), how do you know whether or not to take the next one? The best way is to know how long the overall market has been moving in a direction, and if it is losing steam. Also, consider the average daily range of the stock as well as the strength (momentum) of the breakout. If the stock often trades a 2 to 3 point daily range, then the subsequent breakouts may still have potential if the range on the day is, for example, only 1 and 1/8 points at that time. Looking at the daily historical chart will show whether the price is breaking out of a daily consolidation area and if daily support or resistance has been broken. This can often lead to a large magnitude move, even if the last few daily bars have been in a narrow price range. Again, the longer the consolidation on the 5 minute bar chart, the better the trade.

Trade setup #7 depicts 2 good trade entry points following extended consolidation. Both of them may be worth taking, even though the first trade is a losing trade. The second breakout to the downside should not necessarily be passed up just because you lost on the first setup on the same stock earlier in the day.

7)

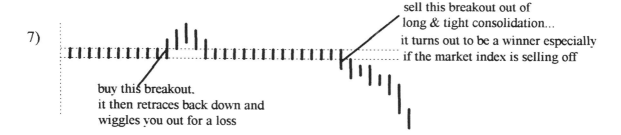

sell this breakout out of
long & tight consolidation...
it turns out to be a winner especially
if the market index is selling off

buy this breakout.
it then retraces back down and
wiggles you out for a loss

8)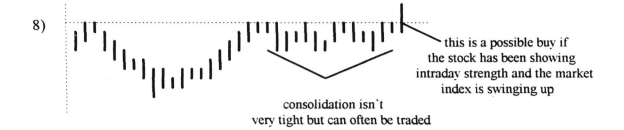

this is a possible buy if
the stock has been showing
intraday strength and the market
index is swinging up

consolidation isn't
very tight but can often be traded

"Wedging" consolidation on the 5 minute chart, especially if it develops over the first 1 to 2 hours of trading, can precipitate strong breakout moves. This pattern usually sets up for a trade on the long side. Consolidation at the high of the day must be present and hugging the upper price boundary as the wedge pattern unfolds. Here is the buy setup:

9)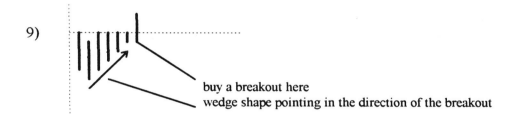

buy a breakout here
wedge shape pointing in the direction of the breakout

So far we've looked at the best and preferred trade setups where you should trade the breakout of the current high or low of the day out of strong consolidation...the longer the consolidation, the better. There are also a few setups that are more aggressive and may be tradable.

LOWER PROBABILITY TRADES:

These are secondary and somewhat lower probability patterns. But when paired with other analysis, such as momentum from the market maker screen, they may be traded successfully.

10)

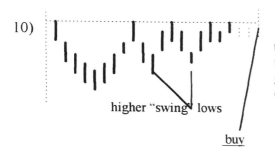

higher "swing" lows

buy

this pattern may well be showing price strength to the upside with successively higher swings down in price as it goes back up to test the <u>same</u> high price. wait for some consolidation before buying a breakout to the upside

11)

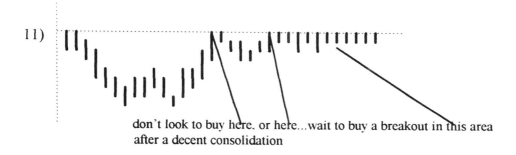

don't look to buy here, or here...wait to buy a breakout in this area after a decent consolidation

The "FLASHBACK" is another morning trade based on a quick reversal in direction of a stock's price. It quickly fakes one direction, then reverses back the other way to break the current high or low of the day. Look for the market index to be moving in the same direction the trade is taken for it to be worthwhile. Here is how it sets up for a buy trade:

12)

buy a breakout of today's high if it happens within the first 10 - 20 minutes of trading and the distance from the low up to the breakout point is 1/2 point or less ...also the overall market must be moving up <u>convincingly</u> (be careful with this one!!)

13)

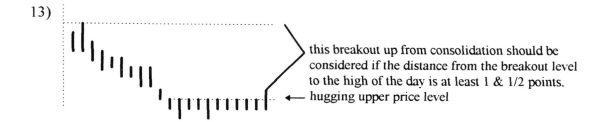

this breakout up from consolidation should be considered if the distance from the breakout level to the high of the day is at least 1 & 1/2 points.
← hugging upper price level

This could be considered if the overall <u>market index begins moving up strongly</u> and there is enough distance to the high from the breakout to make a decent profit. This is because the stock will usually meet resistance at the day's high. You could expect the stock to attempt to reach the day's earlier high. In order for the trade to yield you money there should be at least 1 & 1/2 points from the breakout point to the high of the day. These trades can be good on a day when the market runs down in the morning and then makes a smooth, rounding bottom that subsequently swings back up.

These examples are often decent trade setups that may be taken for a reasonable percentage of success. The rationale is to get in early on a strong move that will provide good follow-through.

<u>LOWEST PROBABILITY TRADES</u>: Be very careful with these patterns

Here are some similar and seemingly desirable price patterns that should <u>usually</u> not be traded unless there is another convincing reason to enter. The first is a "dip and rally" consolidation that is not quite at the high of the day:

14)

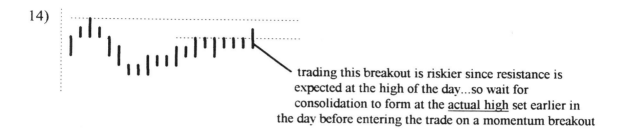

trading this breakout is riskier since resistance is expected at the high of the day...so wait for consolidation to form at the <u>actual high</u> set earlier in the day before entering the trade on a momentum breakout

These other patterns are all further examples of price action that <u>probably</u> should not be traded, even though they may look enticing:

15)

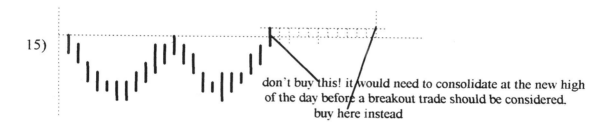

don't buy this! it would need to consolidate at the new high of the day before a breakout trade should be considered. buy here instead

16)

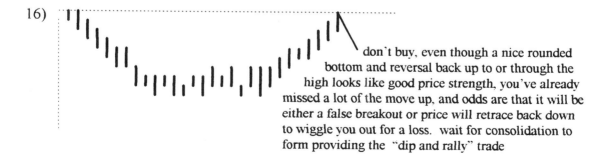

don't buy, even though a nice rounded bottom and reversal back up to or through the high looks like good price strength, you've already missed a lot of the move up, and odds are that it will be either a false breakout or price will retrace back down to wiggle you out for a loss. wait for consolidation to form providing the "dip and rally" trade

17)

don't buy or sell a breakout of the high or low, even though you have definite support and resistance areas, this is <u>not</u> consolidation

18)

great consolidation but it's not at the <u>high</u> or <u>low</u> of the day. since you expect resistance at the high and support at the low of the day. odds are that a breakout trade will not move far enough to give you a profit. or it will reverse off the high or low and wiggle you out for a loss

SUMMARY

These have been a few graphic <u>intraday</u> price patterns to give you a feel for what to look for. They cover the best setups and higher risk trades, as well as what typically not to trade. Obviously these are drawn as textbook examples. Actual stock charts, as they unfold during the day, will vary somewhat.

CONCLUSION: What about yesterday's intraday price chart?

Finally, there are occasions to consider yesterday's intraday price chart, especially as it finished the last hour or two of the day. Here you are looking for stocks that traded in a tight consolidation pattern into yesterday's close at or near the high or low of that day. Today, if the stock opens in the same consolidation price range, you are looking at the possibility of an even more powerful breakout trade. Here is how it should look:

yesterday   today

This presents a great breakout trade of <u>today's current high or low</u>. Refer to the daily bar price chart for analysis to get a better idea of whether a breakout to the upside or to the downside is the best trade to take. This price pattern also enhances the success of trades in the next section covering <u>daily</u> setups (w/r bars w/extreme close, and reversal bars). We'll cover daily price bar analysis next, looking at the past few day's price bars and how to react to today's market price movement based on them. You will see how they can be used together to better choose which stocks to trade and also when to trade them as the current day unfolds.

INTRADAY CHART EXAMPLES

The next several pages show actual 5 minute bar charts for over 100 stocks. Each page has 4 stock charts with each chart providing two days of trading activity. The vertical dotted line through the center of each chart represents the end of the prior day and the beginning of the current day's trading session. Knowing the intraday price action of a stock for 1 or more prior days helps give you a better feel for that stock's personality. These intraday chart examples are marked to show consolidation at the high or low of the day and the breakout point. Commentary is also provided. While most of these are good intraday trade setup examples, don't forget to look at the daily chart when you are actually trading. The daily chart will help you see where price support and resistance levels are. You are looking for trades that have room to run 1 + points during the day.

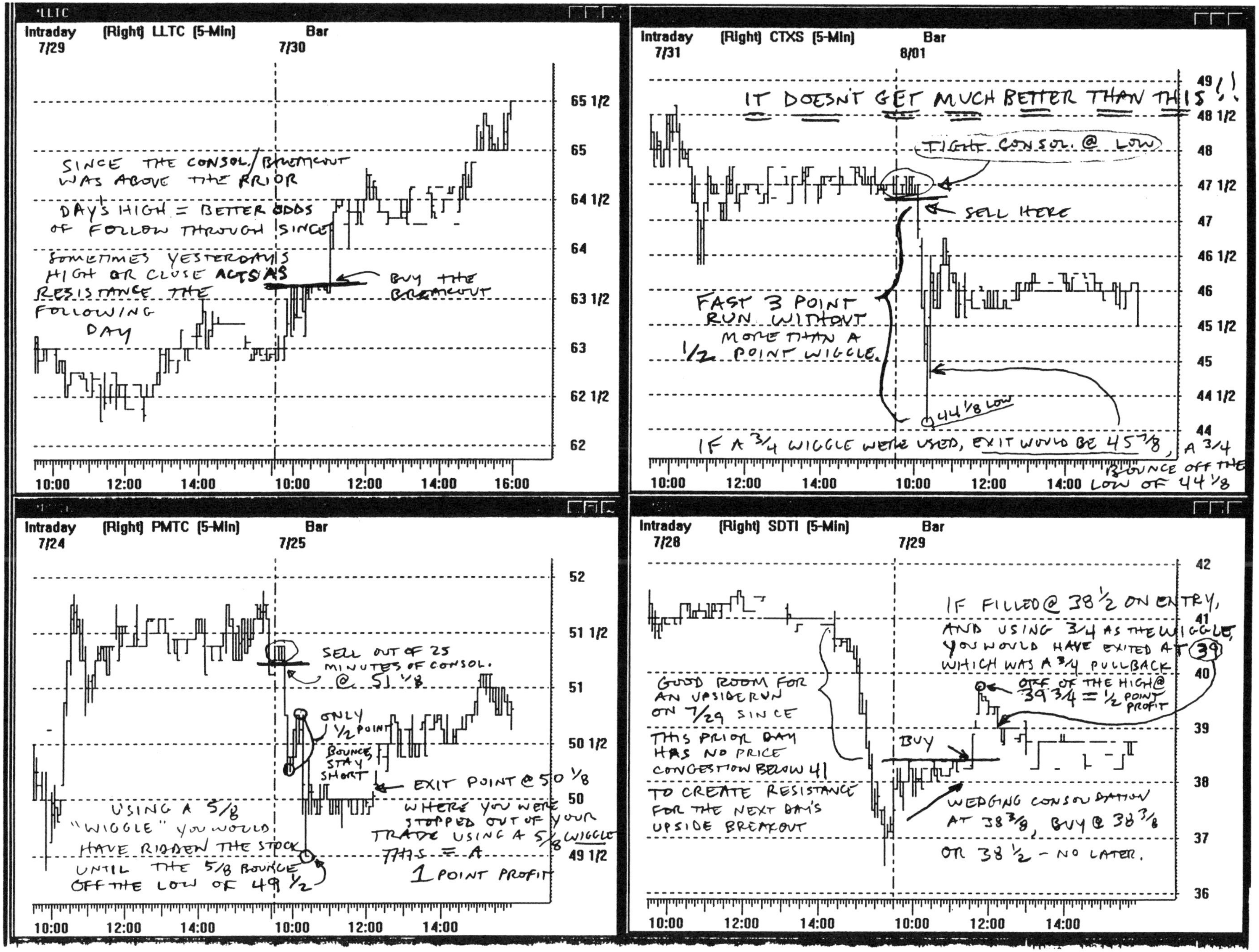
Intraday 7/29 (Right) LLTC (5-Min) Bar 7/30
65 1/2
65
64 1/2
64
63 1/2
63
62 1/2
62
10:00 12:00 14:00 10:00 12:00 14:00 16:00
SINCE THE CONSOL/BREAKOUT WAS ABOVE THE PRIOR DAY'S HIGH = BETTER ODDS OF FOLLOW THROUGH SINCE
SOMETIMES YESTERDAY'S HIGH OR CLOSE ACTS AS RESISTANCE THE FOLLOWING DAY
BUY THE BREAKOUT
Intraday 7/31 (Right) CTXS (5-Min) Bar 8/01
49
48 1/2
48
47 1/2
47
46 1/2
46
45 1/2
45
44 1/2
44
10:00 12:00 14:00 10:00 12:00 14:00
IT DOESN'T GET MUCH BETTER THAN THIS!!
TIGHT CONSOL. @ LOW
SELL HERE
FAST 3 POINT RUN WITHOUT MORE THAN A 1/2 POINT WIGGLE.
44 1/8 LOW
IF A 3/4 WIGGLE WERE USED, EXIT WOULD BE 45 7/8, A 3/4 BOUNCE OFF THE LOW OF 44 1/8
Intraday 7/24 (Right) PMTC (5-Min) Bar 7/25
52
51 1/2
51
50 1/2
50
49 1/2
10:00 12:00 14:00 10:00 12:00 14:00
SELL OUT OF 25 MINUTES OF CONSOL. @ 51 1/8
ONLY 1/2 POINT BOUNCE, STAY SHORT
EXIT POINT @ 50 1/8 WHERE YOU WERE STOPPED OUT OF YOUR TRADE USING A 5/8 WIGGLE
THIS = A 1 POINT PROFIT
USING A 5/8 "WIGGLE" YOU WOULD HAVE RIDDEN THE STOCK UNTIL THE 5/8 BOUNCE OFF THE LOW OF 49 1/2
Intraday 7/28 (Right) SDTI (5-Min) Bar 7/29
42
41
40
39
38
37
36
10:00 12:00 14:00 10:00 12:00 14:00
IF FILLED @ 38 1/2 ON ENTRY, AND USING 3/4 AS THE WIGGLE, YOU WOULD HAVE EXITED AT 39 WHICH WAS A 3/4 PULLBACK OFF OF THE HIGH @ 39 3/4 = 1/2 POINT PROFIT
GOOD ROOM FOR AN UPSIDE RUN ON 7/29 SINCE THIS PRIOR DAY HAS NO PRICE CONGESTION BELOW 41 TO CREATE RESISTANCE FOR THE NEXT DAY'S UPSIDE BREAKOUT
BUY
WEDGING CONSOLIDATION AT 38 3/8, BUY @ 38 3/8 OR 38 1/2 - NO LATER.

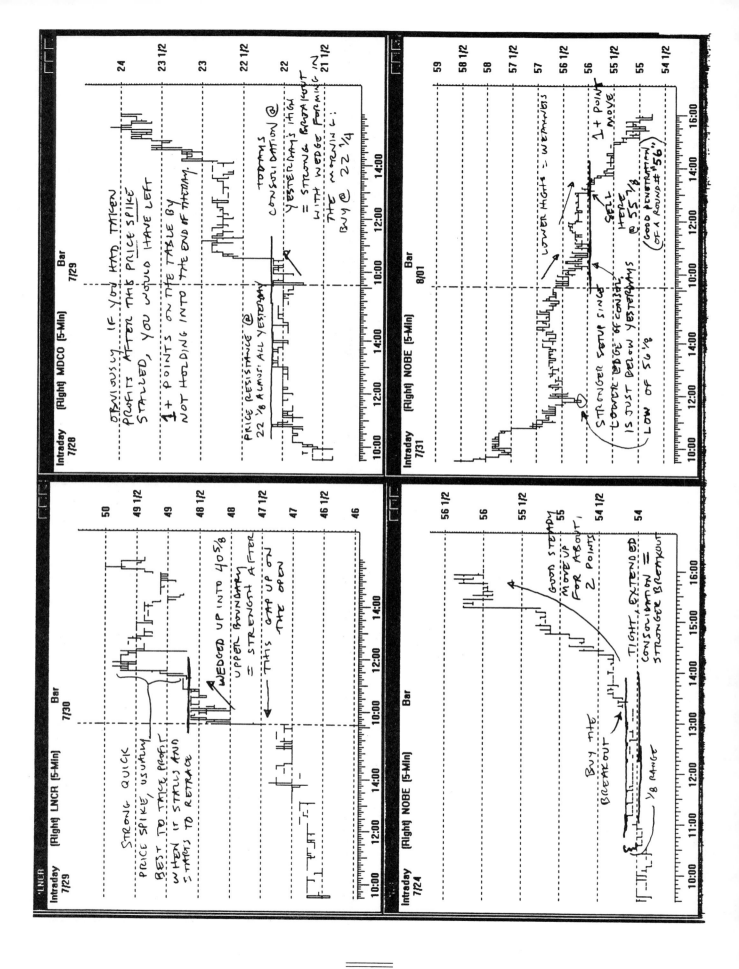

Intraday [Right] MDCO [5-Min]
7/28

Bar 7/29

OBVIOUSLY IF YOU HAD TAKEN
PROFITS AFTER THIS PRICE SPIKE
STALLED, YOU WOULD HAVE LEFT
1+ POINTS ON THE TABLE BY
NOT HOLDING INTO THE END OF THE DAY.

PRICE RESISTANCE @
22 1/8 ALMOST ALL YESTERDAY

TODAY'S
CONSOLIDATION @

YESTERDAY'S HIGH
= STRONG BREAKOUT
WITH WEDGE FORMING IN
THE MORNING.:
BUY @ 22 1/4

Intraday [Right] NOBE [5-Min]
7/31

Bar 8/01

LOWER HIGHS = WEAKNESS

1+ POINT
MOVE

SELL 1/2
@ 55 1/8
HIGH

(GOOD PENETRATION
OF A ROUND # "56")

STRONGER SETUP SINCE
LOWER EDGE OF PRICE
CONSOLIDATION IS JUST
8/05 OF 56
LOW

Intraday [Right] LNCR [5-Min]
7/29

Bar 7/30

STRONG QUICK
PRICE SPIKE, USUALLY

BEST TO TAKE PROFIT
WHEN IT STALLS AND
STARTS TO RETRACE

WEDGED UP INTO 40 5/8
UPPER BOUNDARY
= STRENGTH AFTER

THIS GAP UP ON
THE OPEN

Intraday [Right] NOBE [5-Min]
7/24

Bar

GOOD STEADY
MOVE UP
FOR ABOUT
2 POINTS

BUY THE
BREAKOUT

TIGHT, EXTENDED
CONSOLIDATION =
STRONGER BREAKOUT

1/8 RANGE

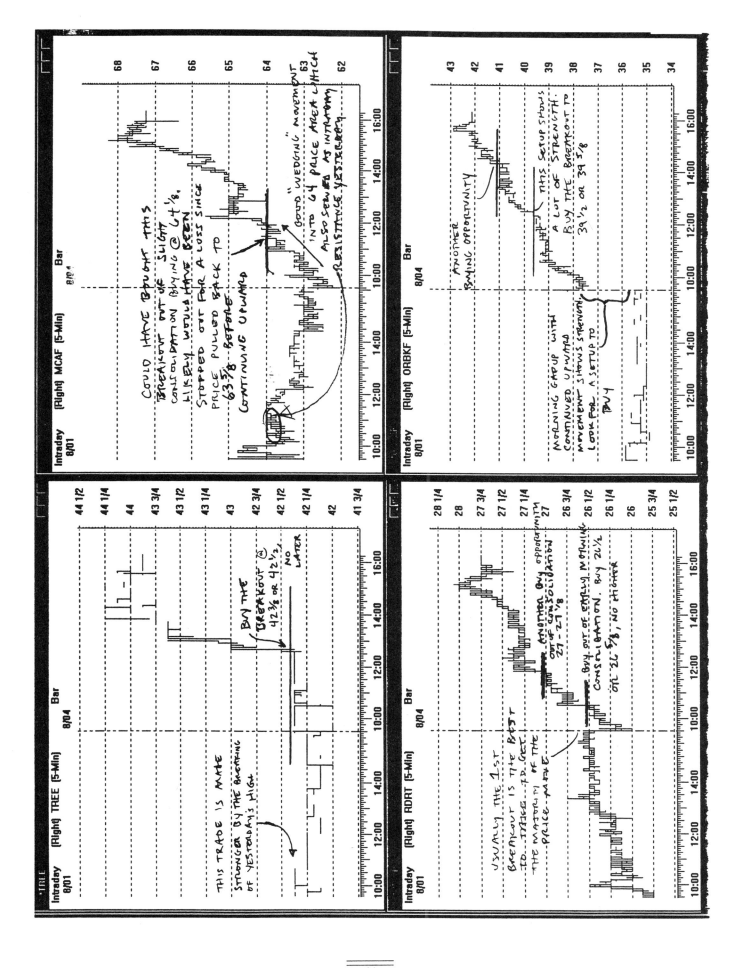

Intraday [Right] TREE [5-Min]
8/01

THIS TRADE IS MADE STRONGER BY THE BREAKING OF YESTERDAY'S HIGH

BUY THE BREAKOUT @ 42⅜ OR 42½. NO LATER

Intraday [Right] MCAF [5-Min]
8/01

COULD HAVE BOUGHT THIS BREAKOUT OUT OF SLIGHT CONSOLIDATION BUYING @ 64⅛. LIKELY WOULD HAVE BEEN STOPPED OUT FOR A LOSS SINCE PRICE PULLED BACK TO 63⅝ BEFORE CONTINUING UPWARD

GOOD "WEDGING" MOVEMENT INTO 64 PRICE AREA WHICH ALSO SERVED AS INTRADAY RESISTANCE YESTERDAY

Intraday [Right] RDRT [5-Min]
8/01

USUALLY THE 1st BREAKOUT IS THE BEST TO TRADE. TO GET THE MAXIMUM OF THE PRICE MOVE

ANOTHER BUY OPPORTUNITY OUT OF CONSOLIDATION 27-27⅛

BUY OUT OF EARLY MORNING CONSOLIDATION. BUY 26½ OR 26⅝, NO HIGHER

Intraday [Right] ORBKF [5-Min]
8/01

ANOTHER BUYING OPPORTUNITY

THIS SETUP SHOWS A LOT OF STRENGTH. BUY THE BREAKOUT TO 39½ OR 39⅝

MORNING GAP-UP WITH CONTINUED UPWARD MOVEMENT SHOWS STRENGTH LOOK FOR A SETUP TO BUY

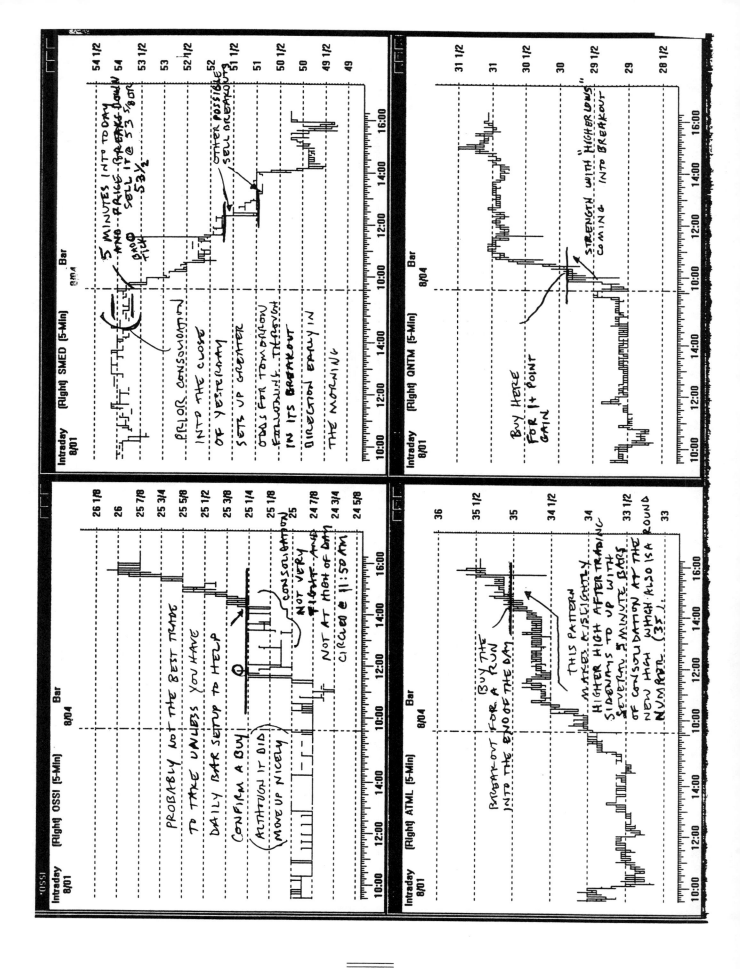

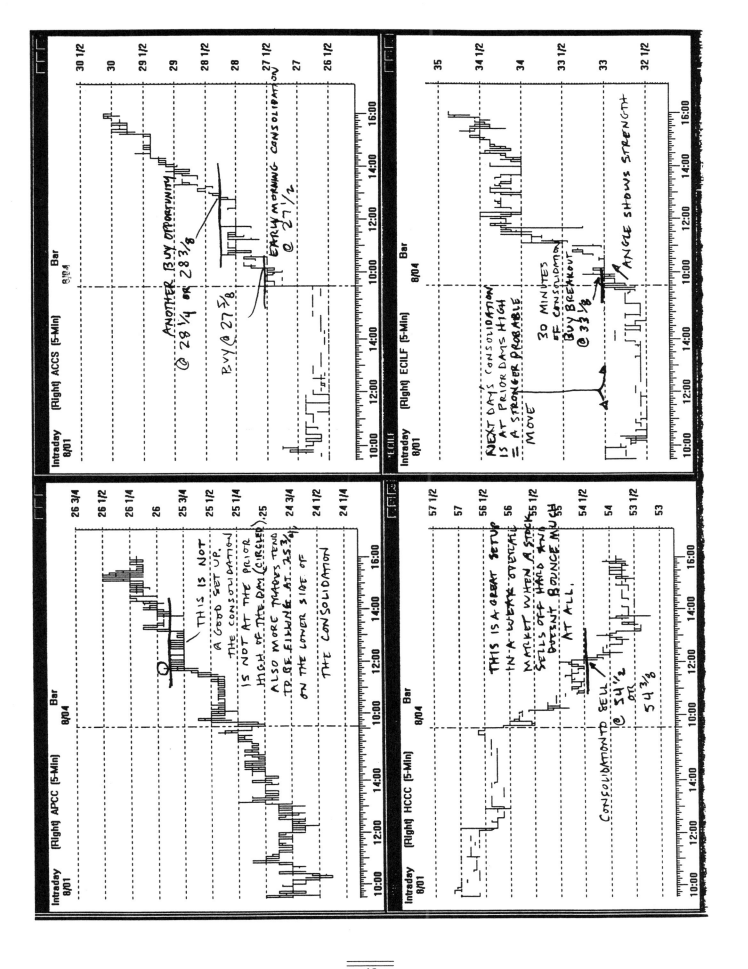

[Right] ACCS [5-Min] Bar 8/01

ANOTHER BUY OPPORTUNITY
@ 28 1/4 OR 28 3/8

BUY @ 27 5/8

EARLY MORNING CONSOLIDATION
@ 27 1/2

[Right] APCC [5-Min] Bar 8/04

THIS IS NOT
A GOOD SET UP.
THE CONSOLIDATION
IS NOT AT THE PRIOR
HIGH OF THE DAY (CIRCLED).
ALSO MORE TRADERS TEND
TO BE FILLING AT 25 3/4
ON THE LOWER SIDE OF
THE CONSOLIDATION

[Right] ECILF [5-Min] Bar 8/04

NEXT DAYS CONSOLIDATION
IS AT PRIOR DAYS HIGH
= A STRONGER PROBABLE
MOVE

30 MINUTES
OF CONSOLIDATION
BUY BREAKOUT
@ 33 1/8

ANGLE SHOWS STRENGTH

[Right] HCCC [5-Min] Bar 8/01

THIS IS A GREAT SETUP
IN A WEAK OVERALL
MARKET WHEN A STOCK
SELLS OFF HARD AND
DOESN'T BOUNCE MUCH
AT ALL.

CONSOLIDATION SELL
@ 54 1/2
OR
54 3/8

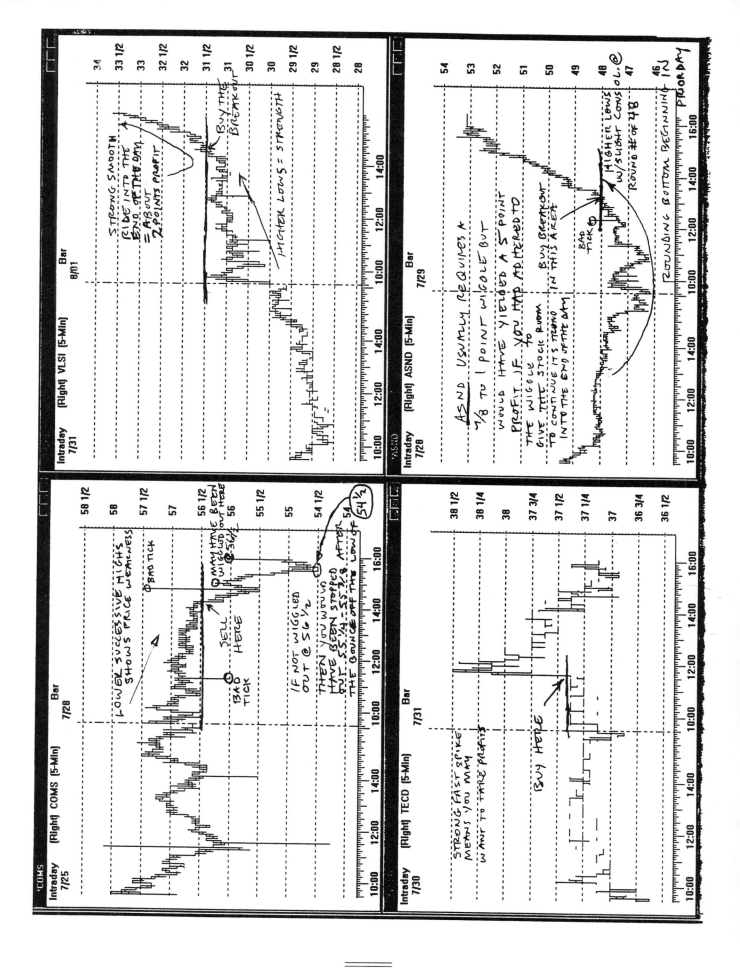

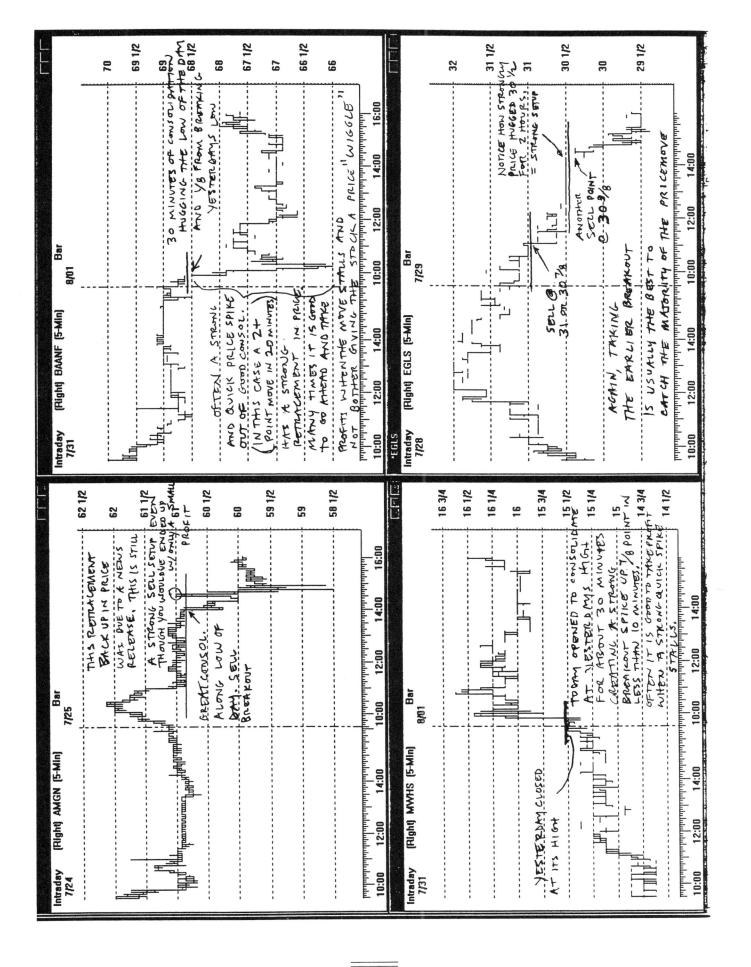

AMGN [Right] [5-Min]   Bar
Intraday 7/24   7/25

THIS RETRACEMENT
BACK UP IN PRICE
WAS DUE TO A NEWS
RELEASE, THIS IS STILL
A STRONG SELL SETUP
THOUGH YOU WOULDVE ENDED UP
W/ONLY A 61 SMALL
PROFIT

BREAKT CONSOL.
ALONG LOW OF
RTN'L SELL
BREAKOUT

BAANF [Right] [5-Min]   Bar
Intraday 7/31   8/01

30 MINUTES OF CONSOLIDATION
HUGGING THE LOW OF THE DAY
AND Y/B FROM B (RUNNING)
YESTERDAYS LOW

OFTEN A STRONG
AND QUICK PRICE SPIKE
OUT OF GOOD CONSOL.
(IN THIS CASE A 2+
POINT MOVE IN 20 MINUTES)
HAS A STRONG
RETRACEMENT IN PRICE.
MANY TIMES IT IS GOOD
TO GO AHEAD AND TAKE
PROFIT WHEN THE MOVE STALLS AND
NOT BOTHER GIVING THE STOCK A PRICE "WIGGLE"

MWHS [Right] [5-Min]   Bar
Intraday 7/31   8/01

YESTERDAY CLOSED
AT ITS HIGH

TODAY OPENED TO CONSOLIDATE
AT YESTERDAYS HIGH
FOR ABOUT 30 MINUTES
CREATING A STRONG
BREAKOUT SPIKE UP 7/8 POINT IN
LESS THAN 10 MINUTES.
OFTEN IT IS GOOD TO TAKE PROFIT
WHEN A STRONG QUICK SPIKE
STALLS.

EGLS [Right] [5-Min]   Bar
Intraday 7/28   7/29

NOTICE HOW STRONGLY
PRICE HUGGED 30 1/2
FOR 2 HOURS;
= STRONG SETUP

SELL @
31.01 30.7/8

ANOTHER
SELL POINT
@ 30.3/8

AGAIN, TAKING
THE EARLIER BREAKOUT
IS USUALLY THE BEST TO
CATCH THE MAJORITY OF THE PRICE MOVE

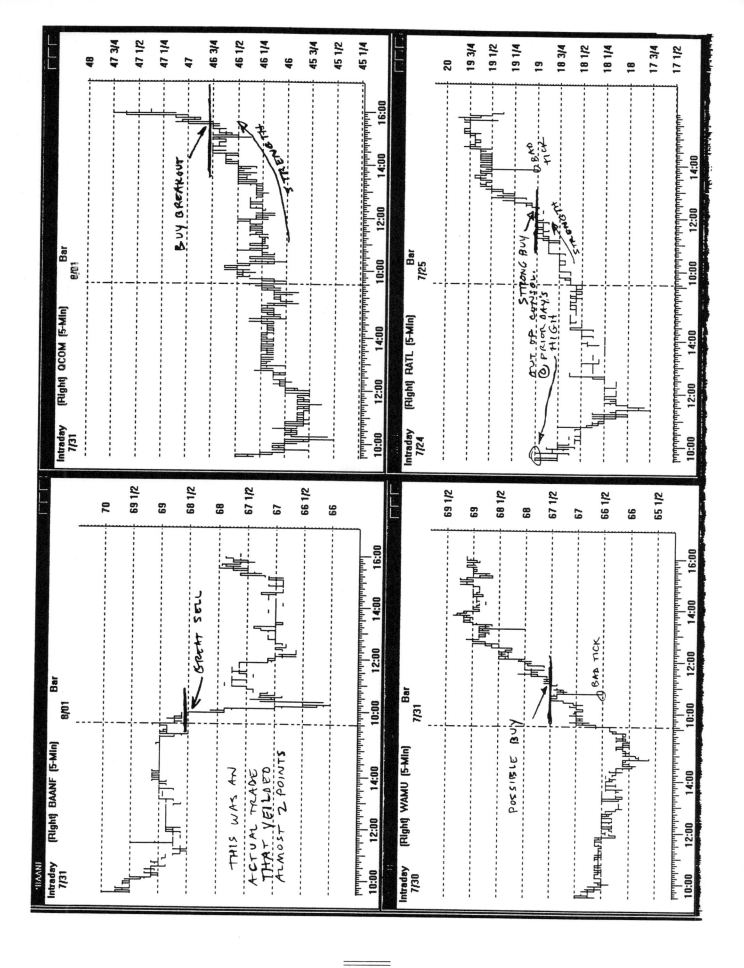

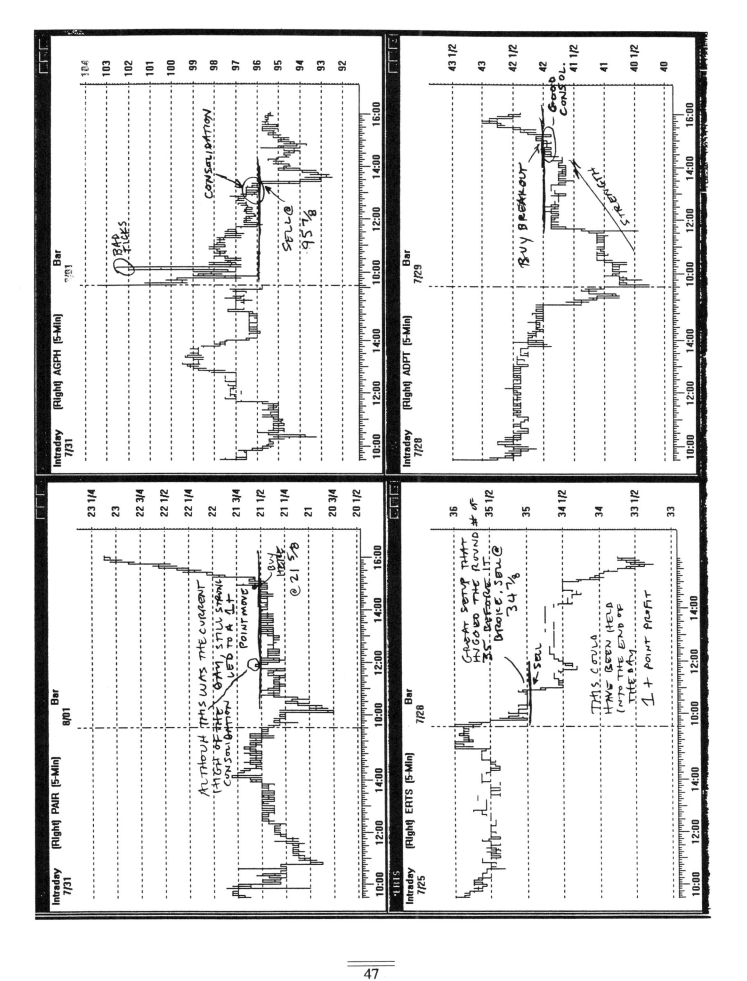

47

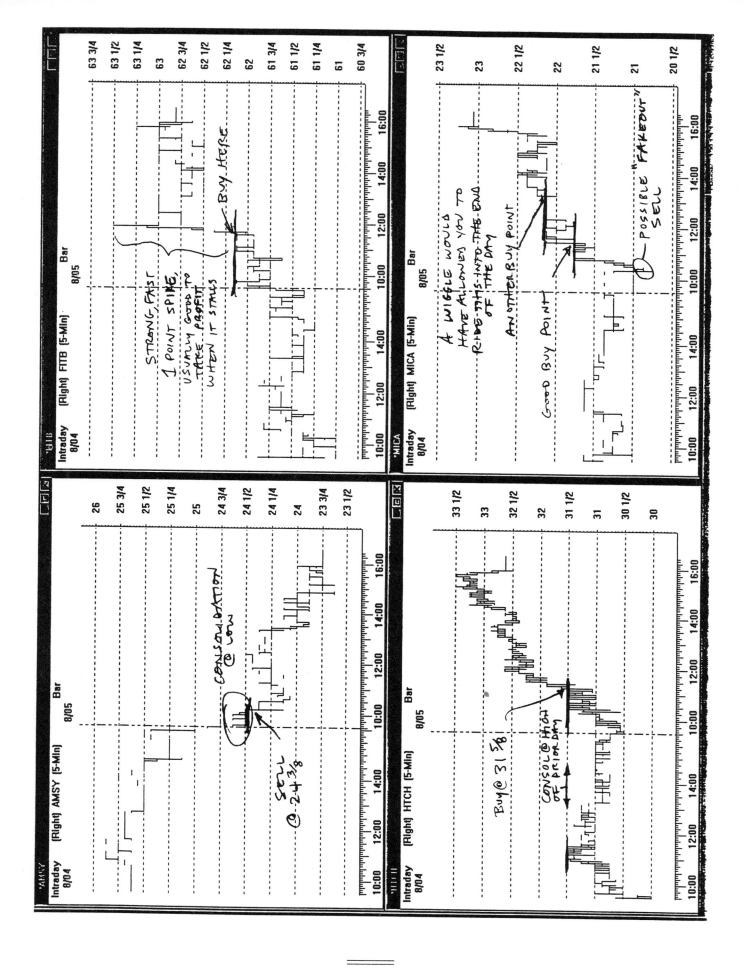

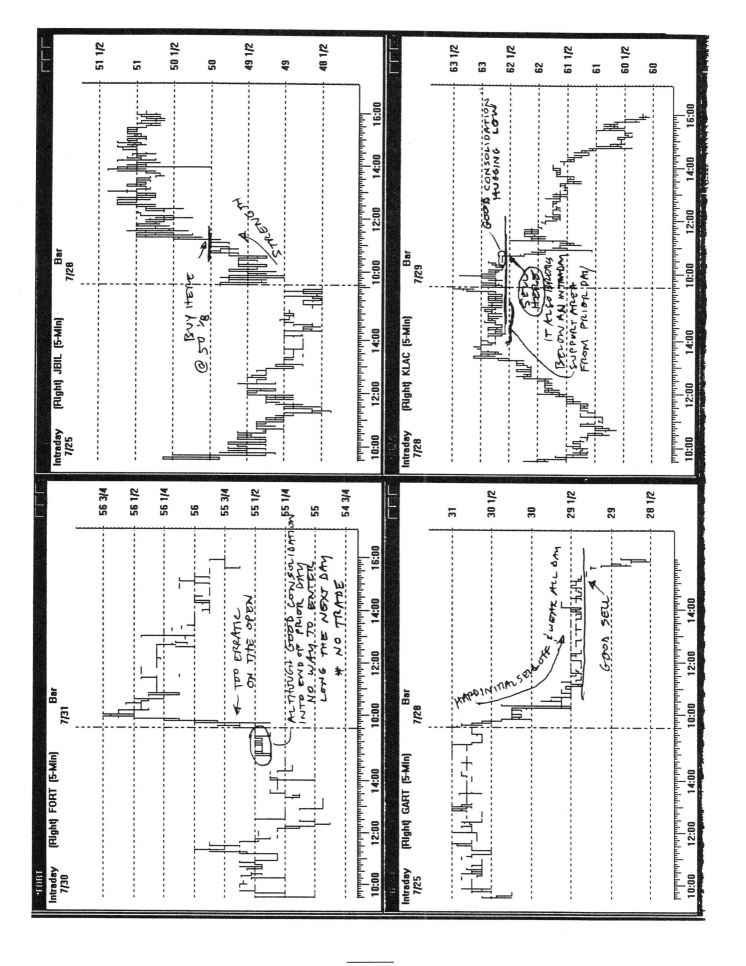

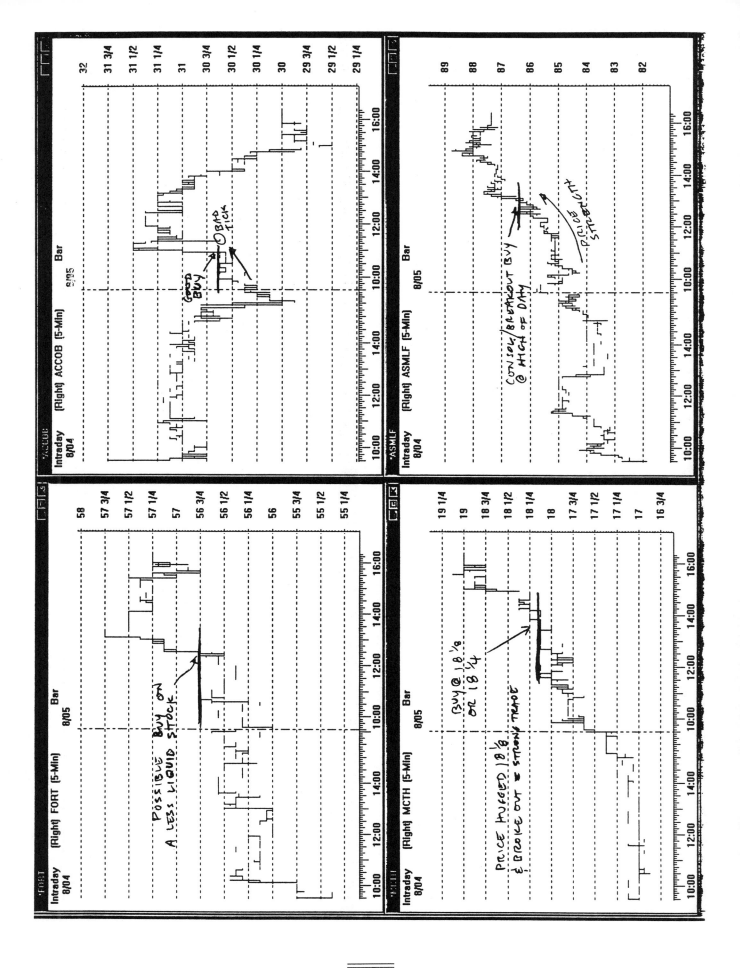

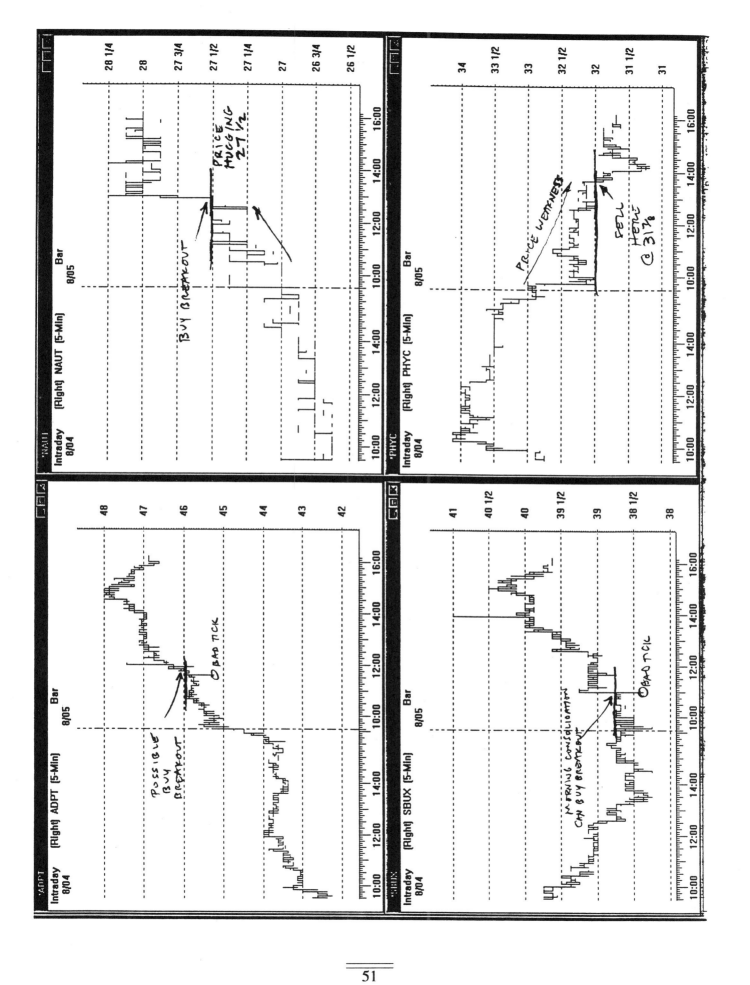

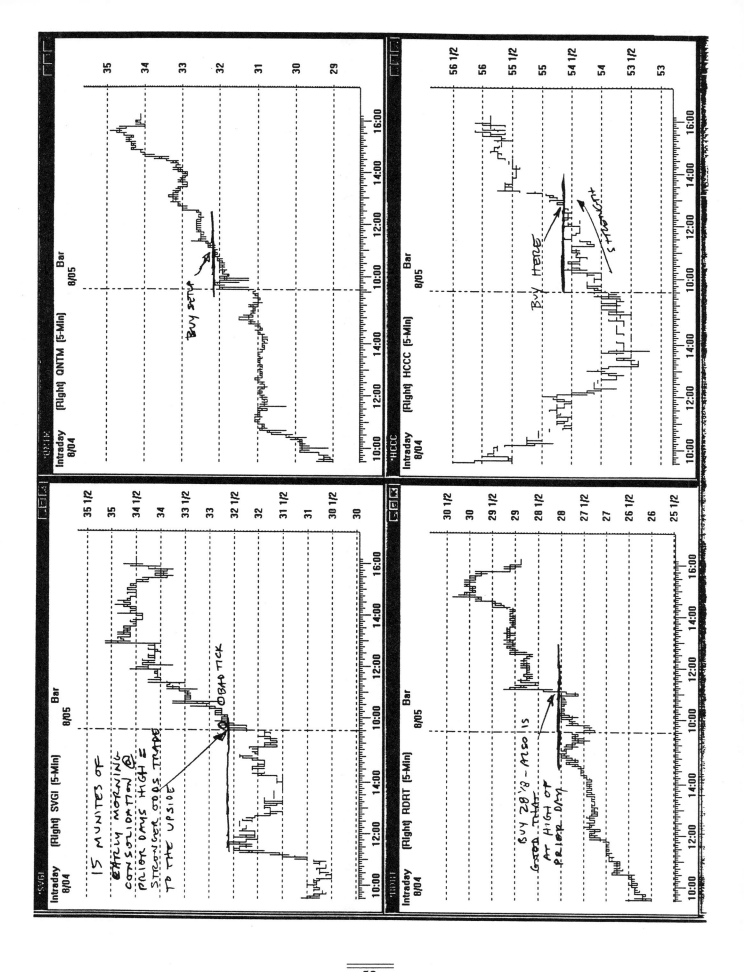

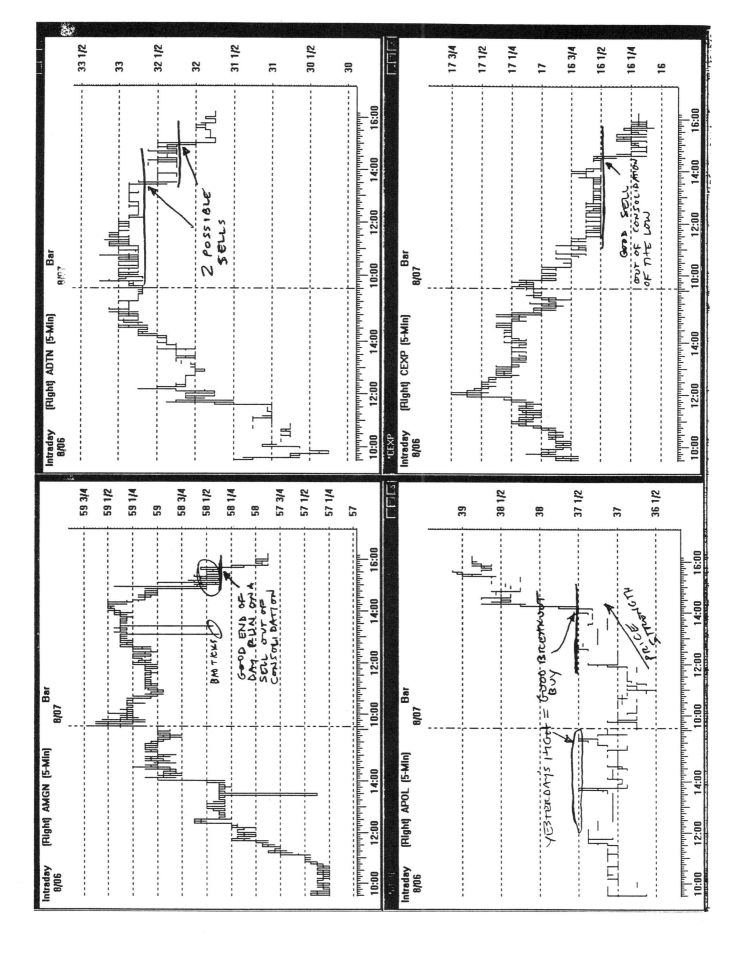

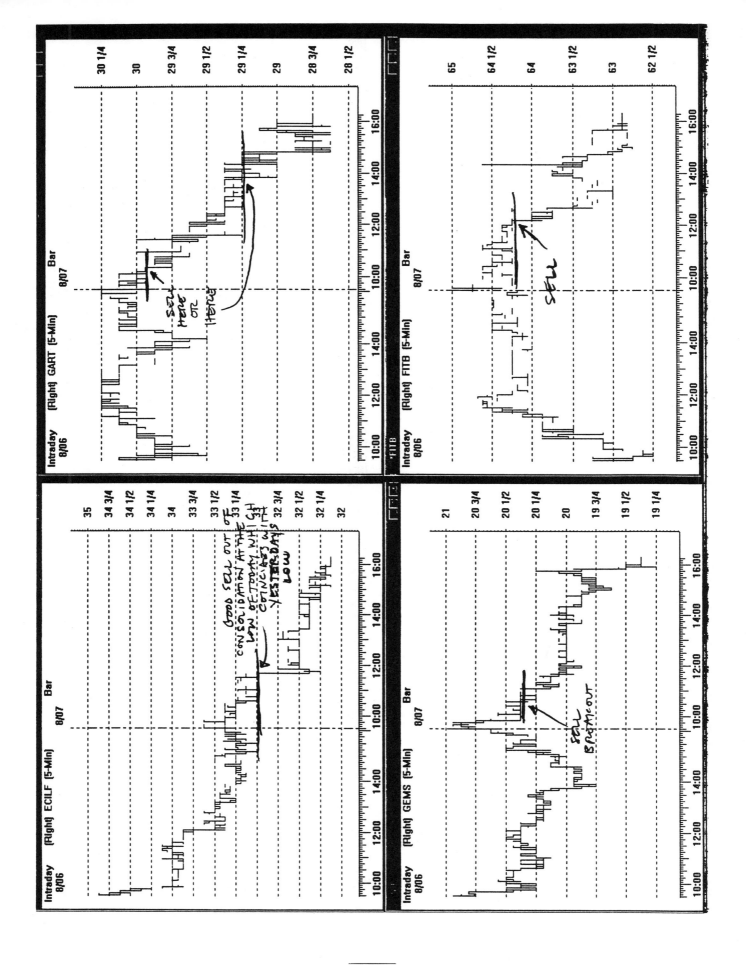

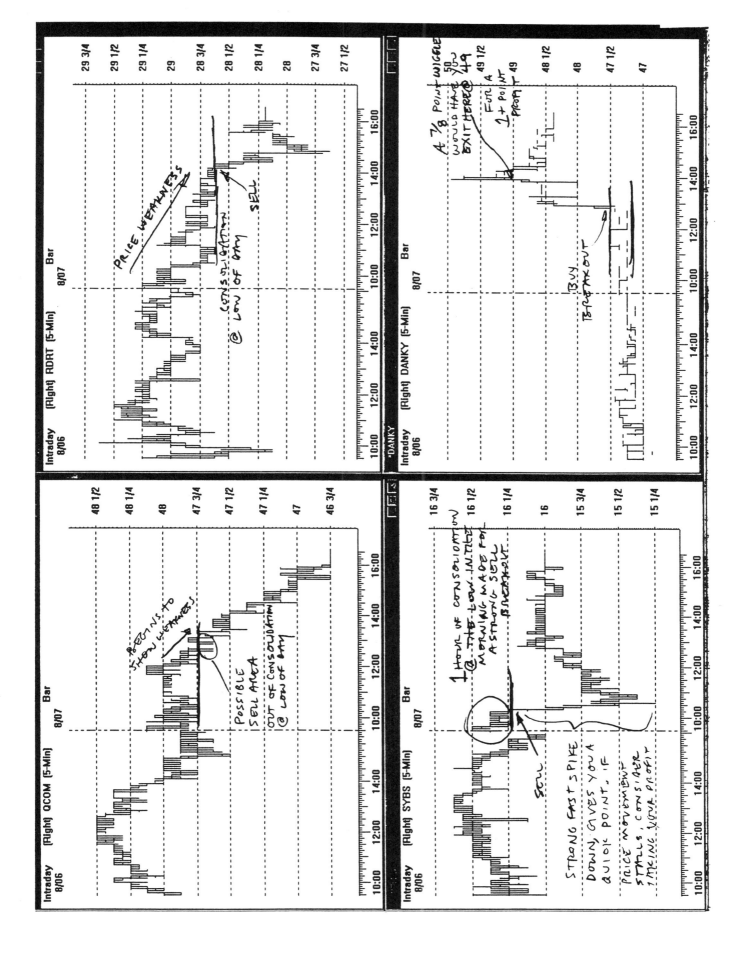

PRICE WEAKNESS

SELL

@ CONSOLIDATION
@ LOW OF DAY

BEGINS TO
SHOW WEAKNESS

POSSIBLE
SELL AREA

OUT OF CONSOLIDATION
@ LOW OF DAY

A 7/8 POINT WIGGLE
WOULD HAVE YOU
EXIT HERE @ 49

FOR A
1 + POINT
PROFIT @ 49

BUY
BREAKOUT

1 HOUR OF CONSOLIDATION
@ THE LOW. ENTIRE
MORNING MADE FOR
A STRONG SELL
BREAKOUT

SELL

STRONG FAST SPIKE
DOWN, GIVES YOU A
QUICK POINT. IF
PRICE MOVEMENT
STALLS, CONSIDER
TAKING YOUR PROFIT

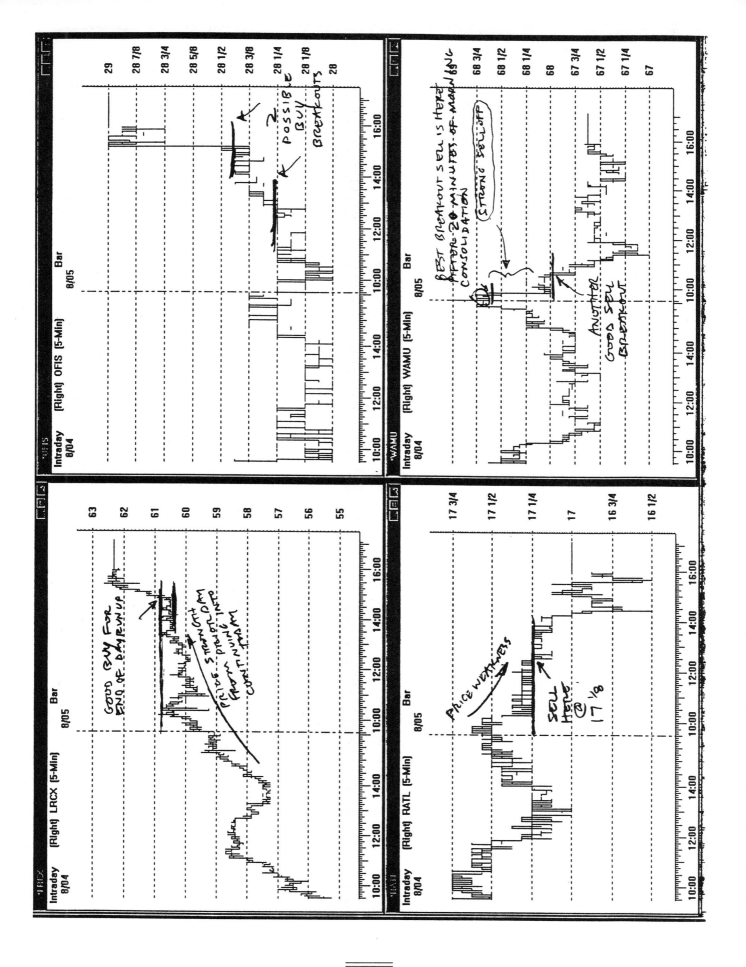

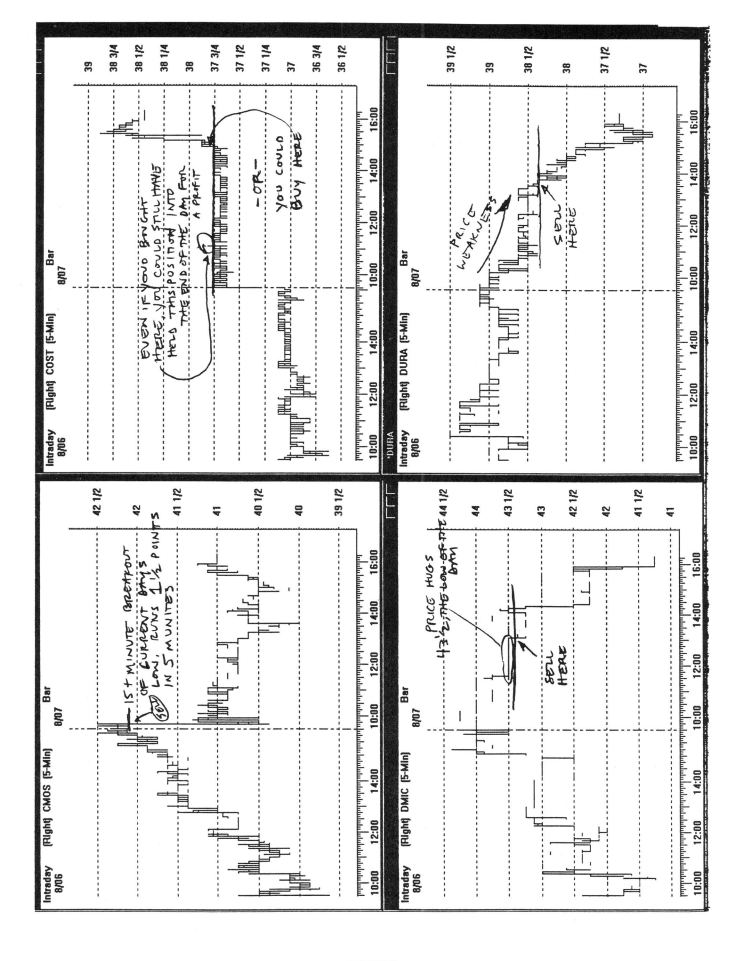

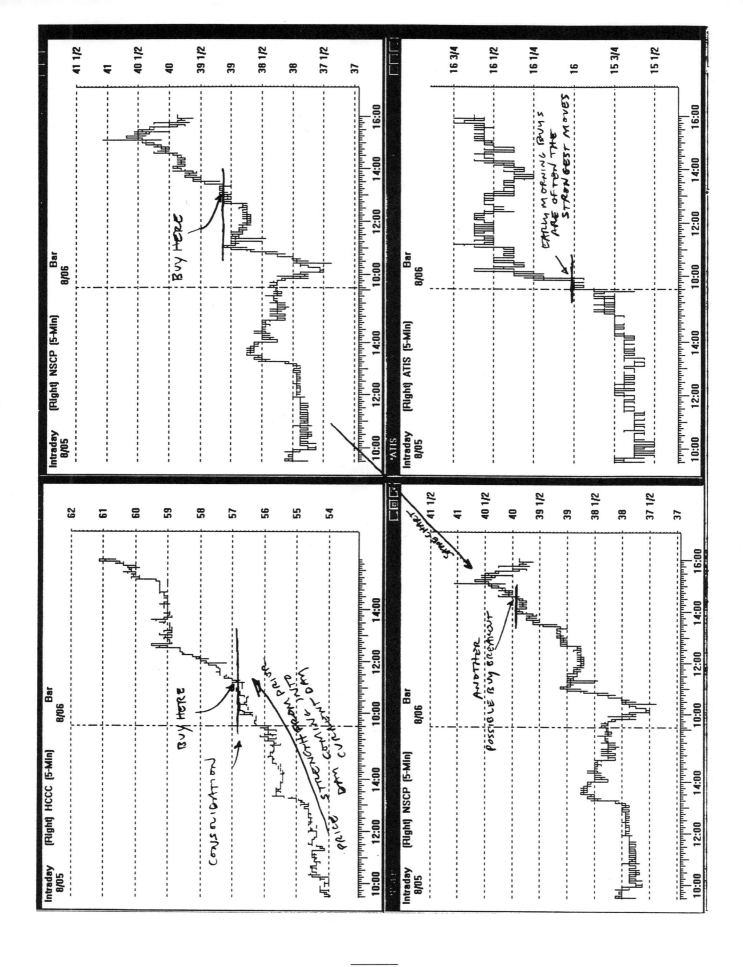

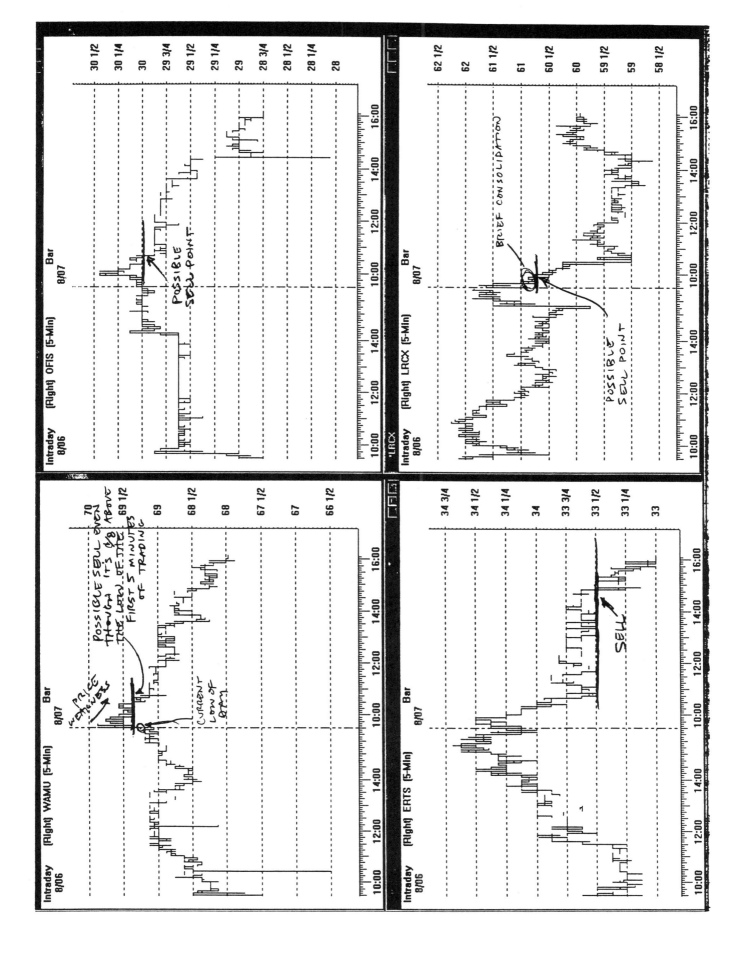

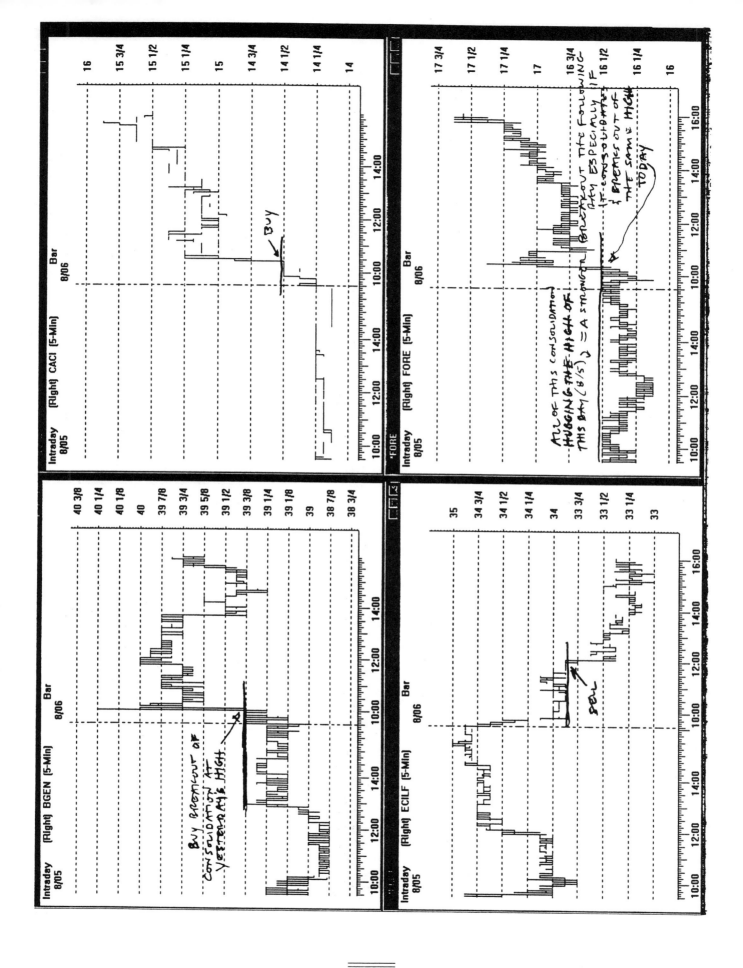

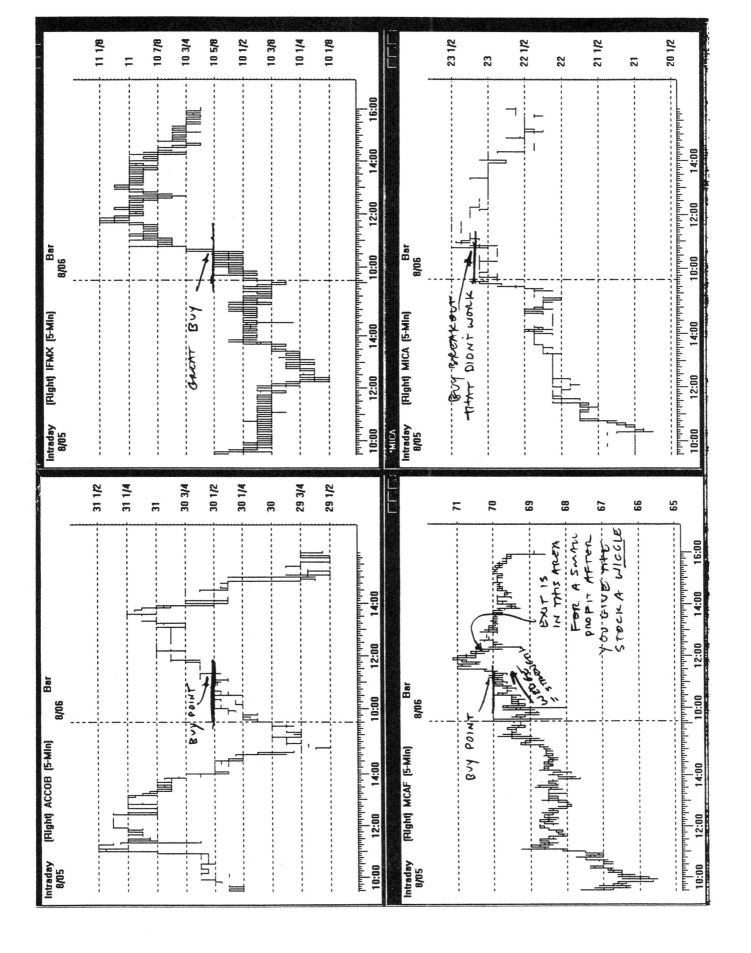

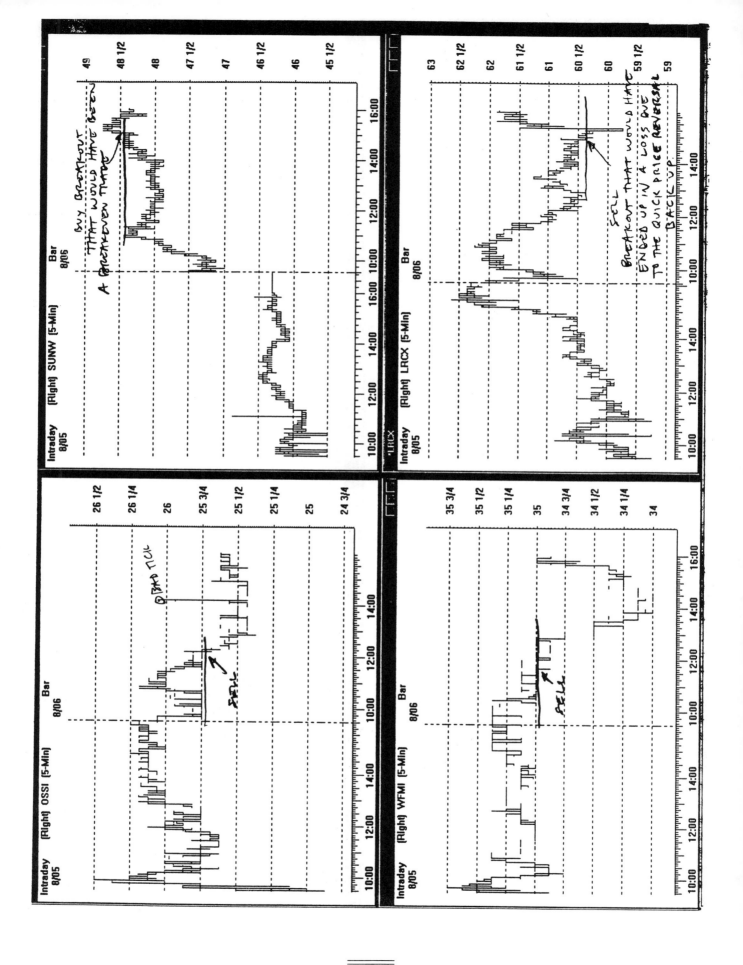

BUY BREAKOUT
THAT WOULD HAVE BEEN
A BREAKEVEN TRADE

SELL
BREAKOUT THAT WOULD HAVE
ENDED UP IN A LOSS DUE
TO THE QUICK PRICE REVERSAL
BACK UP

@ BAD TICK

SELL

SELL

Intraday   [Right] SUNW [5-Min]   Bar
8/05   8/06

Intraday   [Right] LRCX [5-Min]   Bar
8/05   8/06

Intraday   [Right] OSSI [5-Min]   Bar
8/05   8/06

Intraday   [Right] WFMI [5-Min]   Bar
8/05   8/06

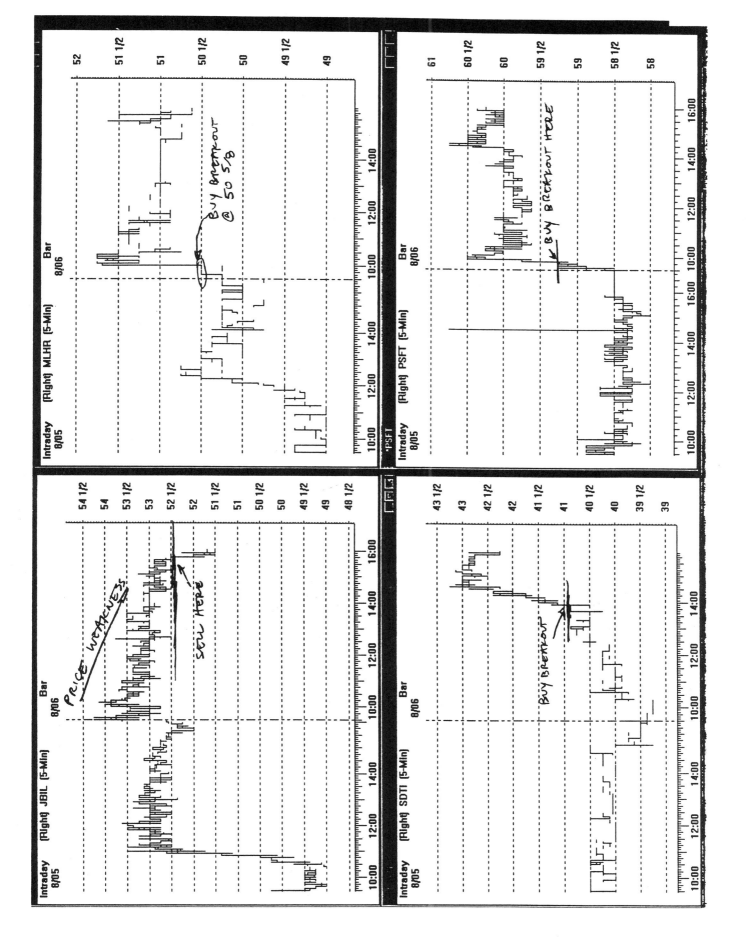

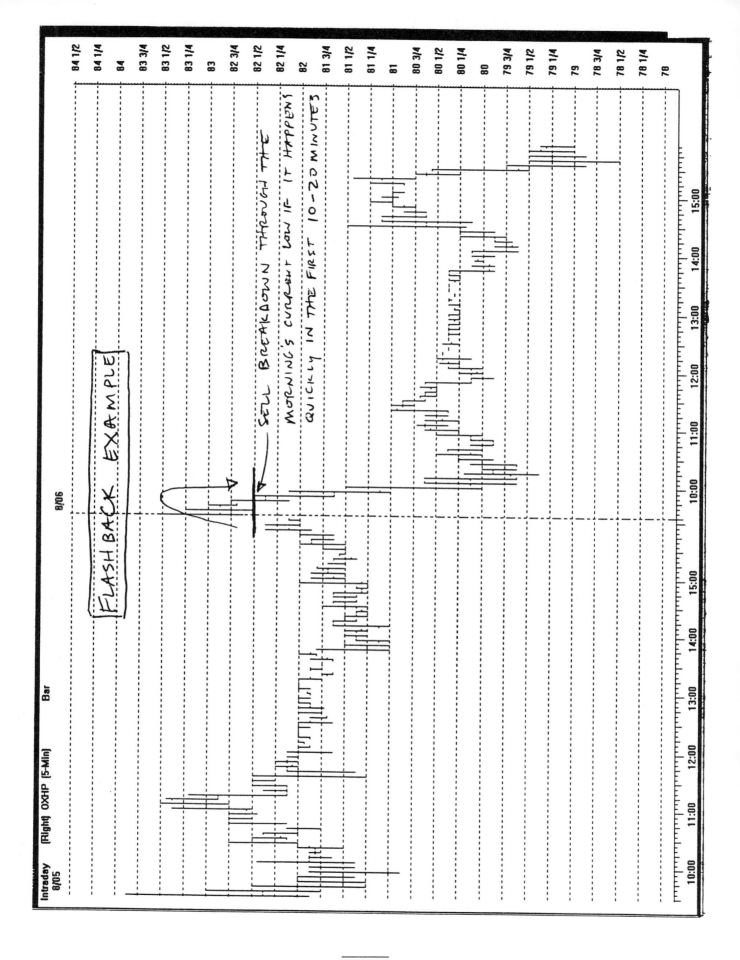

FLASH BACK EXAMPLE

SELL BREAKDOWN THROUGH THE MORNING'S CURRENT LOW IF IT HAPPENS QUICKLY IN THE FIRST 10-20 MINUTES

1 TO 3 DAILY BAR SETUPS
(for day trading)

INTRODUCTION:

In this section we'll be looking at a stock's daily historical bar chart and isolating high probability day trades by analyzing yesterday's price bar. In some cases the past 2 or 3 daily bars will also be part of the setup. Knowing in advance which stocks have these setups prepares you to react quickly once the market opens. These trades are geared primarily for entering soon after the morning bell rings as price chooses its direction. You will not be "predicting" the stock's direction. Instead, you'll be <u>reacting</u> to the price movement depending on where the stock opens today in relation to yesterday's price bar. Three primary setups are presented. Several scenarios are depicted that yield "high-odds" trades.

W/R BAR, EXTREME CLOSE

This is a bar that has a <u>W</u>ide <u>R</u>ange (from high to low) and also closes <u>at or very near</u> its high or low of the day. You can pick each of these out relatively easily just by comparing its size to the average bar size on the stock's daily historical chart. Often these days are followed by 1 or more days of strong price movement providing a good day trading opportunity. Here is how this basic setup looks:

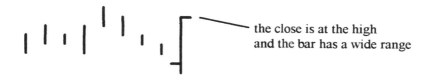

This is the same principle when inverted:

Bars which open at the low and close at the high (or vice versa) are the strongest setups.

There are 4 trade setups that depend on where the stock opens the next day in relation to the close of the W/R bar. The first 2 setups have rather clear cut entry rules. The other 2 setups can be a bit trickier during the first 10 - 15 minutes of trading. These second 2 setups are described in more detail and also offer an alternative entry point based on the 5 minute bar chart.

The first setup is for an open <u>slightly</u> above the high of the W/R bar. #19-A is a buy setup (followed by the sell setup). On this type of open, price often swings down toward the high of the previous W/R day initially. This should happen quickly with price immediately reversing back upwards through the morning's current high. Buy the breakout of the high if this scenario plays out within the first 15 minutes of trading.

19-A)

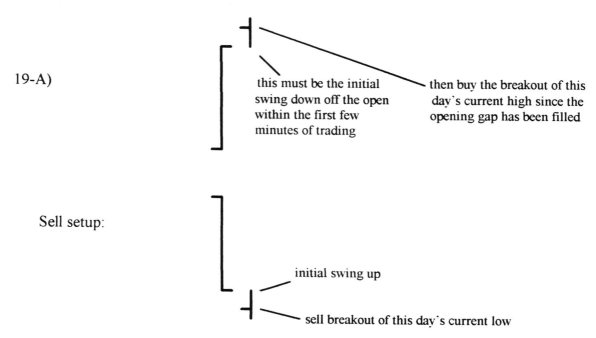

this must be the initial swing down off the open within the first few minutes of trading

then buy the breakout of this day's current high since the opening gap has been filled

Sell setup:

initial swing up

sell breakout of this day's current low

The above trade is even better if the stock has an established daily trend. You increase the odds of this trade when you are trading in the direction of the longer term trend.

The second setup, 19-B, is a substantial gap up on the open. If it moves down at all, consider quickly selling it short.

19-B)

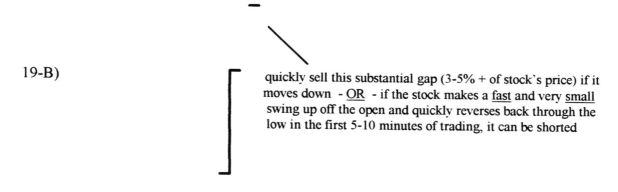

quickly sell this substantial gap (3-5% + of stock's price) if it moves down - <u>OR</u> - if the stock makes a <u>fast</u> and very <u>small</u> swing up off the open and quickly reverses back through the low in the first 5-10 minutes of trading, it can be shorted

The reverse scenario:

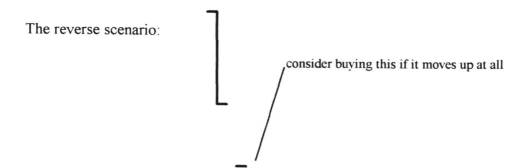

consider buying this if it moves up at all

There are 2 other setups. One occurs when price opens even with yesterday's close. The other is when price opens <u>slightly</u> below the close of a W/R bar that closed near its high (or price opened <u>slightly</u> above the close of a W/R bar that closed near its low). These may be played either long or short depending on several factors. The first consideration is if the W/R day sets up after a strong 3 - 5 day run up in the stock, or if it is the 1st or 2nd day of a strong move up. If it is only the 1st or 2nd day then the tendency is to the buy side on these 2 opening setups. After a 3 - 5 day run up, the tendency leans toward the sell side as a correction is probably due.

The converse of this is true with a W/R day that closes at its low. If this is the 1st or 2nd strong day down, then odds favor a continuation of this short term price swing. 3 - 5 strong days down and these 2 setups favor a bounce to the long side as a correction. Therefore, a trade setup for early morning entry is provided as well a more conservative entry based on waiting a little longer into the morning and keying off of the 5 minute bar chart. The other factor to consider is whether you are in the midst of a bull or bear swing in the overall market. This also influences the odds behind which direction the stock is more likely to move.

These are the 2 setups with a W/R day that closed near its high:

Here are the examples of the 2 setups with a W/R day closing near its low.

On a W/R day where price opens even with yesterday's close, you can consider buying a move up off the open.

You may instead want to wait for the stock to move one direction or the other and show consolidation at the current session's high or low for 2 to 3 bars on the 5 minute intraday chart. If the stock has not moved too far in price you can then enter a trade on the consolidated breakout of the high or low. This is the alternative entry. You may miss some of the price move (or miss it entirely), but it lowers your risk of an early morning fake out. If you are convinced the initial move off the open (up or down in this setup) is the direction the stock will take for the day then you can buy or sell this stock no more than 3/8 points from the open. Remember, also consider the odds of the direction based on what was mentioned earlier. Ask yourself how many days has this stock run up strongly, what is the overall market direction of the last few days, and how is the market index moving on its intraday chart (gap up or down, moving up or down strongly etc.).

The last W/R bar sets up when the next day's open is just slightly below the close of the W/R bar up. It is usually a short sell trade, but occasionally may also go long. Do not buy this immediately off the open if it begins moving up. It will probably meet resistance at yesterday's close or high. If you are convinced that it is going to be a down move and retrace yesterday's bar then you can sell it early in the morning no more than 3/8 points off the open. If you are unsure of the true direction, then a more conservative approach is to wait for a few bars of consolidation on the 5 minute chart at the current day's high or low. You could then enter on a breakout in either direction. This is especially true on the buy side since resistance is expected at yesterdays close and high. Preferably the 5 minute consolidation should be at or above yesterday's close and high for buying this stock.

Once again look at how many days this stock has run up or down. Also consider the overall market trend daily and intraday #19-D shows the setup with a W/R bar up.

19-D)

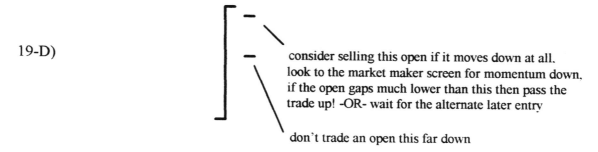

consider selling this open if it moves down at all. look to the market maker screen for momentum down. if the open gaps much lower than this then pass the trade up! -OR- wait for the alternate later entry

don't trade an open this far down

The W/R bar down setup: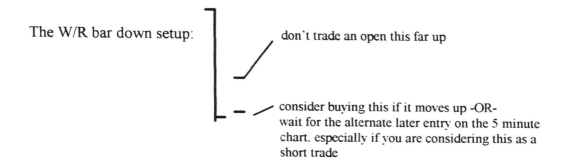

don't trade an open this far up

consider buying this if it moves up -OR-
wait for the alternate later entry on the 5 minute
chart. especially if you are considering this as a
short trade

* NOTE: If you had intraday consolidation into yesterday's close (refer to last example in intraday section of manual) then the W/R bar setups are much stronger. If this is the case then you may wish to take the initial trade entry off the open on the above 4 setups. In these instances you probably will not want to wait for the alternate trade entries later in the morning.

Although I've mentioned probabilities of the direction to play 1 to 2 day versus 3 to 5 day price runs with a W/R day, they are simply guidelines. These rules are not set in stone. Sometimes even a 1 day W/R bar will have the next day retrace it. You have to listen (react) to the market and to what the market indexes are telling you about how a stock's W/R day should play out the following day. Once again, this is part of the art of trading. The most important point is that a W/R day is often followed by another day of significant movement where profit may be had. Be sure to rely on the 5 minute charts, and wait for an intraday setup if you are not convinced of the initial move off of the open the next day.

REVERSAL BAR SETUP

This 3 bar pattern when completed resembles this:

The setup consists of only the first two bars. The key here is
1) The close of bar 1 must be near its low
2) Bar 2's high must not be much above the low of bar 1
3) Bar 2 must close at or near its high (and preferably have opened near its high as well)
4) Bar 1's high should be 1+ points above the close (or high) of bar 2 to provide a decent profit -- the expectation is for day 3 to attempt to trade up to day 1's high

Bar 2 thus sets up as a potential reversal bar, and you look for a trade on day 3. If day 3 opens at or near the close of day 2 and begins moving up, this may be a good buy at anytime during the trading session of day 3. At this point the 5 minute intraday bar chart can play an additional role if you see consolidation and then a breakout to the upside. This way you have 2 time frames working for you at once (daily and intraday). Buy the breakout. The wider the range of bar 1, the better the trade.

Here is setup #20:

20)

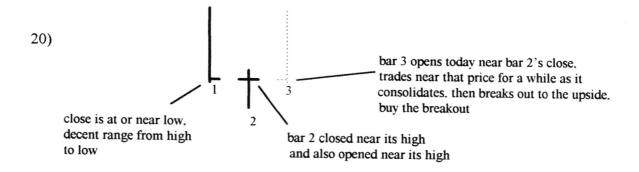

bar 3 opens today near bar 2's close, trades near that price for a while as it consolidates, then breaks out to the upside. buy the breakout

close is at or near low, decent range from high to low

bar 2 closed near its high and also opened near its high

This setup can also have the following look to bar #2 (the reversal bar):

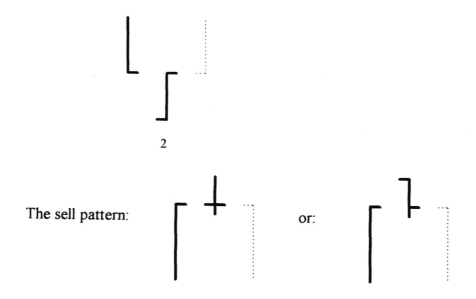

The sell pattern: or:

DELAYED REVERSAL SETUP

This is a variation on the 1 bar reversal. It is a 4 bar pattern with 3 bars setting up the trade for the fourth day. Day 1 must close at or near the bottom of that day's range. Day 2 opens at or near the close of day 1 and continues the prior day's sell off. Day 2 must also close at or near the low of that day's range. Day 3 must open at or near the close of day 2 and retrace back up to (or very near) the high of day 2. Also, day 3 must close at or near its high of the day. If the stock opens on day 4 near the close of day 3 and begins to move up, buy it. The wider the range of bar 1, the better the trade.
Here is setup #20-A:

20-A)

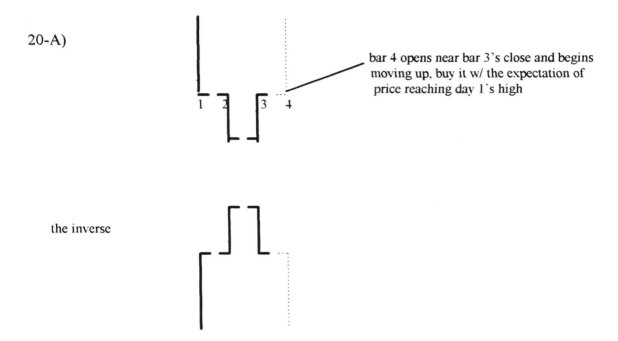

bar 4 opens near bar 3's close and begins moving up, buy it w/ the expectation of price reaching day 1's high

the inverse

So, how do you find these reversal setup of bars? By trading and reviewing charts daily you will learn to pick out possible setups and earmark those stocks in your mind. A daily analysis worksheet is provided later in the manual. When one of those particular stocks comes across the ticker, you go to that stock's screen and automatically know what you are looking for. If the setup is there, and you're getting a breakout, consider taking the trade. The sell setup is an inverted reversal pattern. In a buy setup the expectation is that the stock will move up to or near the high of bar 1. In the inverted reversal sell setup you would expect the stock to sell off down to or near the low of bar 1.

SUMMARY

Obviously you need to be aware of the "W/R day" and "reversal" setups before the market opens, and be ready to act quickly when the daily chart and market maker screen tell you it's "time to trade". Being aware that a stock's longer term trend is up can be important when you have a buy setup and vice versa. Also, keeping tabs on the daily and intraday trend of the NASDAQ market index helps. But these are trades you must act on quickly and decisively. The idea is to catch a good magnitude move at the earliest possible point and to get filled at the price you want.

CONCLUSION

The 1 to 3 day bar chart patterns are very powerful trades to be aware of. Entry timing and speed are critical. Reviewing a list of stocks that currently have these daily trade setups prepares you to react to the market using the highest probability trading patterns. Since they are mostly early morning trades, look to the daily chart and then market maker screen for market entry. The intraday 5 minute bar screen may also be useful this early in the trading day (especially if you are looking for consolidation during the end of the prior day to confirm your trade).

How far will a stock move in price once you've entered the market on one of these trade setups (or one of the intraday trade setups from the last section)? This is an important question. Using daily support and resistance areas, trendlines, trend channels, and some other common-sense analysis, you can get some idea of how far price might go before the close of the day. Probably the most significant reason to know this is to keep you out of some apparent "good trade entry setups" that don't have much room to move.

Some actual daily chart examples follow to show the 1 - 3 daily bar setups and how they appear in actual trading.

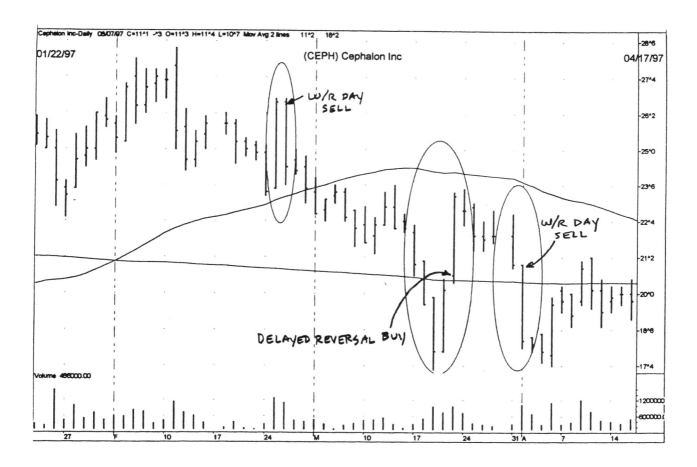

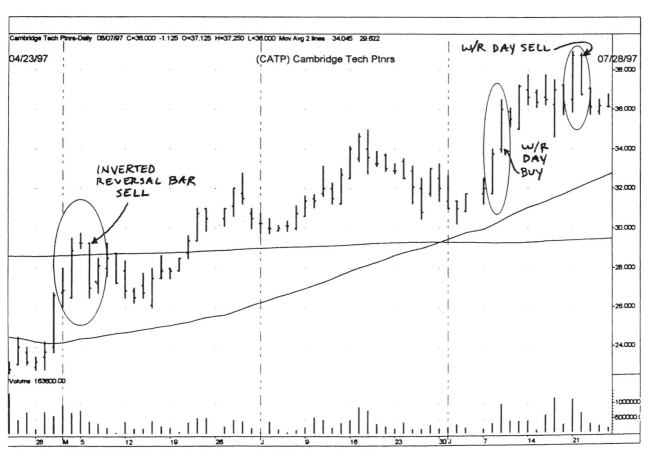

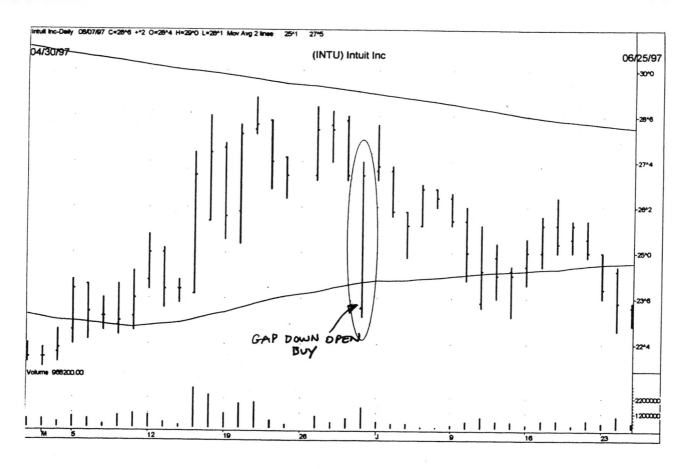

Intuit Inc-Daily 06/07/97 C=26^6 +^2 O=26^4 H=29^0 L=26^1 Mov Avg 2 lines   25^1   27^5

04/30/97   (INTU) Intuit Inc   06/25/97

GAP DOWN OPEN
BUY

Volume 966200.00

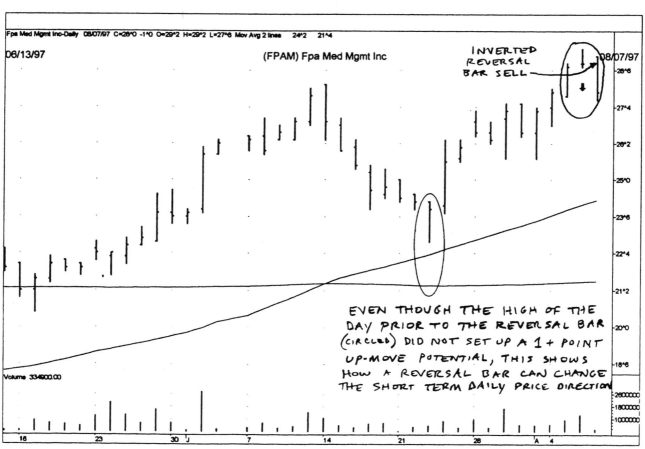

Fpa Med Mgmt Inc-Daily 08/07/97 C=26^0 -1^0 O=29^2 H=29^2 L=27^6 Mov Avg 2 lines   24^2   21^4

06/13/97   (FPAM) Fpa Med Mgmt Inc   08/07/97

INVERTED
REVERSAL
BAR SELL

EVEN THOUGH THE HIGH OF THE
DAY PRIOR TO THE REVERSAL BAR
(CIRCLED) DID NOT SET UP A 1 + POINT
UP-MOVE POTENTIAL, THIS SHOWS
HOW A REVERSAL BAR CAN CHANGE
THE SHORT TERM DAILY PRICE DIRECTION

Volume 334900.00

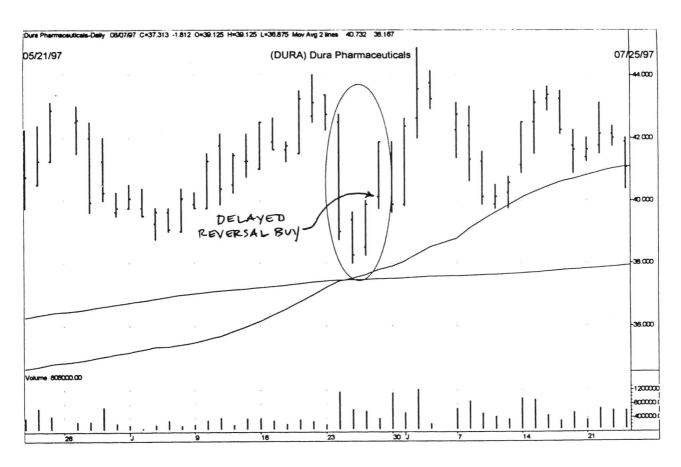

Dura Pharmaceuticals-Daily 08/07/97 C=37.313 -1.812 O=39.125 H=39.125 L=36.875 Mov Avg 2 lines 40.732 38.167

05/21/97   (DURA) Dura Pharmaceuticals   07/25/97

DELAYED
REVERSAL BUY

Volume 808000.00

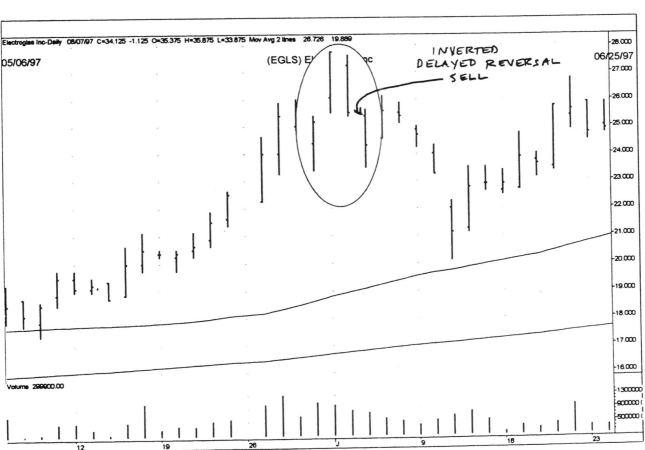

Electroglas Inc-Daily 08/07/97 C=34.125 -1.125 O=35.375 H=35.875 L=33.875 Mov Avg 2 lines 26.726 19.889

05/06/97   (EGLS) E_____c   06/25/97

INVERTED
DELAYED REVERSAL
SELL

Volume 299900.00

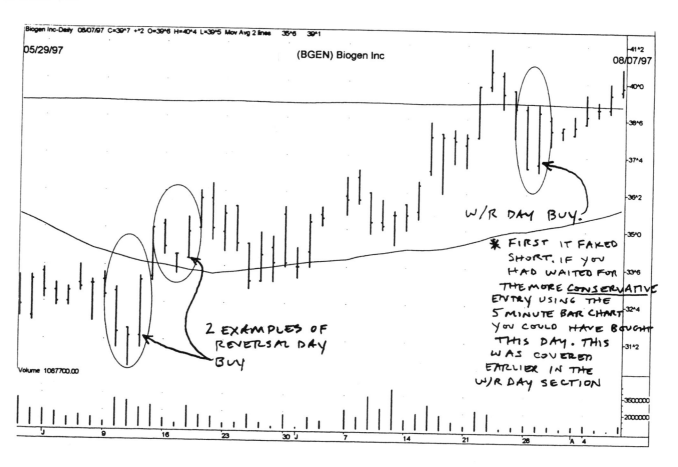

Biogen Inc-Daily 08/07/97 C=39^7 +^2 O=39^6 H=40^4 L=39^5 Mov Avg 2 lines 35^6 39^1

05/29/97   (BGEN) Biogen Inc   08/07/97

W/R DAY BUY.

✱ FIRST IT FAKED SHORT. IF YOU HAD WAITED FOR THE MORE <u>CONSERVATIVE</u> ENTRY USING THE 5 MINUTE BAR CHART YOU COULD HAVE BOUGHT THIS DAY. THIS WAS COVERED EARLIER IN THE W/R DAY SECTION

2 EXAMPLES OF REVERSAL DAY BUY

Volume 1087700.00

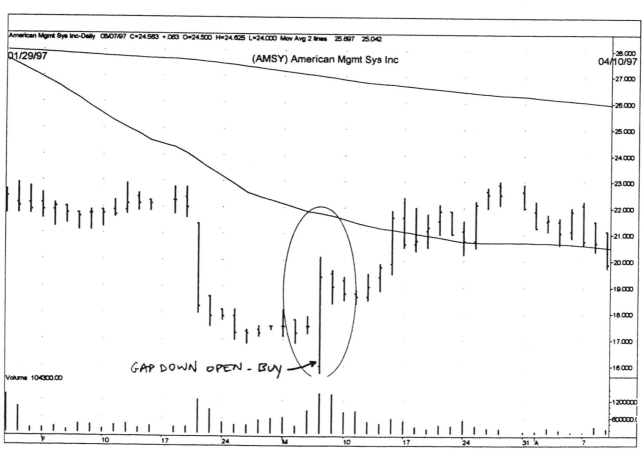

American Mgmt Sys Inc-Daily 08/07/97 C=24.563 +.063 O=24.500 H=24.625 L=24.000 Mov Avg 2 lines 25.697 25.042

01/29/97   (AMSY) American Mgmt Sys Inc   04/10/97

GAP DOWN OPEN - BUY

Volume 104300.00

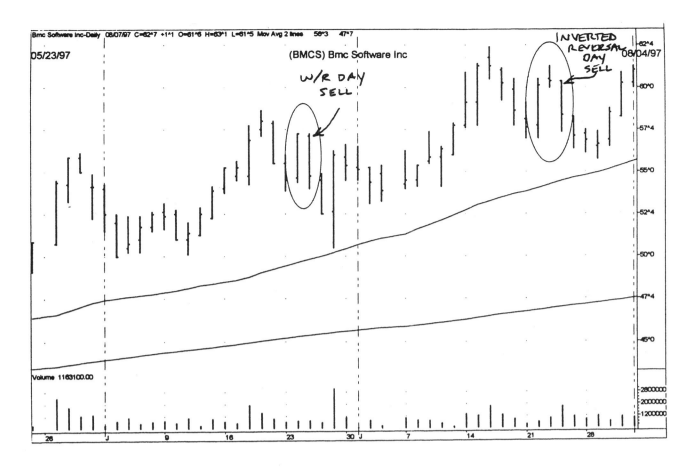

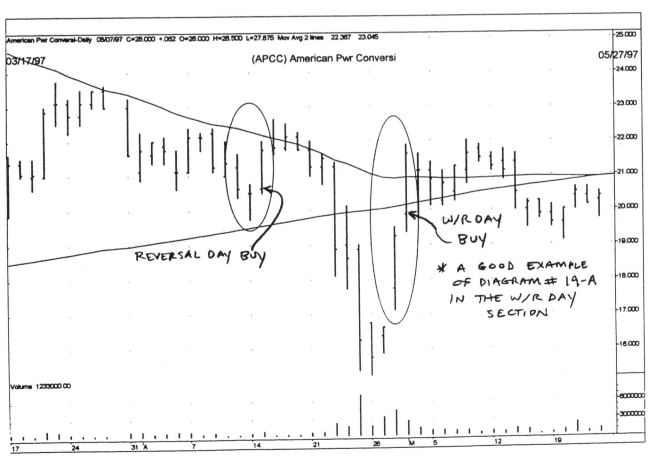

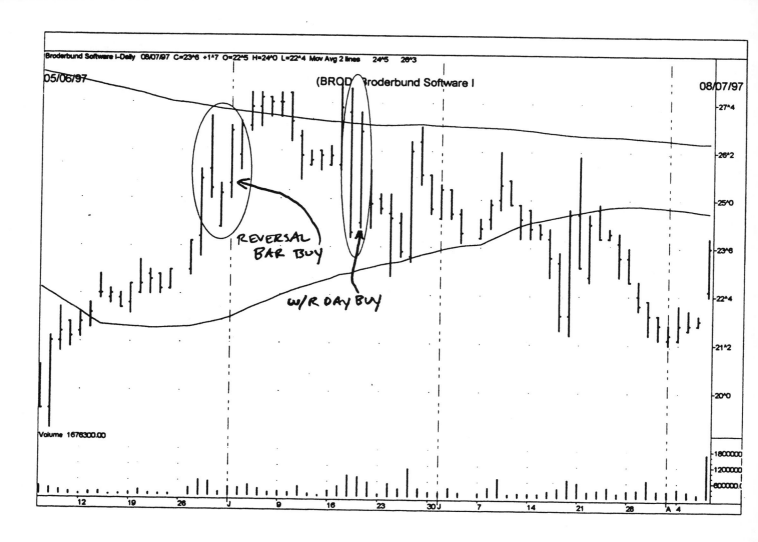

LONGER TERM DAILY BAR PATTERNS
(for day trading)

INTRODUCTION:

Most of these price formations take more than just a few days to form up on the historical daily bar chart. They usually reflect price consolidation or a narrowing of daily price range. Many times these patterns will be followed by a day that breaks out strongly in one direction or the other. When you see one of these formations developing, catalog that stock in the back of your mind. If the day comes when price does make the breakout move, you'll be there for a potential day trade. Using intraday price patterns in conjunction with this longer time frame can increase your odds for a good trade entry. Trading in the direction of the stock's trend and the overall market trend (daily and intraday) enhances the success of these trades.

WEDGE

A wedge is a contraction in a stock's daily range. Each day will typically have a narrower range as it completes a shape that looks like a "wedge". This compression in price over the course of several days to a couple of weeks may be followed by a strong breakout day. A wedge will look similar to this:

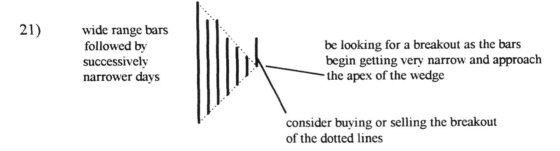

21) wide range bars followed by successively narrower days

be looking for a breakout as the bars begin getting very narrow and approach the apex of the wedge

consider buying or selling the breakout of the dotted lines

A wedge does not have to be exactly symmetrical. It may be tilted to one side or the other. For example:

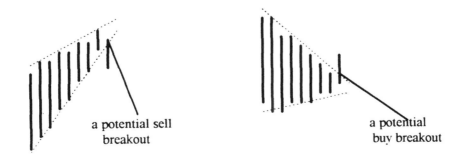

a potential sell breakout

a potential buy breakout

FLAG

The flag is similar to the wedge in that it is a consolidation pattern. Usually a flag forms after a strong run up or down in a stock. After this strong movement which can last several days, the stock takes a breather and may tend to trade sideways. This is where a flag will often form on the daily chart. It should look something like this:

22)

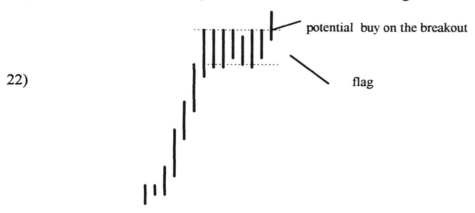

The flag will usually have a relatively tight formation and smaller daily trading ranges. Typically a strong breakout will occur in the direction of the earlier trend. This is especially important if the flag forms at or near a recent or long term high for the stock. The upper boundary of the flag serves as price resistance, and the lower boundary is support. A price breakout in either direction may be a good trade entry, especially when paired with analysis from the 1 to 3 day bar, and/or intraday trade setups(consolidation).

CONSOLIDATION OF DAILY HIGHS OR LOWS

If you have 3 - 5 + daily highs or lows clustered together at the same price (daily consolidation) then you have the potential for a breakout day trade. Here is how it might look for a buy setup:

23)

Be ready for a breakout to the long side for a strong intraday run up in price. The inverse pattern works for the downside sell setup. These often make for some very strong day trade moves.

NEW HIGHS / LOWS

New highs and lows are important to watch for. This is signifying strength or weakness in a stock. The most significant are all time highs and 52 week highs or lows. If you find a stock that is trading very near one of these areas (especially if you have several daily bars of consolidation), be ready for a day that may break through and run. Also, shorter term (6 to 8 week) new highs or lows can provide a substantial day trade or swing trade (several day) opportunity. These stocks may be traded on the actual day of the breakout or on the following day(s). Again, look at the 1 to 3 bar and intraday setups to determine when and where to enter. The reason these work is that price is breaking through a significant and natural price support or resistance area. Other traders and fund managers also monitor and trade these longer term breakouts. This adds extra follow through and offers opportunities for day trading.

One variation on the new high or low setup tends to be an especially strong pattern. When a stock first breaks out to a new high of the past several months, sometimes it will pull back slightly and trade sideways from several days to a week or two. Often you will see a consolidation type of pattern as it is preparing to challenge the new high again. On the day the stock breaks out to penetrate the prior high, you will usually see very heavy buying come into the stock that may drive it up several points. If today appears to be the day of the breakout, rely on your daily and intraday setups to enter the trade.

SUMMARY:

The longer term daily chart patterns help you to recognize consolidation patterns that lead to good breakout day trades. Also recognizing when you are in sideways price congestion will keep you from trading a stock while it is choppy and less predictable. Don't use these setups to blindly fire off a trade. Rather, use them to alert you to monitor the stock for a price breakout and thus a high probability trade. At that point go to your 1 to 3 day and intraday analysis to time your entry. Trading with the trend in these instances increases your odds of success. Be aware of the overall market indexes; you'll want them on your side as well.

CONCLUSION:

You've seen how to recognize and anticipate high probability trading patterns in several time frames. Putting them all together only increases the odds of a successful trade. Trading with the stock's trend and with the market direction (both daily and intraday) only enhances your win rate. Time your entry with the momentum on the market maker screen, and enter the market at the price you want. But remember, it is better to miss a good trade than to get a poor fill and subsequently lose $$$$. There will always be another good trade setup, so wait for it and take only the best trades.

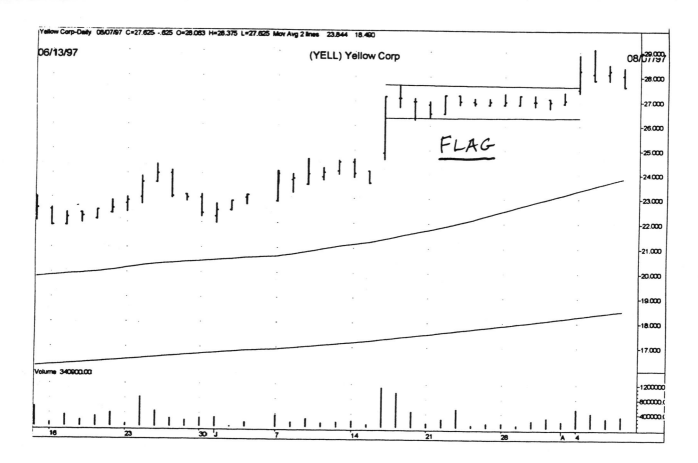

06/13/97   (YELL) Yellow Corp   08/07/97

FLAG

Volume 340900.00

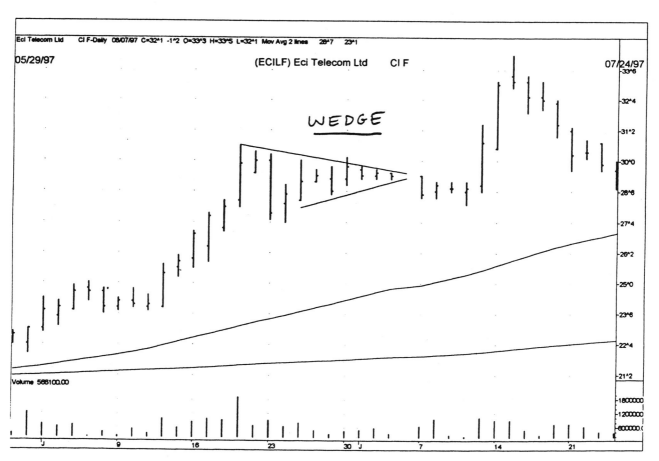

05/29/97   (ECILF) Eci Telecom Ltd   Cl F   07/24/97

WEDGE

Volume 565100.00

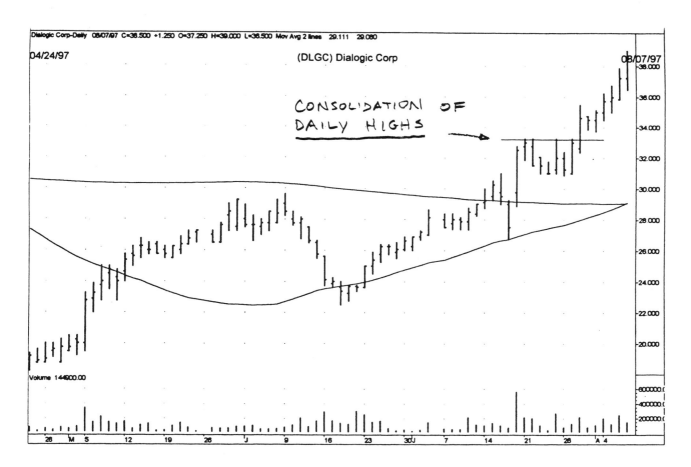

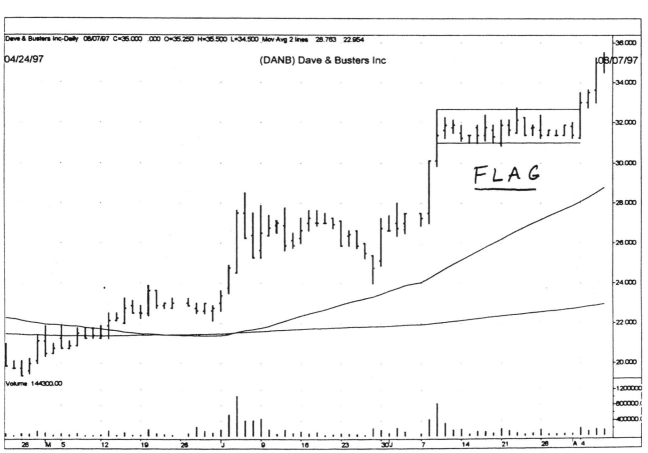

SUPPORT AND RESISTANCE
(S/R)

SUPPORT AND RESISTANCE

Know where the price support and resistance areas are on a chart. These are areas that have halted the movement of the stock in the past. The more times a particular price has stalled the stock's movement, the stronger that support or resistance area becomes. Price support lines can be drawn horizontally through lows on a bar chart where price tended to bounce up. Thus this price level is "supporting" the stock. Price resistance lines can be drawn horizontally through highs on a chart which the stock resists moving up through. Very often you will find that a support area which the stock penetrates to the downside will become a resistance area in the future. And likewise, a resistance area that a stock finally penetrates to the upside becomes a support area in the future.

The daily chart's support and resistance areas will help you better decide whether a trade setup is worth entering. If there is a lot of resistance just above where you would buy the stock, then you may want to pass up the trade. On the other hand, if a price resistance area is being broken or has recently been broken through to the upside, a buy trade setup has a better chance of success with the stock moving up further. Look for these areas on the daily and intraday charts to find the nearest upside resistance level up if you are buying or the next support level down if you are selling. If there is enough room for a 1+ point move, you have enhanced the odds for a successful day trade. Also, if the daily chart shows good support at a price level, and you have a "wide range bar w/extreme close" or a "reversal bar" setup long that held at a price support area, then this might present a strong buying opportunity. Remember not to impose your ideas on the market, but instead react to what it tells you with the daily and intraday setup patterns. The S/R levels will help you find the best trades to enter.

"Trading congestion" is something to stay away from. If a stock is not trending, has narrow range daily bars (from high to low), or is just chopping sideways, then avoid it. Wait until it breaks out of congestion and begins some good daily price swing activity. This is when you look for the trade setups to act upon. Also, look at the recent average range of a daily price bar (from high to low). If that stock doesn't trade over a point or more on a regular basis then you probably won't want to trade it. Look for the bigger profit opportunities with stocks that are currently in a "trader-friendly" mode.

You'll also notice that many times the 50 and 200 day moving averages act as price support and resistance. This is because many fund managers monitor these averages and use them in their buying and selling decisions. Being aware of where these lines are can aid your analysis. This is especially true if a stock has traded up or down to one of these averages at a point which also coincides with a price support or resistance level.

Support and resistance levels aid your decision making for day trades. They show <u>how far a stock can be expected to move</u> up or down on both an intraday and daily time frame. This is the final step (or filter) to confirm a potential trade, or to rule it out.

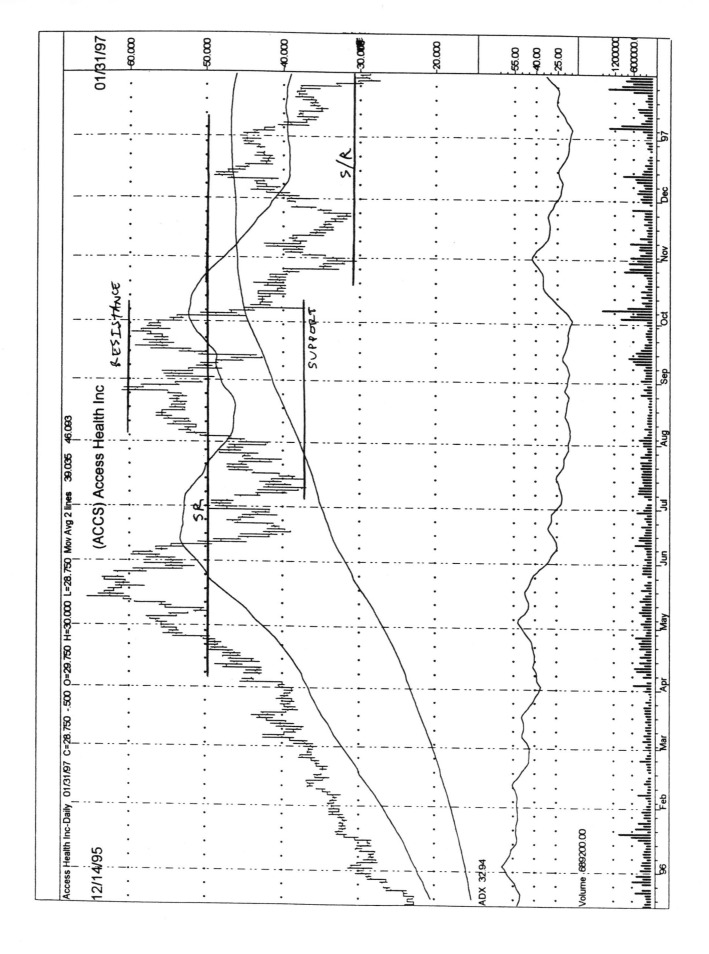

Access Health Inc-Daily 01/31/97 C=28.750 -.500 O=29.750 H=30.000 L=28.750 Mov Avg 2 lines 39.035 46.093

(ACCS) Access Health Inc

12/14/95

01/31/97

RESISTANCE

SUPPORT

S R

S/R

ADX 32.94

Volume 689200.00

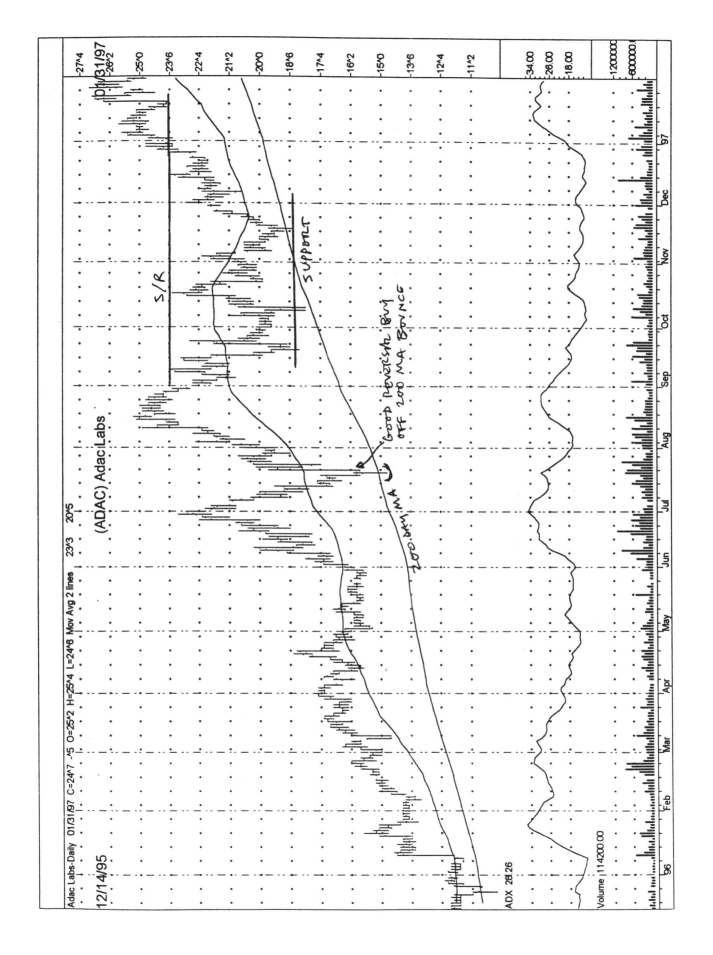

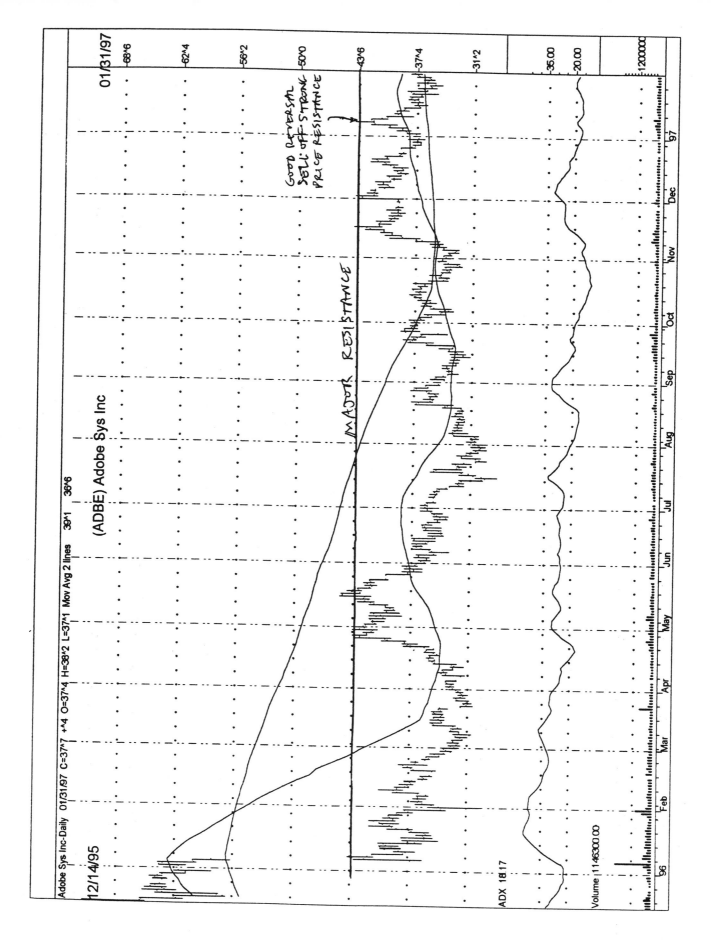

Adobe Sys Inc-Daily 01/31/97 C=37^7 +^4 O=37^4 H=38^2 L=37^1 Mov Avg 2 lines 39^1 36^6

(ADBE) Adobe Sys Inc

12/14/95

01/31/97

68^6
62^4
56^2
50^0
43^6
37^4
31^2

35.00
20.00

ADX 18.17

Volume 11146300.00

120000

96 Feb Mar Apr May Jun Jul Aug Sep Oct Nov Dec 97

MAJOR RESISTANCE

GOOD REVERSAL
SELL OFF STRONG
PRICE RESISTANCE

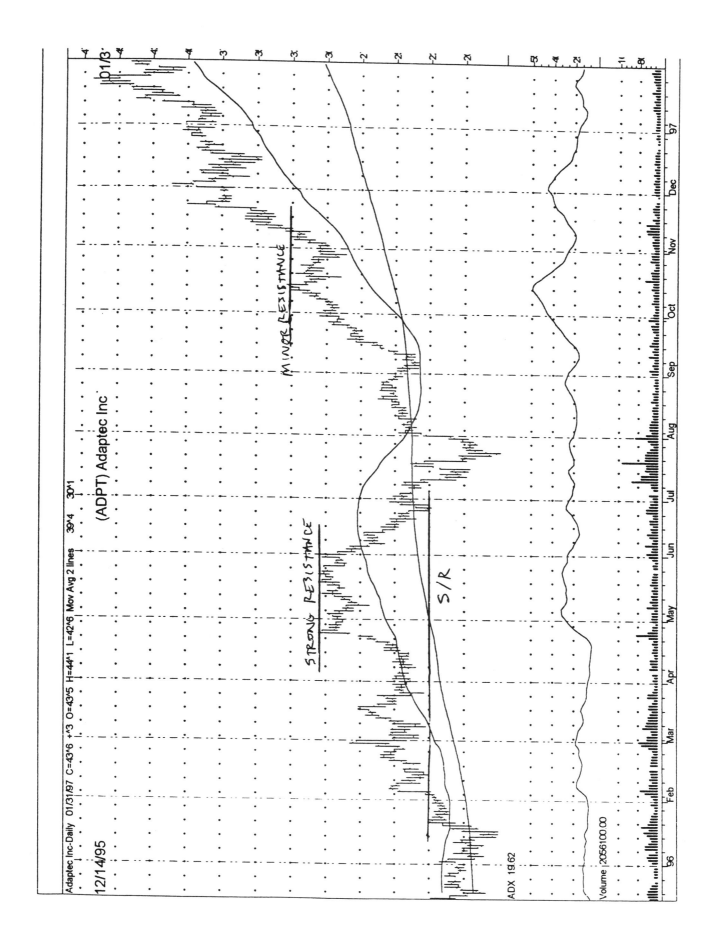

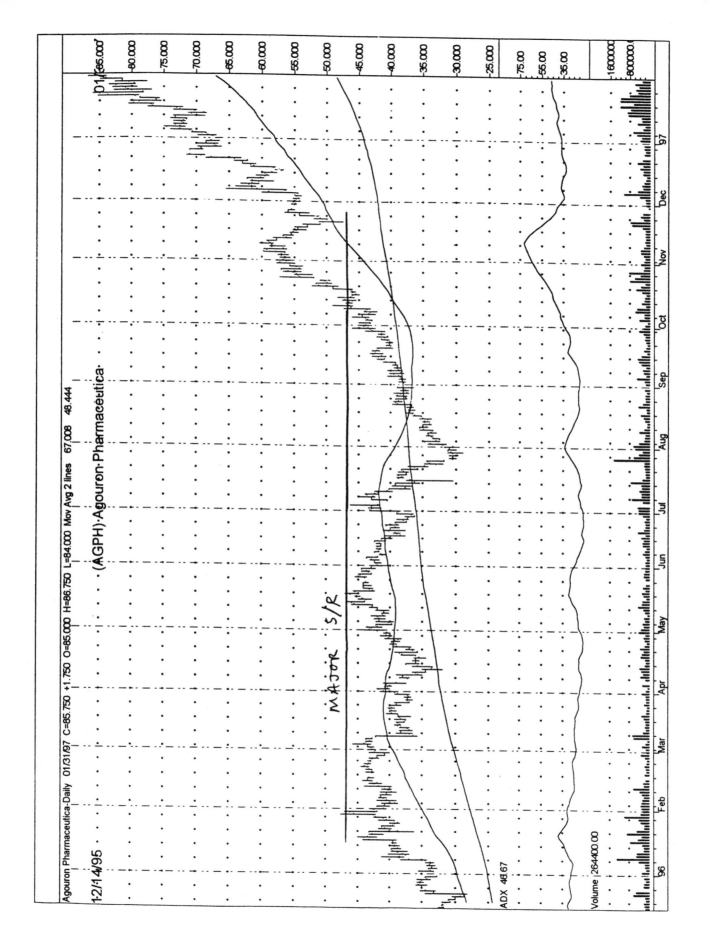

Agouron Pharmaceutica-Daily 01/31/97 C=85.750 +1.750 O=85.000 H=86.750 L=84.000 Mov Avg 2 lines 67.008 48.444

(AGPH) Agouron Pharmaceutica

12/14/95

MAJOR S/R

ADX 46.67

Volume 264400.00

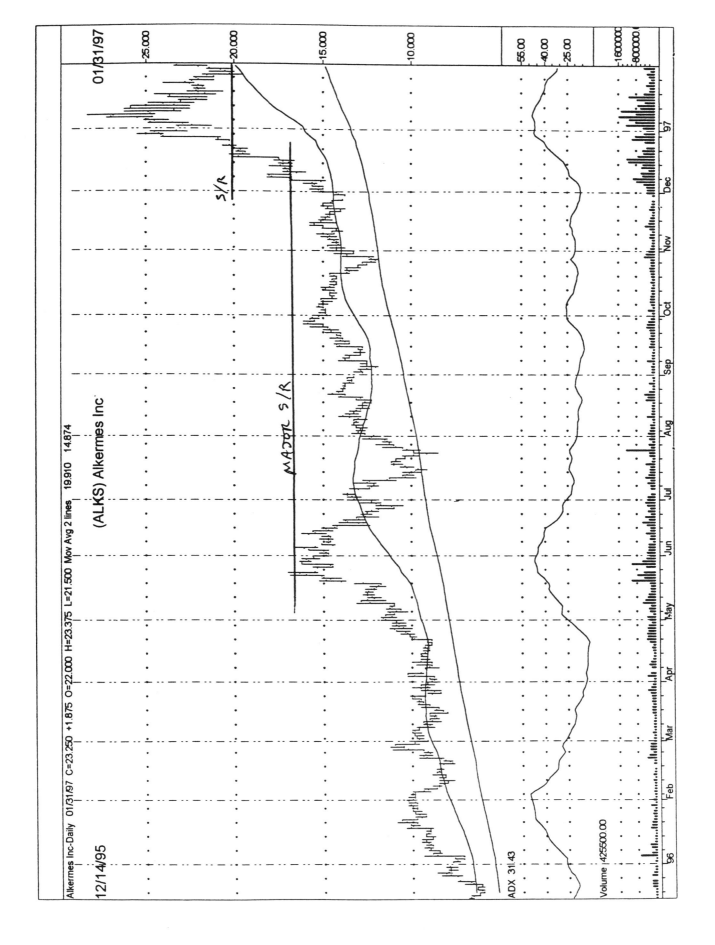

Alkermes Inc-Daily   01/31/97   C=23.250   +1.875   O=22.000   H=23.375   L=21.500   Mov Avg 2 lines   19.910   14.874

(ALKS) Alkermes Inc

12/14/95

01/31/97

S/R

MAJOR S/R

ADX 31.43

Volume 425500.00

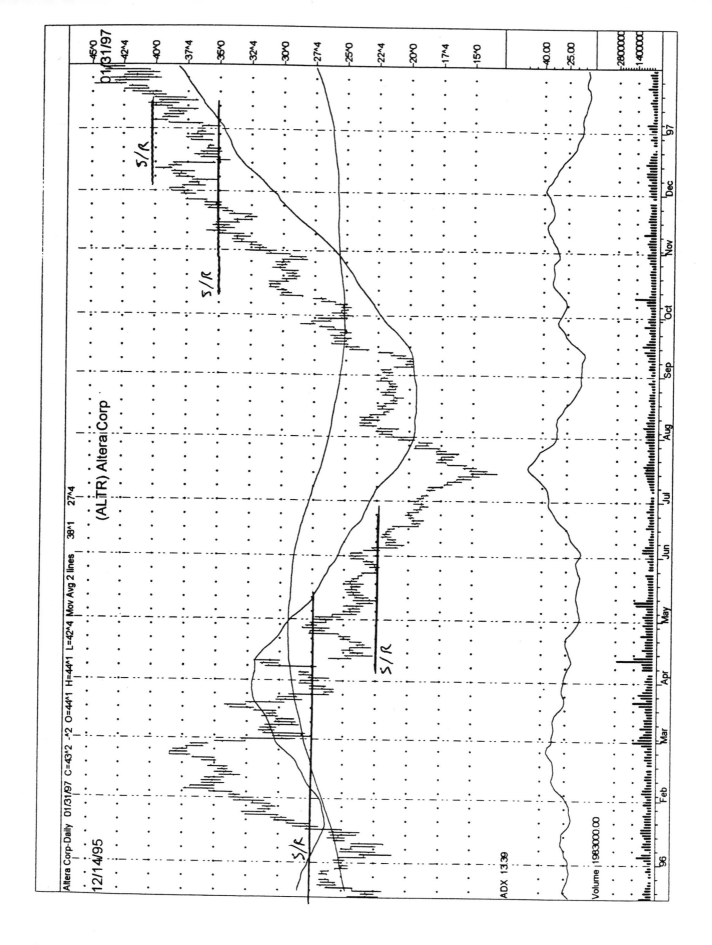

Altera Corp-Daily 01/31/97 C=43^2 .^2 O=44^1 H=44^1 L=42^4 Mov Avg 2 lines 38^1 27^4

(ALTR) Altera Corp

12/14/95

ADX 13.39

Volume 19830000.00

01/31/97

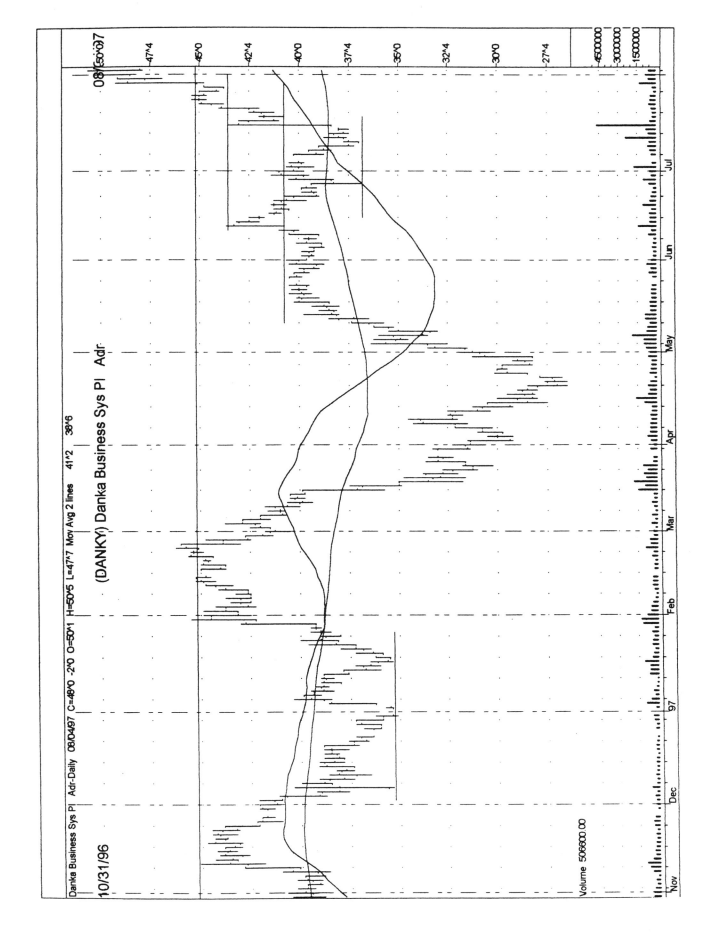

Danka Business Sys Pl   Adr-Daily   08/04/97   C=48^0 -2^0 O=50^1   H=50^5   L=47^7   Mov Avg 2 lines   41^2   38^6

(DANKY) Danka Business Sys Pl   Adr

10/31/96

Volume 506600.00

MARKET MAKER
T.O.S.
AND
TICKER SCREENS

MARKET MAKER AND T.O.S. SCREENS

INTRODUCTION:

This section describes the "market maker" and "time of sale" (T.O.S.) screens as well as the stock "ticker" screen. The market maker screen will help with 2 things:

1) To determine which stocks you are willing to trade, and therefore which stocks you want as part of the ticker of stocks that you follow

2) To aid in timing the best moment for entering and exiting trades that are described in the 5 minute and daily bar chart setups.

The time of sale (T.O.S.) screen is used in conjunction with the market maker screen for timing trade entry and exit.

The "ticker" is the screen loaded with the stocks you have chosen to follow. This is the screen that immediately shows if a market maker has changed his bid up or down for one of your stocks as well as when the inside bid or offer has changed and whether it was up or down in price.

You will have your market maker, T.O.S., daily chart and 5 minute chart screens all linked together so that when you type in a stock symbol, all of this information for that particular stock immediately pops up on your computer monitor. By watching the ticker scroll along, you are immediately alerted to a stock's uptick or downtick (usually color coded) and can then quickly type in the stock symbol to access the market maker, T.O.S, daily and 5 minute bar information. These are the 4 screens that are used in conjunction to find the price pattern setups and to time your trade entry and exits.

MARKET MAKER SCREEN

This screen shows you the current "inside" bid and offer (or ask) price for a stock. It also shows you how many market makers are bidding and offering at each price level. You will see the other bid/offer price levels as well. The difference between the bid and ask price is known as the "spread". You will be looking for stocks that regularly have 1/8 spreads. Some 1/4 spread stocks may also be tradable. Also, you want the number of market makers at each price level to typically be 4 <u>or more</u>. The more "depth" per price level, the safer that stock is to trade. Avoid stocks with 1 - 3 market makers per price level. These thin price levels can quickly cost you much more than a 1/4 loss if you are wrong about the trade.

* Before entering a stock long or short ask yourself this question: "If the market immediately reverses against me when I enter the trade, what is my probable exit price?"

This means if you buy the inside ask on a stock to go long, look at the price and depth on the bid side to determine where you are likely to get filled if you have to exit the trade right away. If it is for more than 1/4 point (or in some cases 3/8) loss, then pass up that trade setup. Another one will come along later. Each stock has its own personality with how the market maker screen moves.

T.O.S. SCREEN

This screen shows actual trades, the time, the # of shares and the price. If you have a trade pattern setup, look at the T.O.S. screen flow of orders to see if they are being filled at the bid or at the ask. If you are set up for a trade to the long side, look for trades coming through at the inside ask price of the market maker screen to help you time your entry. Also, the inside price level of market makers will start to move up. This is especially true if you see 1000 lot trades coming through the T.O.S. screen. These are other computer day traders that are buying the stock and help assist the momentum into the upside move. The reverse scenario is true of a downside move.

Together the market maker and time of sale screens are fundamental to help you time your entries and exits for the best trade setups. Only actual experience will enable you to hone this ability. This is why "paper trading" is very important initially. But remember, the actual timing is learned when you begin "live" trading. This is why I recommend using only 500 share trades when you first start with real money. 500 shares cuts your "tuition" in half as you first learn the typical fill time and price for each stock under varying market circumstances. "Live" trading is very different from paper trading when it comes to actual entries and exits (and actual dollars won or lost).

Have the "big 4": the market maker, T.O.S., daily, and 5 minute screens viewed together on your computer monitor for each stock that you type into your keyboard. This will provide all of the information needed to execute and manage the best trades.

TICKER

This is the screen which contains your collection of stocks that scroll through with any bid or ask adjustments up or down by a market maker. It also shows when the inside bid or ask has changed. As mentioned earlier, your group of stocks are chosen based on several factors. Look for average volume of at least 100,000 shares per day. These stocks should have only 1/8 point (and occasionally 1/4) bid/ask spreads on the market maker screen. In addition, the market maker screen should typically have an average of at least 4+ market makers per price level. Also, consider the daily and 5 minute charts to see if the stock provides the daily and intraday price setups from this manual which regularly follow through with the setup's trade expectations. Look for stocks that often show good daily price range or movement on a regular basis. This means setups with an opportunity of a 1+ point move during the day.

Your ticker may contain as many stocks as you can reasonably follow. That may mean 60, 150, or 200+ stocks. Be aware that each stock does have its own price movement and market maker/T.O.S. screen personality. Be aware that each stock tends to cycle in and out of a "trader-friendly" mode. You can always add or delete stocks from your ticker to keep it updated.

SUMMARY

Tying together the daily and intraday price pattern setups with the learned timing of the market maker and T.O.S. screens are <u>essential</u> to your success. Leave one component out and you reduce your odds for even the best price pattern setups. Only through experience with your universe of stocks will you improve your bottom line. This is the art to trading.

CONCLUSION

Now that you have the price pattern setups paired with the timing principles in this section, you possess the fundamentals for day trading. The next few pages show market maker screens for both "good" stocks as well as higher risk stocks. These examples are labeled to help you get a better understanding of the basic elements that you are looking for in a tradable stock.

COST CURRENTLY HAS A 1/16 BID/ASK SPREAD 37 5/8 BY 37 11/16

T.D.S. SCREEN

COST					
Hi	37 13/16	Lo 37 5/8	+5/8	down	Vl 2222800
Bid →	37 5/8	Ask 37 11/16	Hst Cl 37 1/16		

Bid	Price	Size		Ask	Price	Size
DLJP	37 5/8 INSIDE BID	10		GSCO	37 11/16 INSIDE	10
INCA	37 5/8	1		INCA	37 11/16 ASK	50
SHWD	37 9/16	10		MLCO	37 3/4	10
LEGG	37 1/2	10		HRZG	37 3/4	10
PWJC	37 1/2	10		NITE	37 3/4	4
WBLR	37 1/2	10		WEED	37 13/16	10
NFSC	37 1/2	5		SALB	37 7/8	10
DEAN	37 1/2	10		FBCO	37 7/8	10
TSCO	37 1/2	10		CHGO	37 7/8	10
OPCO	37 1/2	10		ABSB	37 7/8	10
RAGN	37 1/2	10		MSCO	37 7/8	10
HRZG	37 1/2	10		DAIN	37 7/8	10
NITE	37 1/2	10		SELZ	37 7/8	10
SALB	37 3/8	10		BEST	37 7/8	10
FBCO	37 3/8	10		JEFF	37 7/8	10
ABSB	37 3/8	10		PWJC	37 7/8	10
MSCO	37 3/8	10		SHWD	37 7/8	10
PRUS	37 3/8	10		MASH	37 7/8	10
DAIN	37 3/8	10		PIPR	37 7/8	10
SELZ	37 3/8	10		SWCO	37 7/8	10
BEST	37 3/8	10		MADF	37 7/8	3
JEFF	37 3/8	10		OLDE	38	10
PACS	37 3/8	10		UBSS	38	10
PERT	37 3/8	10		DMGL	38	10

TYPICALLY GOOD "DEPTH" TO PRICE LEVELS

1/8 DIFFERENCE BETWEEN PRICE LEVELS

COST

Time	Price	# of shares
13:34	37 11/16	100
13:33	37 11/16	1400
13:33	37 11/16	100
13:32	37 5/8	300
13:30	37 11/16	100
13:29	37 5/8	200
13:28	37 11/16	100
13:26	37 11/16	300
13:24	37 11/16	1000
13:23	37 11/16	100
13:23	37 11/16	1000
13:21	37 11/16	100
13:20	37 5/8	600
13:17	37 11/16	500
13:16	37 11/16	300
13:15	37 11/16	400
13:12	37 5/8	1000
13:12	37 5/8	500
13:12	37 5/8	1000
13:11	37 5/8	1000
13:11	37 5/8	1000
13:11	37 5/8	1000
13:11	37 5/8	200
13:11	37 5/8	2000
13:11	37 3/4	200
13:11	37 3/4	200
13:10	37 3/4	75000
13:09	37 5/8	1000
13:09	37 11/16	1500
13:08	37 5/8	1000
13:08	37 11/16	400
13:08	37 11/16	500

TIME PRICE # OF SHARES (ACTUAL TRADES)

IF YOU HAD A BUY SETUP, YOU WOULD LIKELY GET FILLED AT 37 11/16 OR 37 3/4. IF THE TRADE IMMEDIATELY WENT AGAINST YOU, YOU WOULD PROBABLY NOT GET FILLED ON YOUR SELL AT 37 5/8 ON 37 9/16. YOU WOULD LIKELY GET 37 1/2 FOR A 1/4 LOSS ASSUMING YOU BOUGHT AT 37 3/4. THIS IS AN EXAMPLE OF A STOCK THAT CURRENTLY HAS A GOOD, SAFE MARKET MAKER SCREEN.

QNTM HAS A 1/8 BID/ASK SPREAD

35 5/8 BY 35 3/4

QNTM

Hi	35 11/16	Lo	+3/16	down
	36 1/2	35 5/16	35 5/16	VI 3417800
Bid	35 5/8	Ask	35 3/4	Hst Cl 35 1/2

		Bid	Size			Ask	Size
O	MSCO	35 5/8	10	O	GSCO	35 3/4	10
O	MONT	35 5/8	10	O	DEAN	35 3/4	20
O	PWJC	35 5/8	7	O	JPMS	35 3/4	10
O	PERT	35 5/8	13	O	SELZ	35 3/4	10
O	OLDE	35 5/8	10	O	JEFF	35 3/4	10
O	PRUS	35 1/2	10	O	GRUN	35 3/4	10
O	SALB	35 1/2	10	O	TSCO	35 3/4	30
O	FBCO	35 1/2	10	O	MADF	35 13/16	3
O	NITE	35 1/2	1	O	RSSF	35 7/8	10
O	DEAN	35 1/2	1	O	DLJP	35 7/8	10
O	SBSH	35 1/2	2	O	BEST	35 7/8	10
O	MADF	35 1/2	13	O	MLCO	35 7/8	10
O	SNDV	35 1/2	10	O	JBOC	35 7/8	20
O	MASH	35 1/2	10	O	HMQT	35 7/8	10
O	INCA	35 1/2	3	O	NITE	35 7/8	8
O	LLCO	35 7/16	3	O	SBSH	35 7/8	2
O	HRZG	35 7/16	10	O	LEHM	35 7/8	10
O	RSSF	35 3/8	10	O	CANT	35 7/8	10
O	RPSC	35 3/8	10	O	MASH	35 7/8	10
O	NAWE	35 3/8	10	O	INCA	35 7/8	20
O	SHRP	35 3/8	5	O	ISLD	35 7/8	13
O	SHWD	35 3/8	2	O	NFSC	35 15/16	4
O	CHGO	35 3/8	10	O	PRUS	36	10
O	NFSC	35 3/8	10	O	GVRC	36	10

GOOD DEPTH @ PRICE LEVELS

QNTM

Time	Price	Size
13:38	35 11/16	1000
13:38	35 3/4	100
13:38	35 11/16	500
13:37	35 3/4	100
13:37	35 3/4	100
13:37	35 11/16	1000
13:37	35 11/16	600
13:37	35 11/16	100
13:36	35 11/16	400
13:36	35 3/4	100
13:36	35 11/16	100
13:36	35 11/16	400
13:36	35 11/16	500
13:35	35 11/16	500
13:35	35 7/8	13000
13:35	35 11/16	3200
13:34	35 5/8	200
13:34	35 5/8	200
13:34	35 3/4	1000
13:34	35 3/4	1000
13:33	35 3/4	100
13:33	35 11/16	1000
13:31	35 5/8	200
13:30	35 11/16	2800
13:30	35 5/8	1000
13:30	35 5/8	1000
13:30	35 5/8	1000
13:30	35 5/8	300
13:30	35 11/16	100
13:30	35 5/8	500
13:30	35 5/8	100
13:30	35 11/16	600
13:29	35 5/8	3000
13:29	35 3/4	300

IF YOU BOUGHT AT 35 3/4 YOU COULD EASILY EXIT AT 35 1/2.

IF YOU SOLD AT 35 5/8 YOU COULD EASILY EXIT AT 35 7/8.

THIS ALLOWS YOU TO STAY WITHIN THE BOUNDARIES OF AN INITIAL 1/4 STOPP-LOSS.

DIGI CURRENTLY HAS A 1/16 BID/ASK SPREAD 28 1/4 BY 28 5/16

DIGI					
Hi	28 5/16	Lo	-15/16	down	Vl 1417800
Bid ↓	28 1/4	Ask	28 5/16		Hst Cl 29 1/4

	MM	Bid	Size		MM	Ask	Size
O	SBSH	28 1/4	10	O	INCA	28 5/16	10
O	RSSF	28 1/4	10	O	NITE	28 3/8	10
O	FBCO	28 1/4	10	O	MLCO	28 3/8	10
O	COWN	28 1/4	10	O	ISLD	28 3/8	10
O	OLDE	28 1/4	5	O	MASH	28 7/16	10
O	SALB	28 1/4	10	O	MSCO	28 1/2	10
O	DLJP	28 1/4	10	O	PWJC	28 1/2	10
O	HRZG	28 1/4	12	O	JPMS	28 1/2	10
O	MASH	28 1/4	10	O	PRUS	28 1/2	10
O	INCA	28 1/4	20	O	HRZG	28 1/2	5
O	MADF	28 1/4	4	O	SNDV	28 9/16	10
O	MONT	28 3/16	10	O	CHGO	28 5/8	10
O	BTRD	28 3/16	8	O	OPCO	28 5/8	10
O	GKMC	28 1/8	10	O	WEAT	28 5/8	10
O	COST	28 1/8	10	O	LEHM	28 5/8	10
O	CANT	28 1/8	10	O	JEFF	28 5/8	10
O	RPSC	28 1/8	10	O	NAWE	28 5/8	10
O	CHGO	28 1/8	10	O	UBSS	28 5/8	10
O	BEST	28 1/8	10	O	TSCO	28 5/8	10
O	RHCO	28 1/8	10	O	MONT	28 11/16	10
O	LEHM	28 1/8	10	O	BTRD	28 11/16	2
O	JEFF	28 1/8	10	O	MWSE	28 11/16	1
O	LEGG	28 1/8	10	O	MADF	28 11/16	10
O	DEAN	28 1/8	10	O	GKMC	28 3/4	10

DIGI

Time	Price	Size
13:36	28 5/16	500
13:33	28 1/4	100
13:33	28 1/4	4000
13:33	28 1/4	1000
13:33	28 1/4	300
13:32	28 1/4	100
13:32	28 1/4	900
13:32	28 1/4	1000
13:31	28 1/4	100
13:31	28 1/4	100
13:30	28 1/4	500
13:30	28 1/4	500
13:30	28 5/16	200
13:30	28 5/16	800
13:28	28 09/32	3000
13:27	28 3/8	25000
13:27	28 5/16	600
13:26	28 5/16	100
13:22	28 5/16	2500
13:21	28 5/16	6000
13:20	28 5/16	7500
13:20	28 5/16	7500
13:20	28 3/8	1000
13:20	28 5/16	400
13:20	28 5/16	10800
13:19	28 5/16	300
13:19	28 5/16	300
13:19	28 5/16	300
13:19	28 5/16	400
13:19	28 3/8	1000
13:15	28 3/8	200
13:15	28 5/16	2500
13:14	28 3/8	1000
13:14	28 3/8	2000

THIS IS ANOTHER EXAMPLE OF GOOD DEPTH OF PRICE LEVELS AND ONLY 1/8 OR 1/16 DIFFERENCE BETWEEN EACH LEVEL. VERY SAFE TO TRADE. WITHOUT RISKING MORE THAN YOUR INITIAL 1/4 STOP-LOSS

CURRENTLY 1/8 BID/ASK SPREAD

28 BY 28 1/8

1000 SHARE LOTS ARE TYPICALLY OTHER DAY TRADERS.

WANT TO SEE IF THEY ARE COMING THROUGH AT THE CURRENT INSIDE BID OR INSIDE ASK.

THE BID WOULD BE SELLS

THE ASK WOULD BE BUYS

1/8 OR 1/16 DIFFERENCE BETWEEN LEVELS IS GOOD DEPTH TO EACH PRICE LEVEL

ANOTHER EXAMPLE OF A SAFE MARKET MAKER SCREEN

APCC	28	Lo	+1/16	up	Vl 975400			
Hi	28 1/2		27 7/8					
Bid ↑ 28		Ask 28 1/8		Hst Cl 27 15/16				

MM	Bid	Size		MM	Ask	Size
INCA	28	10		SHWD	28 1/8	10
SBSH	27 15/16	10		LEHM	28 1/8	10
NFSC	27 7/8	10		MSCO	28 1/8	10
PRUS	27 7/8	10		JPMS	28 1/8	10
BEST	27 7/8	10		JEFF	28 1/8	10
ADVS	27 7/8	10		NITE	28 1/4	10
OLDE	27 7/8	10		FACT	28 1/4	10
MASH	27 7/8	2		HRZG	28 1/4	10
MLCO	27 7/8	10		DEAN	28 1/4	10
CANT	27 3/4	10		NAWE	28 1/4	10
PWJC	27 3/4	8		INCA	28 1/4	100
FACT	27 3/4	10		WEED	28 1/4	10
HRZG	27 3/4	10		SBSH	28 3/8	10
TUCK	27 3/4	10		TSCO	28 3/8	10
JBOC	27 3/4	10		MASH	28 3/8	10
WEED	27 3/4	10		BARR	28 3/8	10
NITE	27 5/8	10		TUCK	28 3/8	10
CHGO	27 5/8	10		JBOC	28 3/8	10
MADF	27 5/8	10		MLCO	28 3/8	10
LEHM	27 5/8	10		NFSC	28 1/2	10
MSCO	27 5/8	10		PWJC	28 1/2	11
TSCO	27 5/8	10		ADVS	28 1/2	10
NAWE	27 5/8	10		CHGO	28 1/2	10
JEFF	27 5/8	10		MADF	28 1/2	17

APCC

Time	Price	Size
13:33	28	600
13:33	28	500
13:32	27 15/16	1000
13:32	27 15/16	3000
13:32	27 15/16	2000
13:32	27 15/16	3000
13:32	28	1000
13:32	28	1000
13:32	28	1000
13:32	28	1000
13:32	28	400
13:32	28	700
13:32	28	800
13:32	28	200
13:31	28	400
13:31	28 1/8	1000
13:31	28 1/8	1000
13:31	28 1/8	1000
13:31	28 1/8	1000
13:31	28 1/8	1000
13:30	28 3/16	200
13:30	28 3/16	300
13:29	28 3/16	100
13:27	28 3/16	200
13:26	28 3/16	200
13:25	28 3/16	100
13:23	28 3/16	500
13:22	28 1/4	100
13:19	28 1/4	200
13:19	28 3/16	133000
13:19	28 3/16	133000
13:19	28 3/16	300

105

CURRENTLY 1/8 BID/ASK SPREAD
47 5/8 BY 47 3/4

IF THE 1 MARKET MAKER AT 47 5/8 BID MOVES AWAY,
- BUT -
THEN IT IS 1/4 SPREAD. YOU HAVE TO BE EFFECTIVE
AT TIMING YOUR ENTRY AND EXIT.

GOOD
1/8 TO 1/16
PRICE LEVELS
WITH DEPTH

ADPT montage:

ADPT						
Hi	48 5/8	Lo 47 3/8	+1/4	47 3/8	down	Vl 749300
Bid	↓47 5/8	Ask 47 3/4			Hst Cl	47 3/8

Bid				Ask		
MSCO	47 5/8	10		DLJP	47 3/4	10
SNDV	47 1/2	10		SHWD	47 3/4	11
CANT	47 1/2	10		NBSI	47 3/4	10
CEUT	47 1/2	10		BEST	47 7/8	10
FBCO	47 1/2	10		SBSH	47 7/8	10
INCA	47 1/2	5		MLCO	47 7/8	10
BTRD	47 7/16	6		LEHM	47 7/8	10
GSCO	47 3/8	10		CHGO	47 7/8	10
PWJC	47 3/8	10		MASH	47 7/8	5
RSSF	47 3/8	10		INCA	47 7/8	5
HRZG	47 3/8	10		BTRD	47 15/16	6
MLCO	47 3/8	10		PWJC	48	10
LEHM	47 3/8	10		RSSF	48	10
SHWD	47 3/8	10		HRZG	48	4
MASH	47 3/8	10		FBCO	48	10
NITE	47 3/8	10		GSCO	48 1/8	10
TSCO	47 3/8	10		PERT	48 1/8	10
BEST	47 1/4	10		MWSE	48 1/8	10
SBSH	47 1/4	10		NITE	48 1/8	10
MADF	47 1/4	10		OLDE	48 1/4	10
NFSC	47 1/4	10		SNDV	48 1/4	10
DLJP	47 1/4	10		CANT	48 1/4	10
MWSE	47 1/4	10		CEUT	48 1/4	10
CHGO	47 1/8	10		MSCO	48 1/4	10

Time & Sales (ADPT):

13:37	47 5/8	500
13:37	47 5/8	500
13:34	47 3/4	500
13:32	47 3/4	300
13:32	47 5/8	300
13:29	47 5/8	1000
13:28	47 11/16	1000
13:27	47 11/16	1000
13:27	47 11/16	300
13:27	47 11/16	1000
13:26	47 11/16	1000
13:26	47 11/16	800
13:23	47 11/16	1000
13:23	47 3/4	100
13:22	47 11/16	200
13:21	47 11/16	400
13:20	47 11/16	200
13:20	47 11/16	300
13:17	47 11/16	500
13:17	47 11/16	3500
13:17	47 11/16	1000
13:17	47 21/32	300
13:13	47 5/8	200
13:12	47 5/8	1000
13:11	47 3/4	2000
13:11	47 3/4	5000
13:10	47 3/4	2000
13:10	47 3/4	5000
13:09	47 3/4	5000
13:09	47 5/8	5000
13:09	47 5/8	1000
13:09	47 5/8	300
13:09	47 5/8	1000
13:09	47 5/8	1200

IF YOU HAD A SELL SETUP AND SOLD THE BID, YOU
WOULD LIKELY GET FILLED AT 47 1/2 INSTEAD OF THE
1 MARKET MAKER (MSCO) AT 47 5/8. IF YOU WERE WRONG AND
HAD TO EXIT IMMEDIATELY YOU MAY BE ABLE TO BUY THE 47 3/4 ASK.
BUT IF SEVERAL OTHER TRADERS ALSO BEGIN BUYING BACK THE STOCK, THEN
YOU MIGHT NOT GET FILLED UNTIL 47 7/8. THIS WOULD BE A 3/8 LOSS (A LITTLE BIT RISKIER, BUT TRADABLE)

1/8 CURRENT BID/ASK SPREAD

ERTS			
Hi	34 1/2	33 9/16	down
Lo	33 1/2	-7/16	Vl 239900
Bid ↓	33 1/2	Ask 33 5/8	Hst Cl 34

O	UBSS	33 1/2	10	INCA	33 5/8	4
O	GSCO	33 1/2	10	TSCO	33 3/4	10
O	PWJC	33 1/2	10	MASH	33 3/4	9
O	LEHM	33 1/2	10	FBCO	33 7/8	10
O	NITE	33 1/2	3	MSCO	33 7/8	10
O	WBLR	33 1/2	10	BEST	33 7/8	10
O	DEAN	33 1/2	10	PIPR	33 7/8	10
O	MASH	33 1/2	11	HMQT	33 7/8	10
O	ISLD	33 1/2	10	HRZG	33 7/8	10
O	FBCO	33 3/8	10	SBSH	33 7/8	10
O	MSCO	33 3/8	10	JEFF	33 7/8	10
O	BEST	33 3/8	10	UBSS	34	10
O	RSSF	33 3/8	10	COWN	34	6
O	CANT	33 3/8	10	RSSF	34	10
O	SHWD	33 3/8	10	GSCO	34	10
O	PIPR	33 3/8	10	PWJC	34	10
O	VOLP	33 3/8	10	WEED	34	9
O	DLJP	33 3/8	10	LEHM	34	10
O	HRZG	33 3/8	1	CANT	34	10
O	PRUS	33 3/8	10	VOLP	34	10
O	SBSH	33 3/8	10	WBLR	34	10
O	MADF	33 6/16	10	OLDE	34	10
O	ABSB	33 1/4	10	JPMS	34	10
O	COWN	33 1/4	4	PRUS	34	10

ERTS		
13:36	33 9/16	300
13:32	33 5/8	1000
13:29	33 5/8	300
13:28	33 5/8	300
13:28	33 1/2	2000
13:26	33 1/2	100
13:24	33 3/4	100
13:24	33 5/8	1000
13:23	33 1/2	100
13:22	33 1/2	100
13:21	33 9/16	400
13:21	33 9/16	500
13:21	33 9/16	100
13:21	33 9/16	100
13:20	33 1/2	900
13:20	33 1/2	900
13:19	33 9/16	900
13:17	33 5/8	100
13:14	33 1/2	500
13:09	33 1/2	100
13:05	33 5/8	1000
13:05	33 5/8	100
13:00	33 3/4	500
13:00	33 5/8	1000
12:58	33 5/8	200
12:50	33 3/4	1000
12:49	33 3/4	1000
12:45	33 3/4	100
12:38	33 3/4	100
12:35	33 5/8	600
12:32	33 3/4	100
12:32	33 3/4	100
12:28	33 5/8	2500
12:24	33 5/8	300

GOOD IF YOU ARE BUYING DUE TO THE THICKNESS OF LEVELS ON THE BID SIDE, IF YOU HAVE TO SELL OUT OF THE POSITION WITH 1/4 LOSS.

BAD IF YOU ARE SELLING THE 33 1/2 BID BECAUSE YOUR LIKELY FILL PRICE IF YOU HAVE TO QUICKLY BUY IT BACK WOULD BE 33 7/8, A 3/8 LOSS.

- BUT IF IT IS A STRONG SELL SETUP WITH PROFIT POTENTIAL OF 1+ POINTS THEN YOU MAY WISH TO RISK 3/8 AS YOUR INITIAL STOP LOSS

OTHER DAYTRADERS ARE CURRENTLY SELLING THE BID.

MANY 1000 SHARE TRADES MEANS LOTS OF DAY TRADERS TRADING THIS STOCK

WAMU	Hi 69 7/8	Lo 68 3/8	−11/16	down
Bid ↓ 68 3/8	Ask 68 5/8	Vl 468400	Hst Cl 69 1/16	

	Bid			Ask	
○	SALB	68 3/8	10	LEHM	68 5/8	10
○	DEAN	68 1/4	10	FPKI	68 5/8	10
○	WEED	68 1/4	9	FBCO	68 5/8	10
○	CANT	68 1/4	10	FBRC	68 5/8	10
○	BEST	68 1/4	10	MSCO	68 5/8	10
○	JEFF	68 1/4	10	TSCO	68 5/8	10
○	PWJC	68 1/4	10	GSCO	68 5/8	10
○	MONT	68 1/4	10	UBSS	68 5/8	10
○	SBSH	68 1/4	10	SHWD	68 5/8	10
○	MLCO	68 1/4	10	BTRD	68 5/8	6
○	BTRD	68 1/4	5	BEST	68 3/4	10
○	DAIN	68 1/4	10	JEFF	68 3/4	10
○	KBWI	68 3/16	10	PWJC	68 3/4	10
○	MASH	68 1/8	10	MONT	68 3/4	10
○	JPMS	68 1/8	10	SBSH	68 3/4	10
○	PIPR	68 1/8	10	MLCO	68 3/4	10
○	LEHM	68 1/8	10	KBWI	68 13/16	10
○	FPKI	68 1/8	10	JPMS	68 7/8	10
○	FBCO	68 1/8	10	PIPR	68 7/8	10
○	FBRC	68 1/8	10	SALB	68 7/8	10
○	MSCO	68 1/8	10	CANT	68 7/8	10
○	TSCO	68 1/8	10	HRZG	68 7/8	10
○	HRZG	68 1/8	10	RAGN	68 7/8	10
○	GSCO	68 1/8	10	NITE	68 7/8	10

WAMU

Time	Price	Size
13:36	68 3/8	1000
13:36	68 3/8	1000
13:36	68 3/8	1000
13:36	68 3/8	100
13:36	68 5/8	1000
13:36	68 1/2	1000
13:36	68 3/8	1000
13:36	68 3/8	1000
13:36	68 1/2	2000
13:36	68 1/2	1000
13:36	68 1/2	1000
13:35	68 3/8	1000
13:35	68 3/8	1000
13:35	68 1/2	500
13:35	68 3/4	300
13:35	68 5/8	1000
13:35	68 5/8	100
13:35	68 3/4	200
13:35	68 5/8	300
13:34	68 5/8	1000
13:34	68 5/8	1000
13:34	68 5/8	1000
13:34	68 5/8	300
13:33	68 7/8	1000
13:33	68 3/4	1000
13:33	68 5/8	1000
13:33	68 5/8	1000
13:33	68 5/8	1000
13:33	68 3/4	1000
13:33	68 5/8	1000
13:33	68 5/8	1000

GOOD DEPTH TO MOST PRICE LEVELS EXCEPT THE INSIDE BID OF 68 3/8. IF YOU WERE BUYING AT 68 5/8, YOU'D BE RISKING 3/8 INITIAL STOP-LOSS. IF THE STOCK WERE TO MOVE AGAINST YOU, THE 68 3/8 PRICE WOULD COME OFF THE BID AND YOU'D HAVE TO EXIT AT 68 1/4. THIS IS STILL A VERY PLAYABLE STOCK. YOU MIGHT WANT TO WAIT UNTIL THE LEVELS MOVED AROUND TO GIVE YOU A BETTER MARGIN OF SAFETY (ie. IF MORE MARKET MAKERS CAME IN AT 68 3/8 BID OR, SOME MARKET MAKERS BEGAN FILLING IN AT 68 1/2 AS A NEW INSIDE ASK

TLAB	62	+5/16	up
Hi	62 7/16	Lo 61 3/4	VI 741800
Bid ↑ 62		Ask 62 1/16	Hst Cl 61 11/16

O	CANT	62	10	INCA	62 1/16	4
O	TSCO	61 7/8	10	GSCO	62 1/8	10
O	SALB	61 7/8	10	MASH	62 1/8	7
O	CHGO	61 7/8	10	WEAT	62 1/8	10
O	SBSH	61 7/8	10	DMGL	62 1/8	10
O	UBSS	61 3/4	10	MLCO	62 3/16	10
O	PRUS	61 3/4	10	DLJP	62 1/4	10
O	PWJC	61 3/4	2	BEST	62 1/4	10
O	MWSE	61 3/4	10	MONT	62 1/4	10
O	MSCO	61 3/4	10	BARD	62 1/4	10
O	MADF	61 11/16	1	FBCO	62 1/4	10
L	WBLR	61 5/8	10	HRZG	62 1/4	2
O	COWN	61 5/8	10	LEHM	62 1/4	10
O	RHCO	61 5/8	10	PWJC	62 1/4	10
O	SNDV	61 5/8	10	OLDE	62 1/4	10
O	RAJA	61 5/8	10	MSCO	62 1/4	10
O	NITE	61 5/8	10	ISLD	62 1/4	2
O	BTRD	61 5/8	4	NFSC	62 5/16	10
O	SHWD	61 5/8	10	BTRD	62 5/16	4
O	DLJP	61 1/2	10	MWSE	62 5/16	10
O	BEST	61 1/2	10	COWN	62 3/8	10
O	MONT	61 1/2	10	RHCO	62 3/8	10
O	JEFF	61 1/2	10	RAJA	62 3/8	10
O	KMSI	61 1/2	10	PRUS	62 3/8	10

TLAB

13:30	62		200
13:29	62		300
13:25	62		1000
13:25	62		3000
13:25	62		1200
13:25	62		1000
13:25	62	1/16	300
13:24	62		1000
13:24	62		1000
13:24	62		1000
13:23	62	1/16	100
13:23	62	1/16	100
13:21	62	1/16	400
13:18	62		200
13:17	62		14000
13:17	62	1/8	1000
13:17	62	1/8	1000
13:17	62	1/8	800
13:17	62	1/8	200
13:17	62	1/8	1000
13:17	62	1/8	1000
13:17	62	1/8	1000
13:17	62	1/8	1000
13:16	62	1/8	1000
13:16	62	1/8	2000
13:16	62	1/8	1000
13:16	62	1/8	1000
13:16	62	1/8	1000
13:16	62	1/8	1000

LESS DEPTH TO PRICE LEVELS

YOU HAVE TO BE MORE NIMBLE TO TRADE THIS STOCK, SINCE IT HAS THINNER LEVELS, PRICE CAN MORE QUICKLY MOVE UP OR DOWN. MAKE SURE THAT YOU ARE ONLY GOING TO BE RISKING 1/4 TO 3/8 BY LETTING THE MARKET MAKER SCREEN PRESENT THE BEST PROBABILITY OF GETTING OUT OF THE STOCK AT YOUR PREDETERMINED STOP-LOSS EXIT, OTHERWISE DON'T GET INTO A TRADE

CURRENT 1/8 BID/ASK SPREAD OF 53 7/8 BY 54 WHEN YOU LOOK AT THE THINNESS OF PRICE LEVELS

1/2 POINT DIFFERENCE WITH 1 MARKET MAKER AT EACH LEVEL

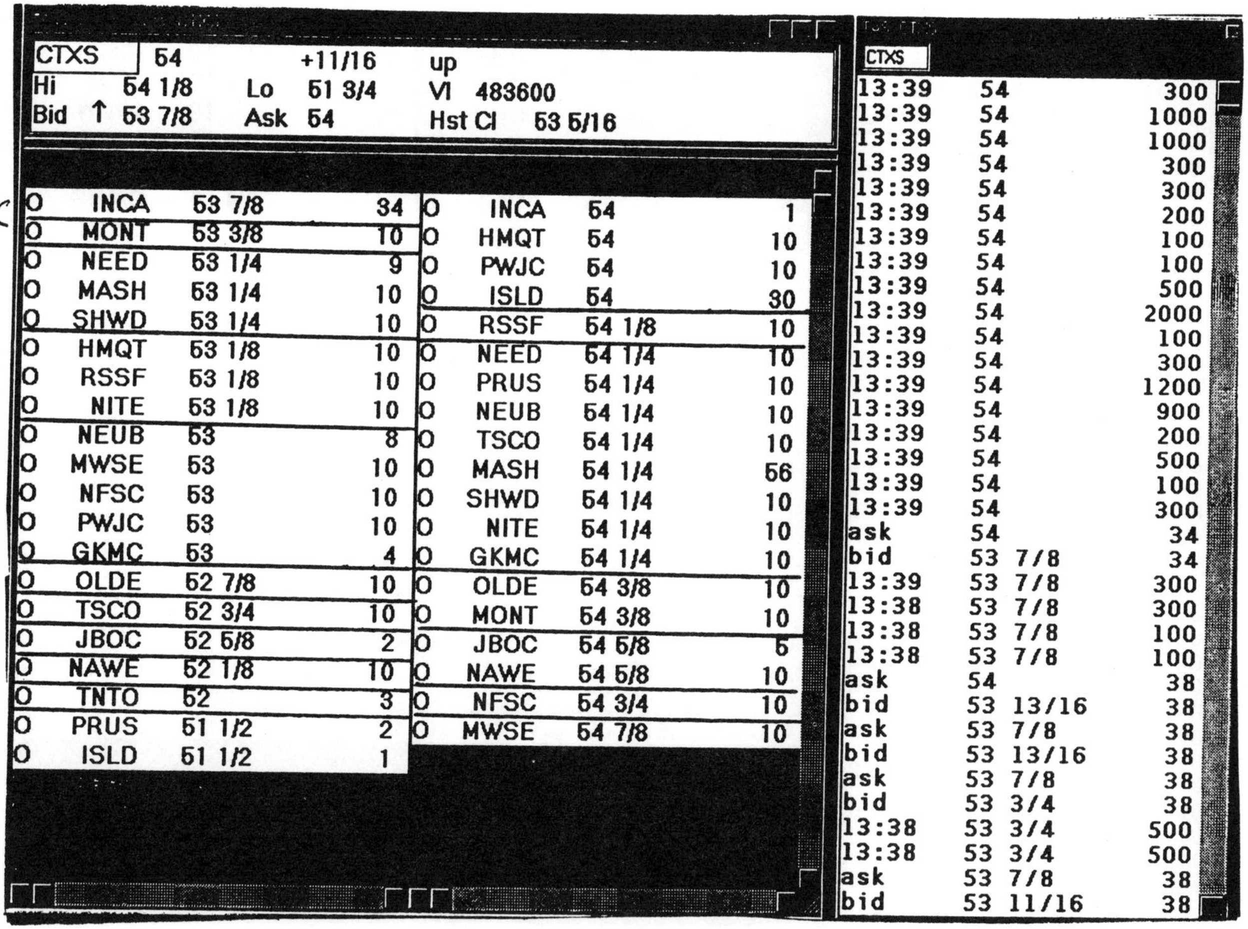

CTXS 54 +11/16 up
Hi 54 1/8 Lo 51 3/4 Vl 483600
Bid ↑ 53 7/8 Ask 54 Hst Cl 53 5/16

O	INCA	53 7/8	34	O	INCA	54	1
O	MONT	53 3/8	10	O	HMQT	54	10
O	NEED	53 1/4	9	O	PWJC	54	10
O	MASH	53 1/4	10	O	ISLD	54	30
O	SHWD	53 1/4	10	O	RSSF	54 1/8	10
O	HMQT	53 1/8	10	O	NEED	54 1/4	10
O	RSSF	53 1/8	10	O	PRUS	54 1/4	10
O	NITE	53 1/8	10	O	NEUB	54 1/4	10
O	NEUB	53	8	O	TSCO	54 1/4	10
O	MWSE	53	10	O	MASH	54 1/4	56
O	NFSC	53	10	O	SHWD	54 1/4	10
O	PWJC	53	10	O	NITE	54 1/4	10
O	GKMC	53	4	O	GKMC	54 1/4	10
O	OLDE	52 7/8	10	O	OLDE	54 3/8	10
O	TSCO	52 3/4	10	O	MONT	54 3/8	10
O	JBOC	52 5/8	2	O	JBOC	54 5/8	5
O	NAWE	52 1/8	10	O	NAWE	54 5/8	10
O	TNTO	52	3	O	NFSC	54 3/4	10
O	PRUS	51 1/2	2	O	MWSE	54 7/8	10
O	ISLD	51 1/2	1				

CTXS

13:39	54	300
13:39	54	1000
13:39	54	1000
13:39	54	300
13:39	54	300
13:39	54	200
13:39	54	100
13:39	54	100
13:39	54	500
13:39	54	2000
13:39	54	100
13:39	54	300
13:39	54	1200
13:39	54	900
13:39	54	200
13:39	54	500
13:39	54	100
13:39	54	300
ask	54	34
bid	53 7/8	34
13:39	53 7/8	300
13:38	53 7/8	300
13:38	53 7/8	100
13:38	53 7/8	100
ask	54	38
bid	53 13/16	38
ask	53 7/8	38
bid	53 13/16	38
ask	53 7/8	38
bid	53 3/4	38
13:38	53 3/4	500
13:38	53 3/4	500
ask	53 7/8	38
bid	53 11/16	38

IF YOU BOUGHT THIS STOCK AT 54, YOU'D BE RISKING AN EXIT PRICE OF 53 1/4 OR 53 1/8 IF YOU WERE WRONG ABOUT THE TRADE. BY THE TIME YOUR SELL ORDER FILLED TO EXIT THE TRADE, THE 53 7/8 AND 53 3/8 ASK PRICES WOULD HAVE PROBABLY MOVED AWAY. THIS LEAVES YOU WITH A 3/4 TO 7/8 LOSS. NEVER BUY A SETUP LIKE THIS.

A SELL WOULD BE OKAY IF YOU WERE ABLE TO HIT THE INSIDE BID OF 53 7/8, YOU COULD BUY BACK AT 54 1/4 OR BETTER IF YOU WERE WRONG

WITH A 3/8 BID/ASK SPREAD, AND SOMEWHAT THINNER PRICE LEVELS, YOU'D BE RISKING 1/2 TO 5/8 LOSS WITH A TRADE IF YOU WERE WRONG.

→ DO NOT TRADE A SETUP IF THE MARKET MAKER SCREEN LOOKS LIKE THIS! TOO MUCH RISK.

HCCC 58 3/4   -2 1/4   down

Hi	60 1/8	Lo	56 1/4	Vl	842800
Bid →	58 5/8	Ask	59	Hst Cl	61

Bid				Ask		
O	MONT	58 5/8	10	O	SALB	59	10
O	MLCO	58 5/8	5	O	GMGS	59	10
O	MASH	58 5/8	10	O	RHCO	59	9
O	DLJP	58 5/8	10	O	MONT	59 1/8	10
O	GSCO	58 1/2	10	O	MLCO	59 1/8	10
O	MSCO	58 1/2	10	O	PIPR	59 1/4	10
O	JEFF	58 1/2	10	O	HMQT	59 1/4	10
O	DAIN	58 1/2	10	O	MSCO	59 1/4	10
O	OLDE	58 1/2	10	O	DAIN	59 1/4	10
O	LEHM	58 3/8	10	O	LEGG	59 1/4	10
O	RHCO	58 3/8	10	O	TSCO	59 1/4	10
O	PIPR	58 1/4	10	O	SHWD	59 1/4	10
O	HMQT	58 1/4	10	O	LEHM	59 3/8	10
O	NITE	58 1/4	10	O	MASH	59 3/8	10
O	TSCO	58 1/4	10	O	MWSE	59 3/8	1
O	SALB	58 1/4	10	O	GSCO	59 1/2	10
O	MWSE	58 1/4	1	O	SCCC	59 1/2	10
O	SCCC	58	10	O	JEFF	59 1/2	10
O	LEGG	58	10	O	OLDE	59 1/2	10
O	GMGS	58	10	O	DLJP	59 5/8	10
O	SHWD	58	10	O	NITE	60	10

HCCC

Time	Price	Size
13:39	58 3/4	900
13:34	59	100
13:33	58 3/4	1000
13:33	58 11/16	1000
13:32	58 5/8	2000
13:28	58 3/4	100
13:28	58 3/4	100
13:28	58 13/16	200
13:28	58 13/16	200
13:28	58 15/16	900
13:25	58 3/4	200
13:15	58 5/8	100
13:12	59	1000
13:12	59	1000
13:12	59	1000
13:09	58 5/8	700
13:09	58 3/4	300
13:09	58 5/8	200
13:07	58 13/16	100
13:07	58 15/16	1000
13:00	59	1000
12:55	58 3/4	1100
12:55	58 3/4	1000
12:55	59 1/8	300
12:54	58 3/4	200
12:54	58 3/4	500
12:53	59	100
12:48	58 3/4	200
12:48	59 1/8	3400
12:46	59 1/16	1000
12:44	59 1/16	1100
12:44	59 1/4	1500
12:44	58 3/4	100
12:43	59 1/8	200

THE ONLY REASONABLE WAY TO TRADE THIS STOCK IF YOU WERE CONVINCED ABOUT THE SETUP WOULD BE TO USE 500 SHARES TO REDUCE YOUR RISK IN THE EVENT YOU ARE WRONG.

111

AGPH | 92 1/4 | -1/8 | down
Hi 93 1/4 | Lo 92 1/4 | Vl 263800
Bid → 92 1/4 | Ask 92 1/2 | Hst Cl 92 3/8

	Bid				Ask	
L	MSCO	92 1/4	10	O	PWJC	92 1/2	10
O	MASH	92 3/16	1	O	NITE	92 7/8	1
O	PERT	92	10	O	PRUS	93	10
O	NITE	92	10	O	ABSB	93 3/8	10
O	TSCO	91 3/4	10	O	ISLD	93 3/8	2
O	LEHM	91 3/4	10	O	HRZG	93 7/16	10
O	SHWD	91 3/4	3	O	INCA	93 7/16	4
O	PWJC	91 3/4	1	O	MONT	93 1/2	10
O	HRZG	91 9/16	10	O	MASH	93 1/2	10
O	MONT	91 1/2	10	L	MSCO	93 5/8	10
O	ISLD	91 1/2	1	O	RSSF	93 5/8	10
O	PRUS	91 1/2	10	O	TSCO	93 3/4	10
O	ABSB	91 3/8	10	O	LEHM	93 3/4	10
O	RSSF	91 3/8	10	O	SHWD	93 3/4	1
				O	PERT	93 7/8	10

APGH

Time	Price	Size
13:35	92 1/4	1000
13:35	92 1/2	200
13:35	92 1/2	1000
13:35	92 3/4	100
13:34	92 7/8	100
13:34	92 5/8	200
13:33	92 11/16	1400
13:33	92 7/8	200
13:31	92 7/8	100
13:30	92 1/2	100
13:25	92 11/16	500
13:25	92 11/16	400
13:23	92 7/8	200
13:23	92 7/8	100
13:21	92 7/8	200
13:19	92 7/8	200
13:18	92 5/8	300
13:17	92 3/4	100
13:17	92 3/4	100
13:15	92 7/8	700
13:14	92 7/8	100
13:11	92 7/8	100
13:08	92 7/8	2500
13:06	92 25/32	100
13:03	92 7/8	100
13:02	92 7/8	200
13:00	92 7/8	100
12:59	92 7/8	100
12:57	92 7/8	500
12:56	92 7/8	100
12:55	92 7/8	100
12:53	92 7/8	100
12:53	92 7/8	500
12:52	92 7/8	500

DON'T EVEN THINK ABOUT IT !!.

WAY TOO MUCH RISK

YOU COULD EASILY LOSE 1 POINT
IN THIS STOCK IF YOU ARE WRONG ABOUT THE TRADE.

PASS IT UP EVEN IF IT HAS
A GREAT BUY OR SELL PRICE PATTERN SETUP

ASMLF

Hi	87 3/8		86 3/8	−1/4	Lo	86
Bid ↑	86 1/4		Ask	86 5/8		

Vl 75700 Hst Cl 86 5/8

	Bid				Ask	
O	INCA	86 1/4	10	O	MLCO	86 5/8	10
O	BEST	86 1/8	10	O	MSCO	86 3/4	10
O	LEHM	86	1	O	RSSF	86 7/8	10
O	FBCO	86	10	O	NEED	87	10
O	ADAM	86	10	O	TSCO	87	10
O	NEED	86	10	O	MONT	87	10
O	SHWD	86	1	O	HRZG	87	10
O	RSSF	85 7/8	10	O	SHWD	87	4
O	OPCO	85 3/4	10	O	CHGO	87 1/8	10
O	TSCO	85 3/4	10	O	LEHM	87 1/4	10
O	MONT	85 3/4	10	O	FBCO	87 1/4	10
O	MSCO	85 3/4	10	O	BEST	87 3/8	10
O	HRZG	85 3/4	10	O	OPCO	87 1/2	10
O	BTRD	85 5/8	1	O	ADAM	87 1/2	10
O	MLCO	85 5/8	10				
O	CHGO	85 5/8	10				

T&S ASMLF

Time	Price	Size
13:33	86 3/8	1000
13:33	86 3/4	1000
13:33	86 3/4	1000
13:33	86 5/8	1000
13:33	86 5/8	1000
13:26	86 3/4	500
13:11	87 1/8	100
13:03	86 3/4	1000
13:01	86 3/4	1000
12:57	86 3/4	1000
12:53	86 11/16	100
12:27	86 5/8	1400
12:25	86 5/8	300
12:24	86 11/16	1000
12:23	86 3/4	4500
12:22	86 9/16	1700
12:16	86 5/8	1100
12:15	86 1/2	1100
12:08	86 7/8	200
12:08	86 7/8	4500
12:07	86 11/16	1000
12:02	86 11/16	1000
11:59	86 13/16	900
11:59	86 5/8	700
11:57	86 3/8	5200
11:55	86 3/4	900
11:55	86 7/16	1000
11:54	86 3/4	100
11:46	86 5/8	1000
11:39	86 3/8	3800
11:37	86 1/8	900
11:36	86 3/8	1100
11:35	86 5/8	300
11:35	87	100

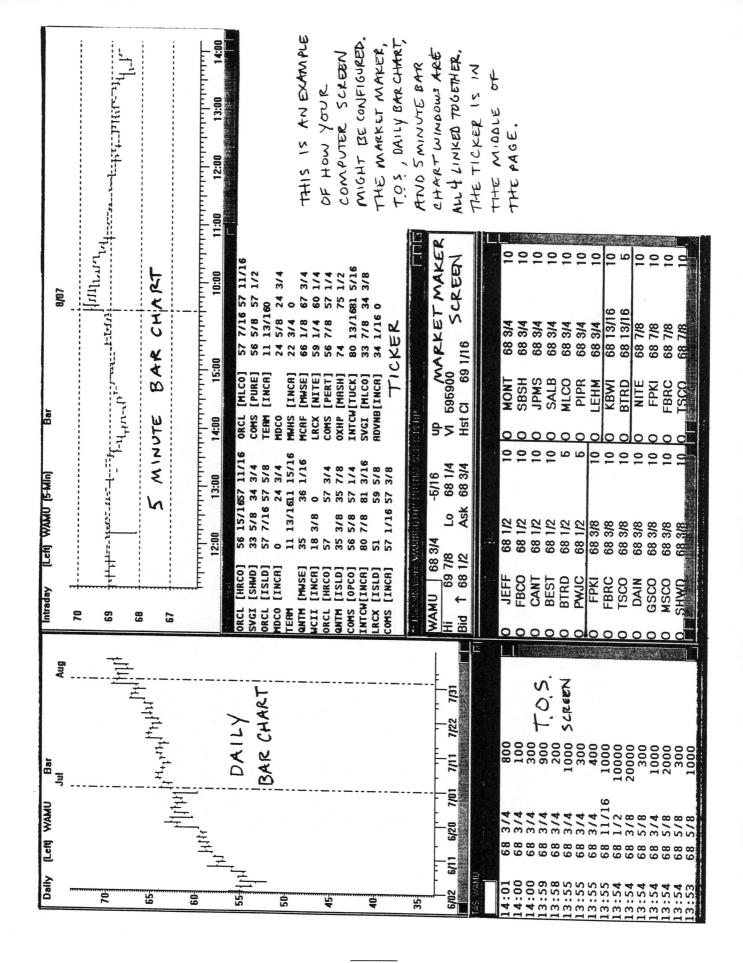

THIS IS AN EXAMPLE OF HOW YOUR COMPUTER SCREEN MIGHT BE CONFIGURED. THE MARKET MAKER, T.O.S., DAILY BAR CHART, AND 5 MINUTE BAR CHART WINDOWS ARE ALL 4 LINKED TOGETHER. THE TICKER IS IN THE MIDDLE OF THE PAGE.

5 MINUTE BAR CHART

DAILY BAR CHART

TICKER

MARKET MAKER SCREEN

T.O.S. SCREEN

SWING TRADES
Trades lasting from 2 to 5 + days

SWING TRADING
(trade setups for 2 to 5 day holds)

INTRODUCTION:

"Swing trades" in this case refers to trades that will typically last from 2 to 5 days. You should be looking to take several points of profit out of the market with each trade. Since holding overnight can be risky, you may wish to hold fewer shares. If you normally day trade 1000 shares at a time, consider trading only 200 to 500 shares on these setups. This limits your loss potential if after-market news on the company causes it to gap open against you. Fewer shares also allow you to use a wider stop-loss (typically 1 to 1&1/4 points) so that you don't get hurt. This also allows more room for price to move around without stopping you out of a good trade. As the stock moves in your favor you can trail the stop-loss anywhere from 1 to 1 & 1/2 points behind it. At some point the stock may trade in your favor to a price level where you want to go ahead and take your profit. Some reasonable exit points are a price support or resistance level, the other side of the channel on a trend channel trade, or if you get a daily "reversal bar" setup counter to the trade direction. Your risk/reward ratio should be good (i.e. 1 to 3 or better). In other words, take the best setups that have the potential to give you 3 to 5 + points. This way you are risking just a few hundred dollars for a profit of 1 to 2 thousand dollars (and sometimes more). Trade these setups along with your regular day trading to add $$$ to the bottom line. A worksheet of potential setups is provided later in the manual. It includes both a day trade and swing trade section for your analysis and stock picks for the upcoming trading day.

TREND CHANNEL (and trendlines)

A trend channel (for an up trending stock) is constructed by drawing a trendline through or very near 2 or more swing lows on a daily bar chart. If a line parallel to the initial trendline can be drawn through at least 2 swing highs on the chart then you have a trend channel (ex. #23). The tighter and more defined the channel is, the better. A stock often continues to trade within the channel if the trendlines are projected into the future on the chart. In an up trend you can buy subsequent dips down to the bottom of the trend channel. Using confirming factors increase the odds of success. For instance, if the dip to the bottom of the trend channel also coincides with a bounce on the 50 day moving average, and / or a bounce on a price support level, and / or you get a "reversal bar" pattern setup to buy, then the odds are stacked strongly in your favor. In a downtrend channel you would sell price rallies at the upper trendline. After entry, expectations are for price to attempt to trade to the other side of the trend channel. Near this area may be a good place to take your profits. Actual examples are presented later, but an up trending channel should look like the diagram at the top of the next page:

23)

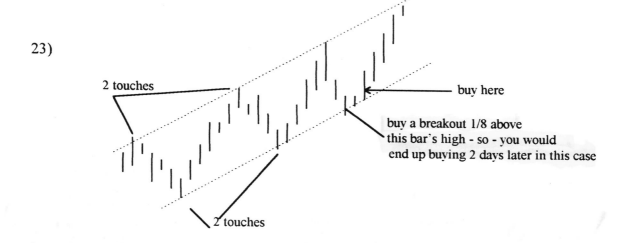

2 touches

buy here

buy a breakout 1/8 above
this bar's high - so - you would
end up buying 2 days later in this case

2 touches

1-2 MONTH BREAKOUTS

If a stock enters into a relatively tight trading range for 1-2 months, be prepared for a breakout to the upside. This is especially true if the prior trend was up, and you are in a bull market environment. The breakout day should close above the highest high of the consolidation range and trade on heavier than average volume. You should expect a several day follow-through in the direction of the breakout. This trade setup is even stronger if the stock price recently bounced up off of the 50 day moving average. Also, if the top side of the price range has a well defined resistance area, then the penetration to the upside will often be even more dramatic. This is a rough sketch of what the setup should look like. Actual examples will be provided later.

24)

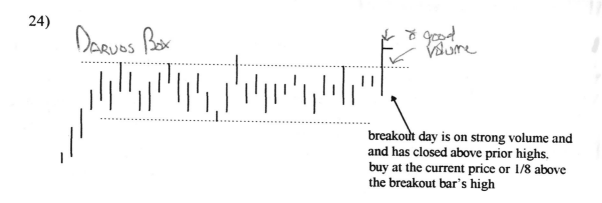

Darvas Box

good
volume

breakout day is on strong volume and
and has closed above prior highs.
buy at the current price or 1/8 above
the breakout bar's high

CUP W/ HANDLE

This name was coined by the founder of *Investor's Business Daily*, William O'Neil. The chart pattern resembles the profile of a coffee cup. The cup part of the pattern can last anywhere from several weeks to several months. The stock initially puts in an intermediate term price high, then begins selling off. After a while, buying comes back into the market pushing price up to, or very near, the earlier intermediate term high. This completes the right side of the cup. At this point the stock sells off again only slightly, trading sideways to down. It then trades back up to the right edge of the cup pattern to complete the handle. Be looking for a day that breaks out of the horizontal resistance area across the top of the cup and handle. This breakout begins an often substantial move up in price. Also keep an eye on volume. The setup is stronger if volume tends to decrease when price is selling off and increase when price is rallying. Here is a diagram of how price might look. Actual examples are included later.

25)

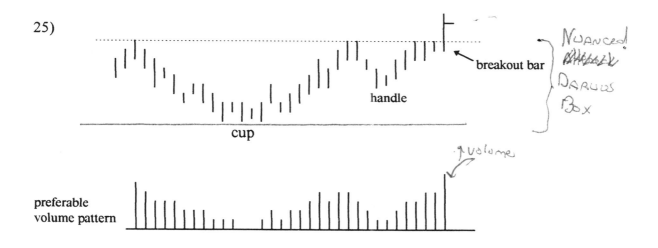

50 & 200 DAY SIMPLE MOVING AVERAGES

Many times the 50 and 200 day moving averages will tend to halt price. As mentioned earlier, fund managers key off of these indicators. This is where the "big money" can come into the market and affect price. If a stock is trading above the 50 day moving average and is selling off, often it will bounce up off of the moving average line (and vice versa). Conversely, a stock that has a day which strongly penetrates up or down through one of the moving averages typically follows through in that direction, at least for the short term (several days or longer). Knowing where the 50 and 200 day lines are for stocks that have trade setups can only help. It may be just one other confirming reason to take the trade, or it may help rule the trade out.

A CURRENTLY PROFITABLE DAY TRADE

As you near the end of a trading session you may have one or more open day trades with profit in them. Before closing them out, evaluate each of them to see if they have a strong chance of continuing their move for several more points over the course of a few days. If so, then consider selling only 700 of your 1000 shares to book the bulk of the profit. This puts money in your pocket but also allows you to participate in more of the price move.

Pull : 63% - 70% of Profit

SUMMARY:

These setups for multiple day trades should be considered separate from your day trading. Sometimes, if you are taking losses in your day trades, you may want to cash in an open and profitable swing trade. Resist the temptation. Let the swing trades stand on their own, and manage them that way. In the long run this will only add to your income. **NOTE OF CAUTION**: Although day trading can be risky, holding stocks overnight can be even <u>more</u> so for a short term trader. A 10 or 20+ point gap against you on the open just once, can really ruin a day, or a week, or a month. Trade only as many shares as you are comfortable with. Always be aware of any upcoming news or earnings on a stock that you are holding for more than one day. Also, know when economic data is being released or when the Fed meets etc... they can cause significant market gaps that may go against your position.

CONCLUSION:

You've seen how to recognize and anticipate high probability trading patterns in several time frames. Putting them all together only increases the odds of a successful trade. Trading with the stock's trend and with the market direction (both daily and intraday) only enhances your win rate. But remember, it is better to miss a good trade than to get a poor fill and subsequently lose $$$$. There will always be another good trade setup, so wait for it and take only the best trades.

CHART EXAMPLES

for
DAY TRADING
and
SWING TRADING

The following daily charts provide numerous examples of labeled trade setups from both the "Day trading" section and the "Swing trading" section of the manual. Support and Resistance (S/R) levels are included as well as commentary. This will help tie together the trading concepts in the manual. A worksheet analysis section is provided subsequent to the charts.

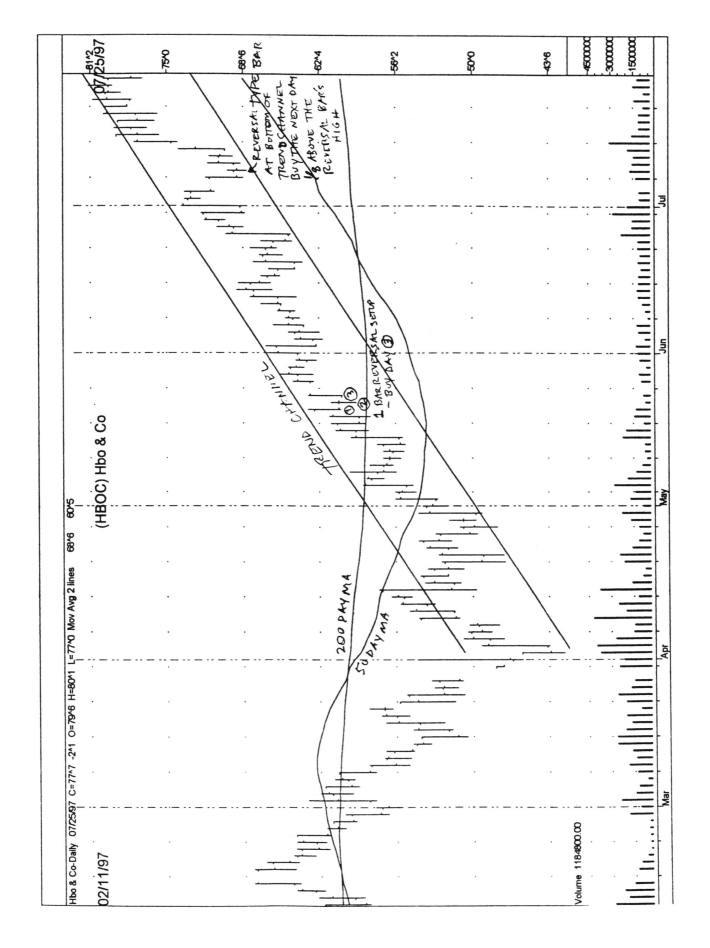

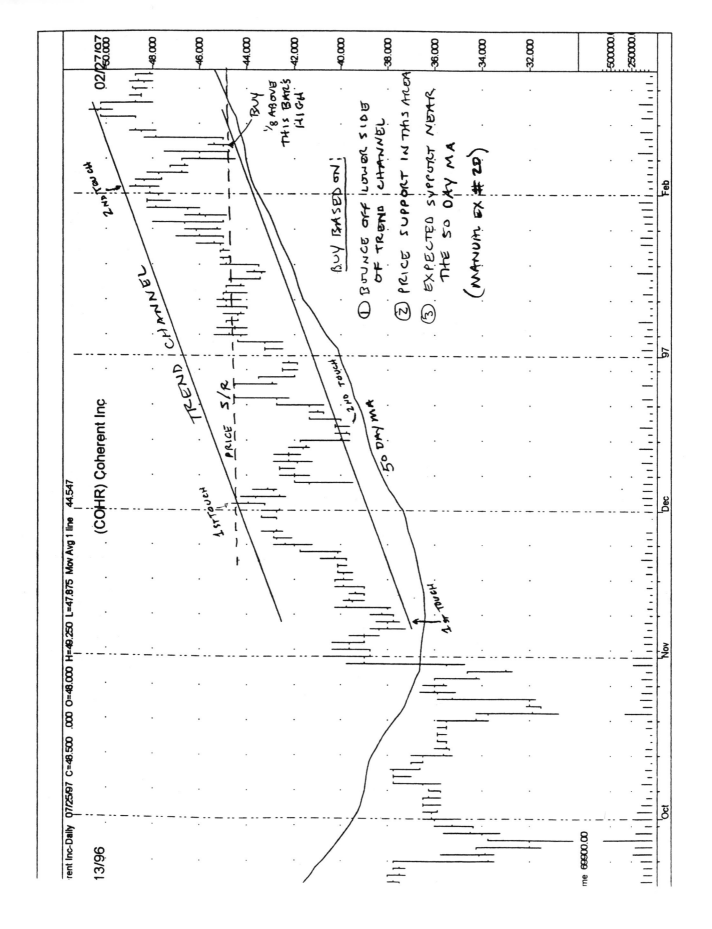

(COHR) Coherent Inc

rent Inc-Daily   07/25/97   C=48.500   .000   O=48.000   H=49.250   L=47.875   Mov Avg 1 line   44.547

13/96

TREND CHANNEL

PRICE S/R

50 DAY MA

1ST TOUCH

1ST TOUCH

2ND TOUCH

2ND TOUCH

BUY
⅛ ABOVE
THIS BARS
HIGH

BUY BASED ON:

① BOUNCE OFF LOWER SIDE
   OF TREND CHANNEL

② PRICE SUPPORT IN THIS AREA

③ EXPECTED SUPPORT NEAR
   THE 50 DAY MA

(MANUAL EX # 20)

me 69900.00

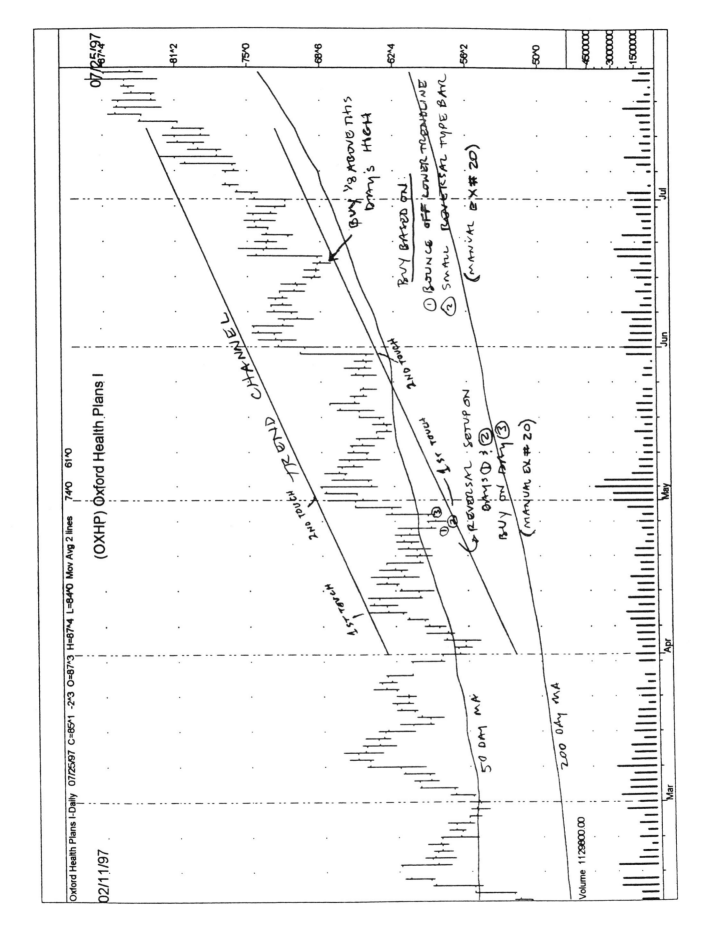

Oxford Health Plans I-Daily 07/25/97 C=85^1 -2^3 O=87^3 H=87^4 L=84^0 Mov Avg 2 lines 74^0 61^0

02/11/97

(OXHP) Oxford Health Plans I

CHANNEL

TREND

2ND TOUCH

2ND TOUCH

2ND TOUCH

1ST TOUCH

1ST TOUCH

50 DAY MA

200 DAY MA

BUY ⅛ ABOVE NHS DAYS HIGH

BUY BASED ON
① BOUNCE OFF LOWER TRENDLINE
② SMALL REVERSAL TYPE BAR
(MANUAL EX # 20)

REVERSAL SETUP ON
DAYS ① & ②

BUY ON DAY ③
(MANUAL EX # 20)

Volume 1129600.00

Mar   Apr   May   Jun   Jul   07/25/97
                                                87^4

81^2
75^0
68^6
62^4
56^2
50^0

4500000
3000000
1500000

125

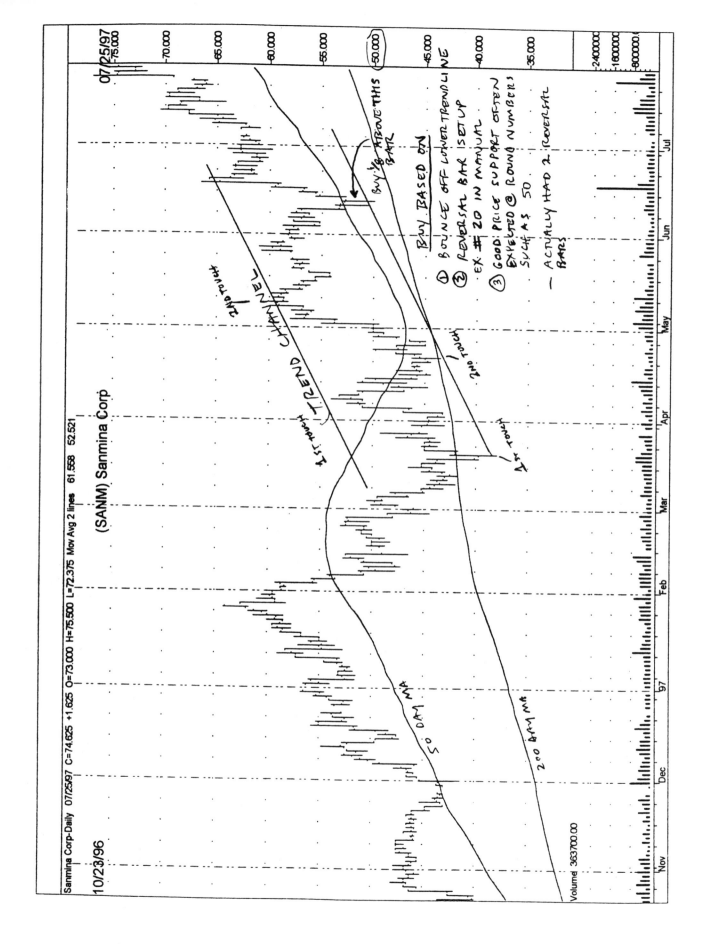

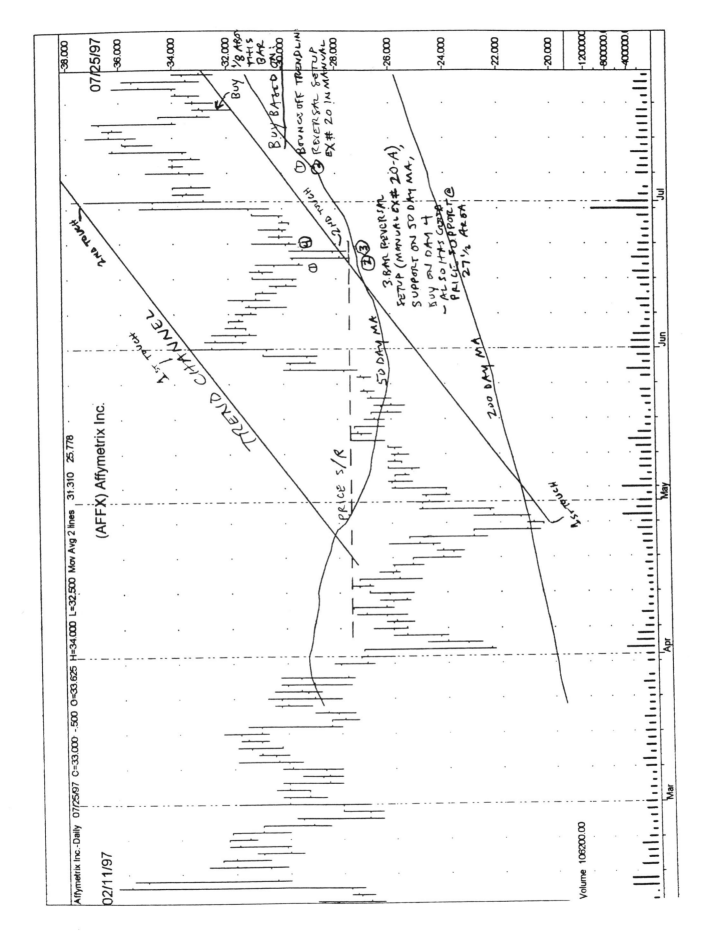

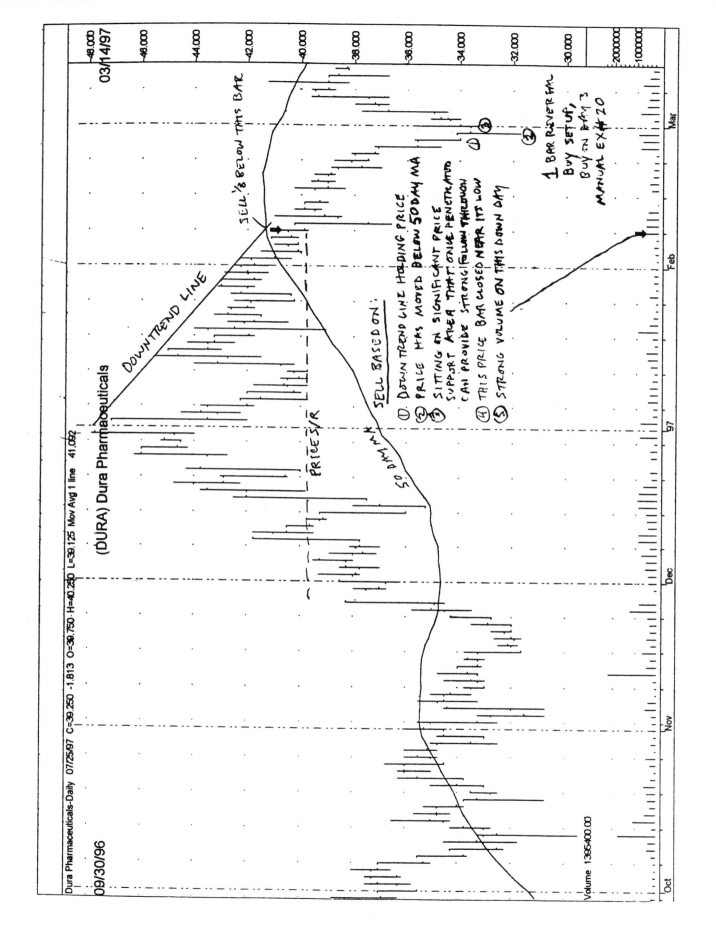

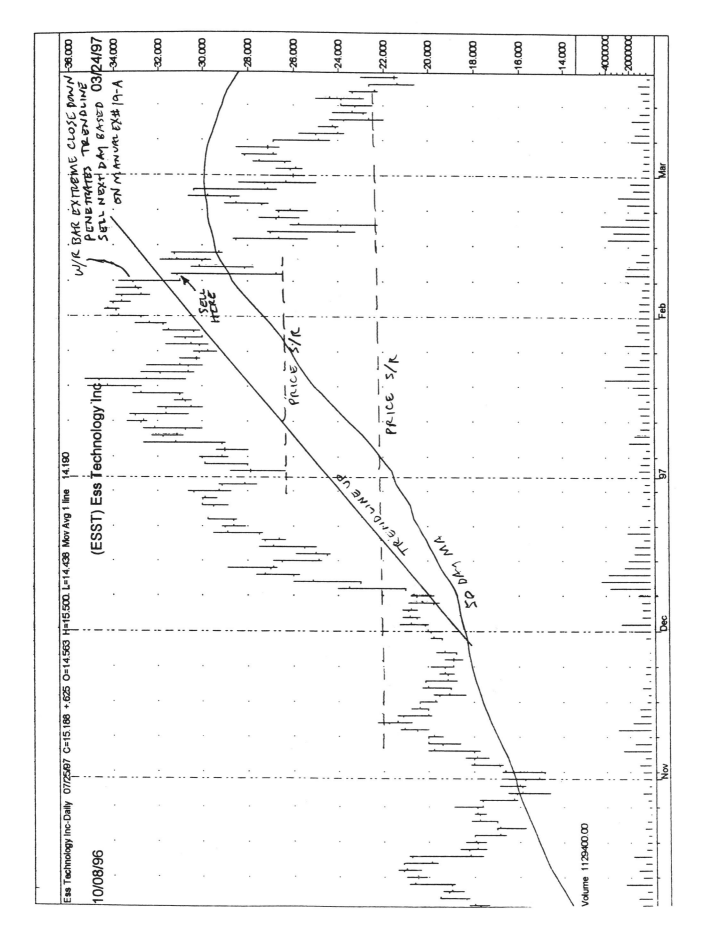

Ess Technology Inc-Daily 07/25/97 C=15.188 +.625 O=14.563 H=15.500 L=14.438 Mov Avg 1 line 14.190

(ESST) Ess Technology Inc

10/08/96

W/R BAR EXTREME CLOSE DOWN
PENETRATES TRENDLINE
SELL NEXT DAY BASED 03/24/97
ON MANUAL EX#19-A

SELL HERE

PRICE S/R

PRICE S/R

TRENDLINE UP

50 DAY MA

Volume 1129400.00

Nov   Dec   97   Feb   Mar

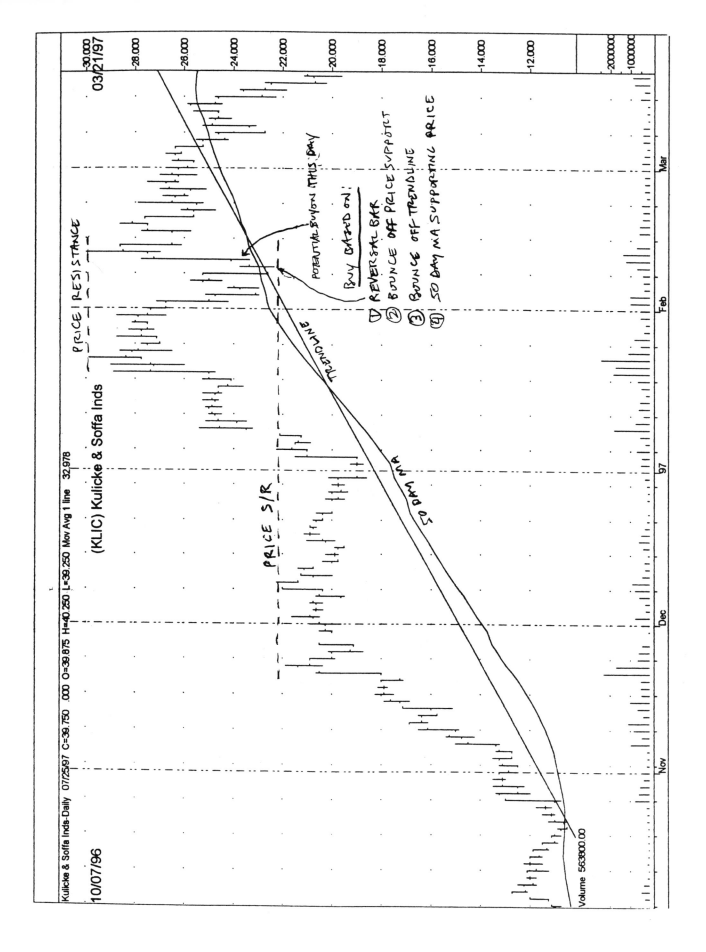

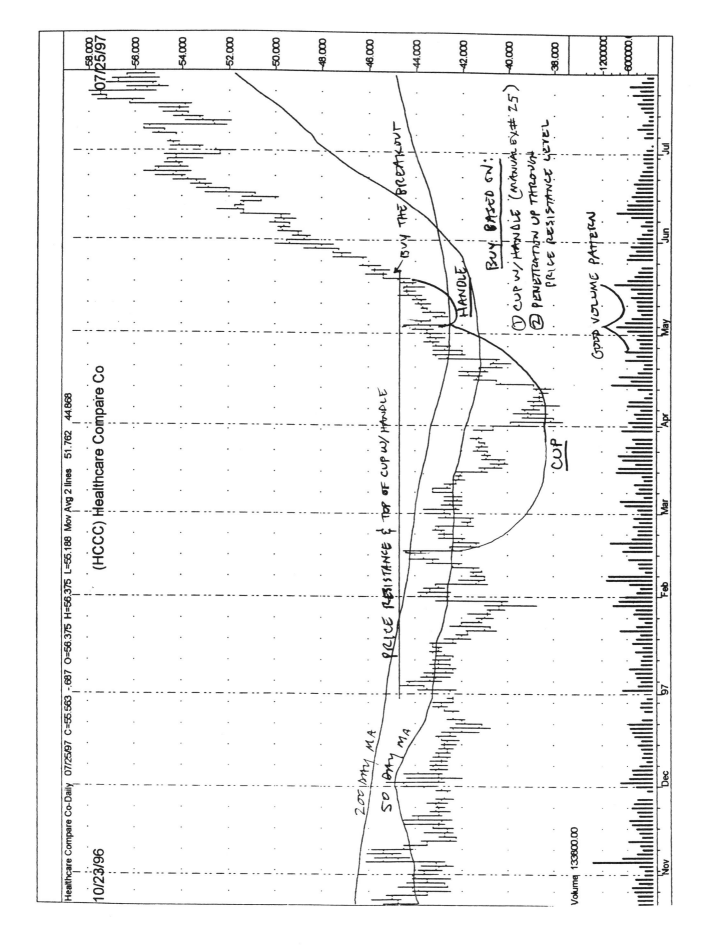

(HCCC) Healthcare Compare Co

Healthcare Compare Co-Daily 07/25/97 C=55.563 -.687 O=56.375 H=56.375 L=55.188 Mov Avg 2 lines 51.762 44.868

10/23/96

07/25/97

BUY BASED ON:
① CUP W/ HANDLE (ANNUAL EX# 25)
② PENETRATION UP THROUGH
    PRICE RESISTANCE LEVEL

BUY THE BREAKOUT

HANDLE

PRICE RESISTANCE & TOP OF CUP W/ HANDLE

200 DAY MA

50 DAY MA

CUP

GOOD VOLUME PATTERN

Volume 133800.00

131

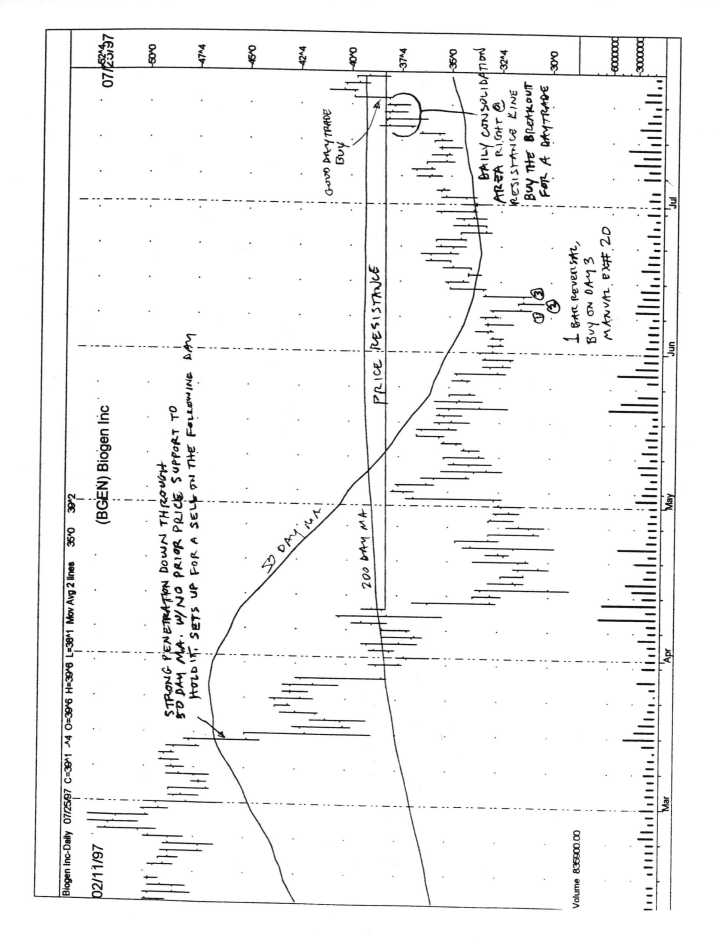

(BGEN) Biogen Inc

GOOD DAY TRADE BUY

PRICE RESISTANCE

50 DAY MA

200 DAY MA

STRONG PENETRATION DOWN THROUGH
50 DAY MA W/NO PRIOR PRICE SUPPORT TO
HOLD IT, SETS UP FOR A SELL ON THE FOLLOWING DAY

DAILY CONSOLIDATION
AREA RIGHT @
RESISTANCE LINE
BUY THE BREAKOUT
FOR A DAYTRADE

1 BAR REVERSAL,
BUY ON DAY 3
MANUAL EX#20

① ② ③

02/11/97

07/25/97

Biogen Inc-Daily 07/25/97 C=39^1 .^4 O=39^6 H=39^6 L=38^1 Mov Avg 2 lines 35^0 39^2

Volume 836500.00

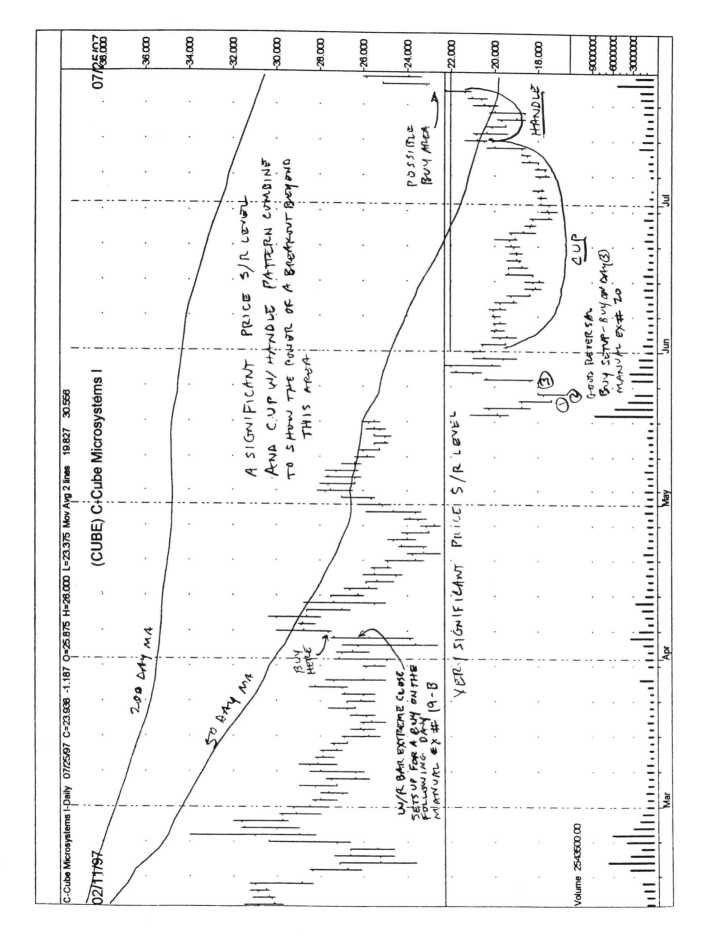

C-Cube Microsystems I-Daily 07/25/97 C=23.938 -1.187 O=25.875 H=28.000 L=23.375 Mov Avg 2 lines 19.827 30.556

(CUBE) C-Cube Microsystems I

200 DAY MA

50 DAY MA

BUY HERE

W/R BAR EXTREME CLOSE
SETS UP FOR A BUY ON THE
FOLLOWING DAY
MANUAL EX # 19-B

A SIGNIFICANT PRICE S/R LEVEL

AND CUP W/ HANDLE PATTERN COMBINE
TO SHOW THE POWER OF A BREAKOUT BEYOND
THIS AREA

VERY SIGNIFICANT PRICE S/R LEVEL

POSSIBLE
BUY AREA

HANDLE

CUP

G-OLD REVERSAL
BUY SETUP - BUY ON DAY ③
MANUAL EX# 20

Volume 2545500.00

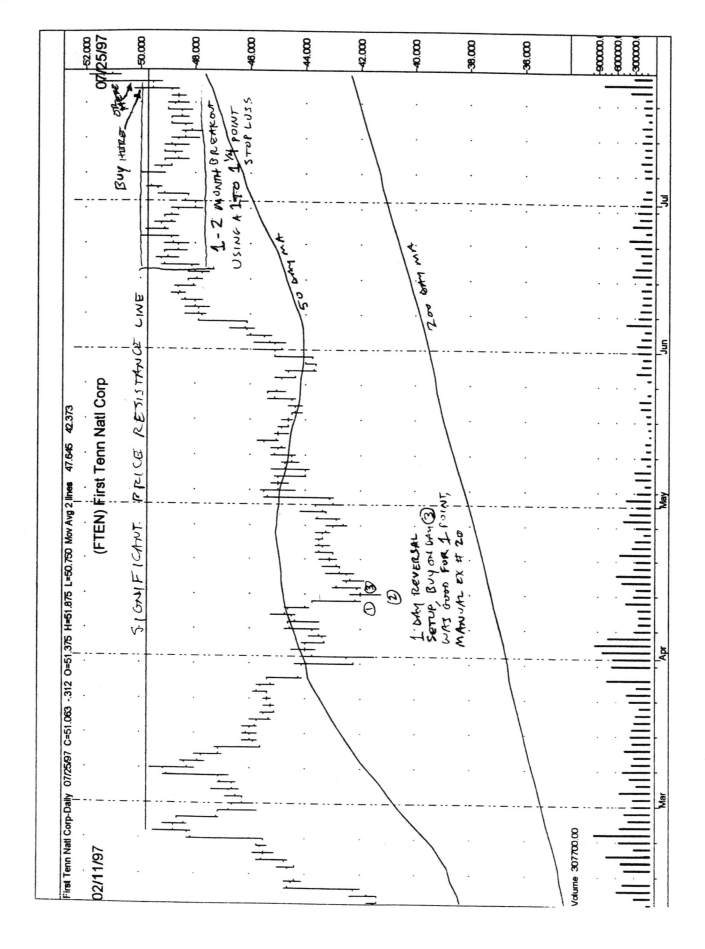

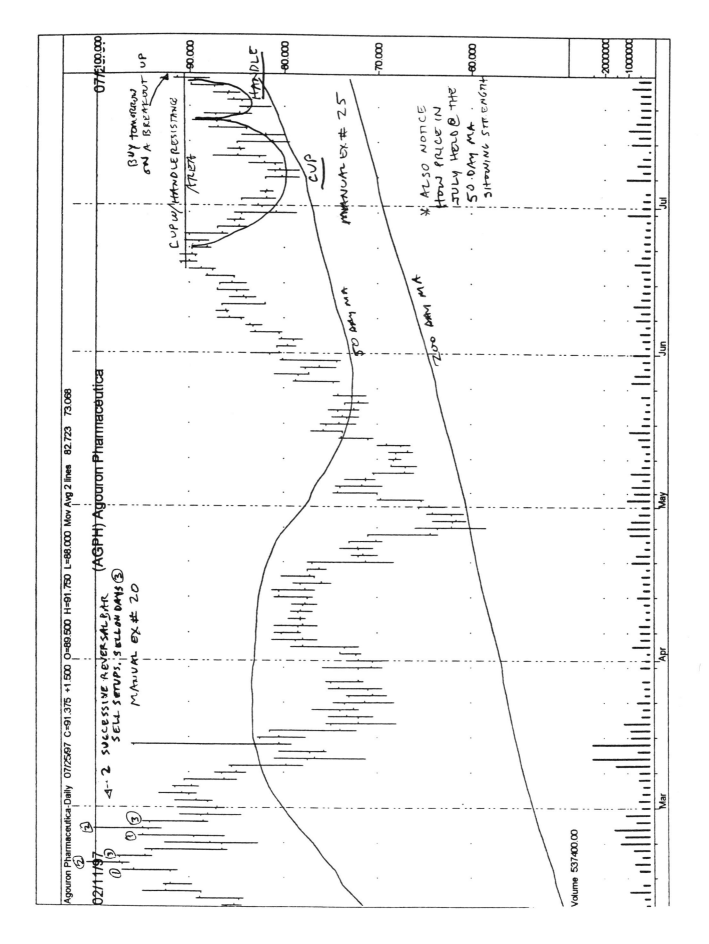

Agouron Pharmaceutica-Daily 07/25/97 C=91.375 +1.500 O=89.500 H=91.750 L=88.000 Mov Avg 2 lines 82.723 73.068

(AGPH) Agouron Pharmaceutica

BUY TOMORROW ON A BREAKOUT UP

CUP W/HANDLE RESISTING AREA

HANDLE

CUP

50 DAY MA

100 DAY MA

MANUAL EX # 25

* ALSO NOTICE HOW PRICE IN JULY HELD @ THE 50.0 DAY MA SHOWING STRENGTH

← 2 SUCCESSIVE REVERSAL BAR SELL SETUPS, SELL ON DAYS ③

MANUAL EX # 20

Volume 537400.00

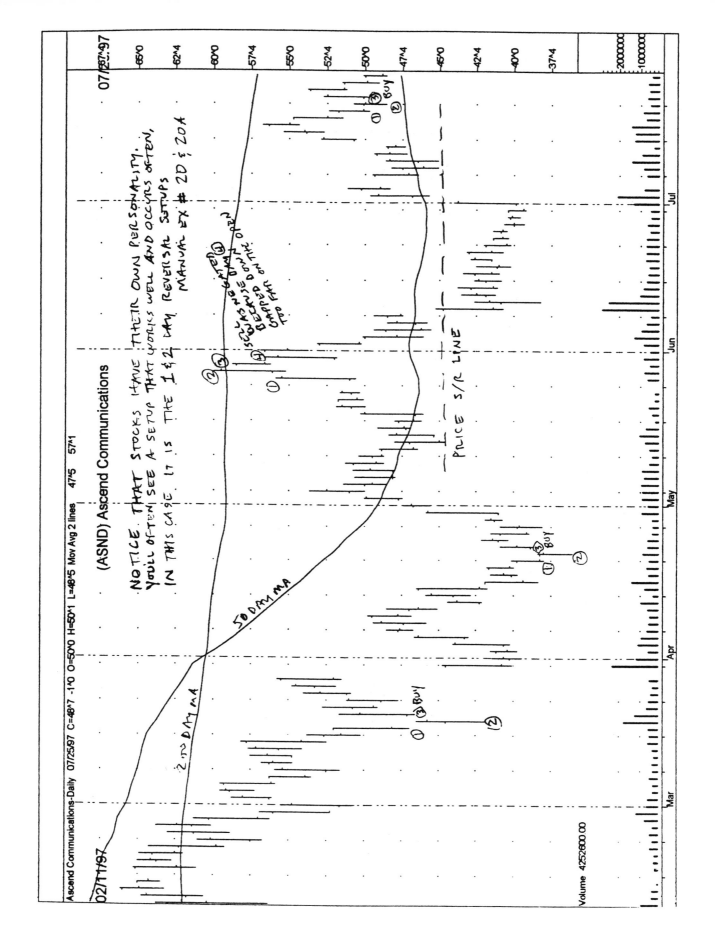

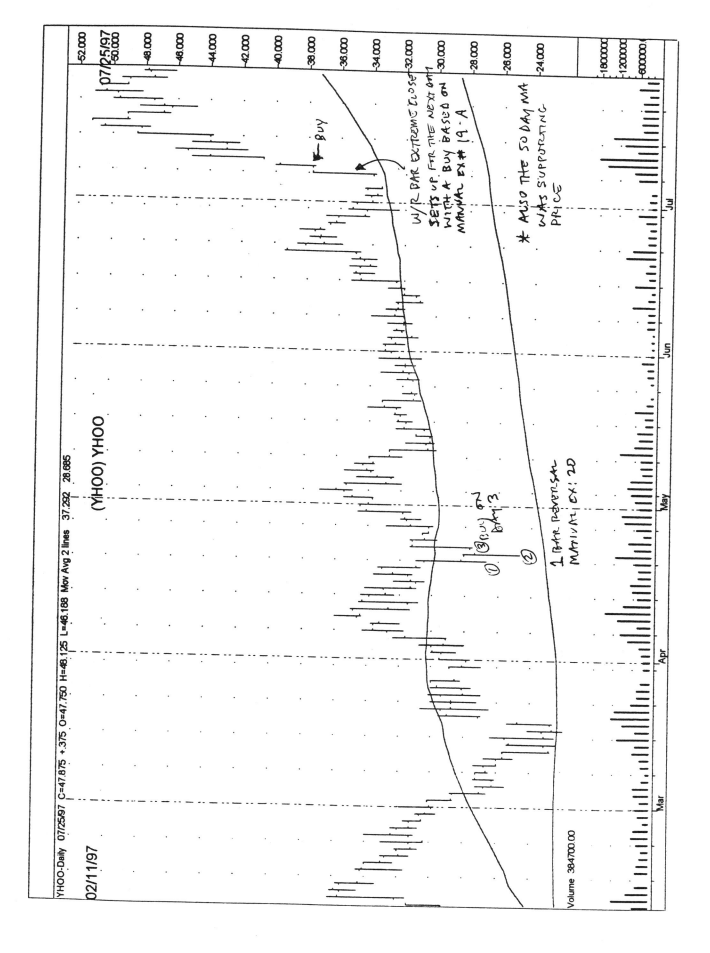

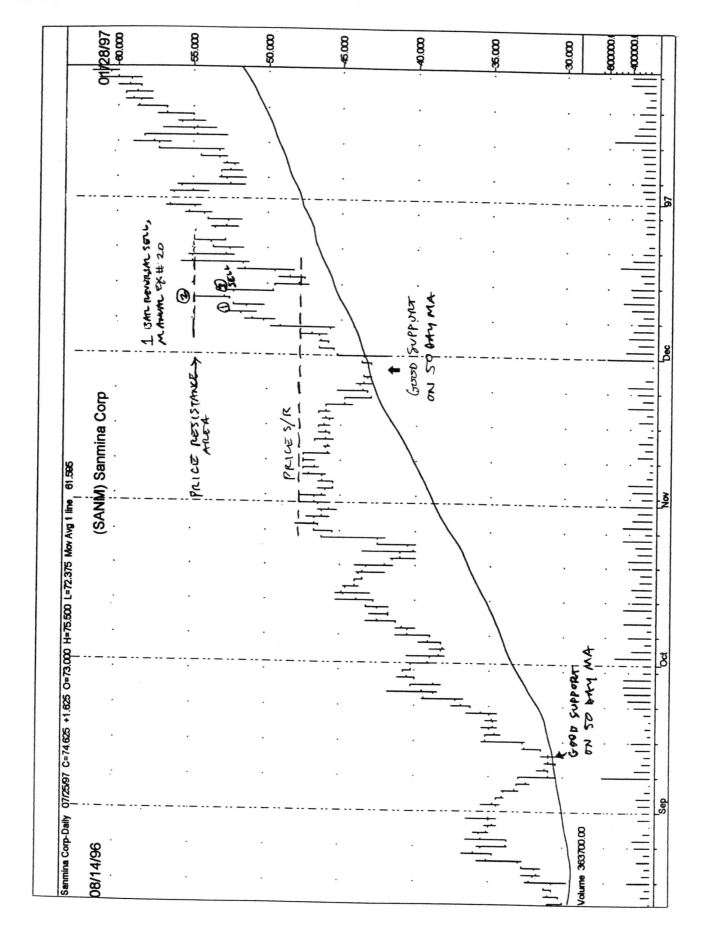

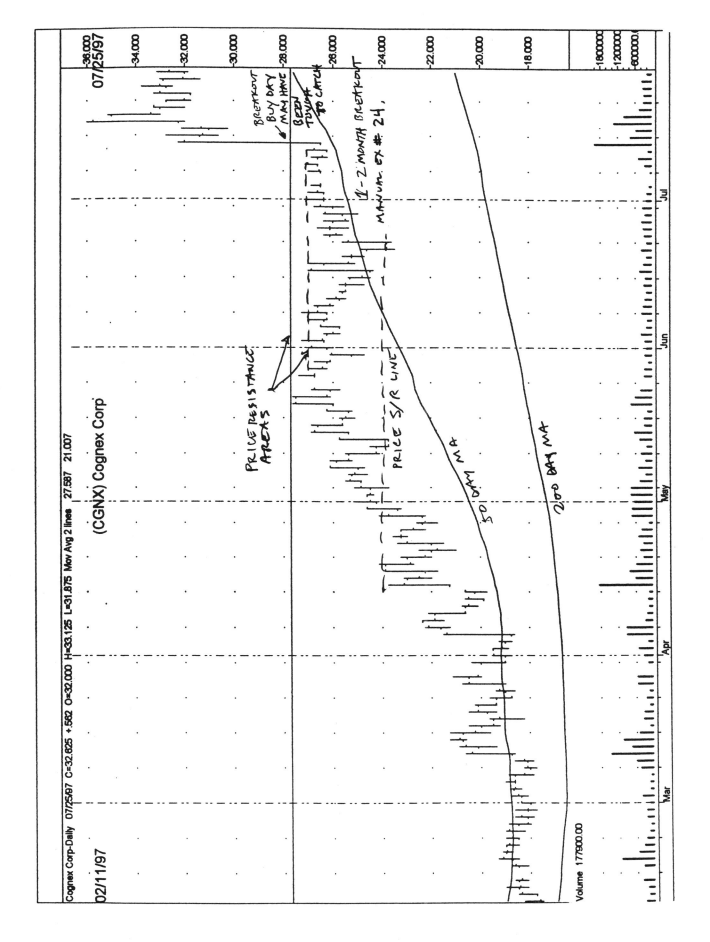

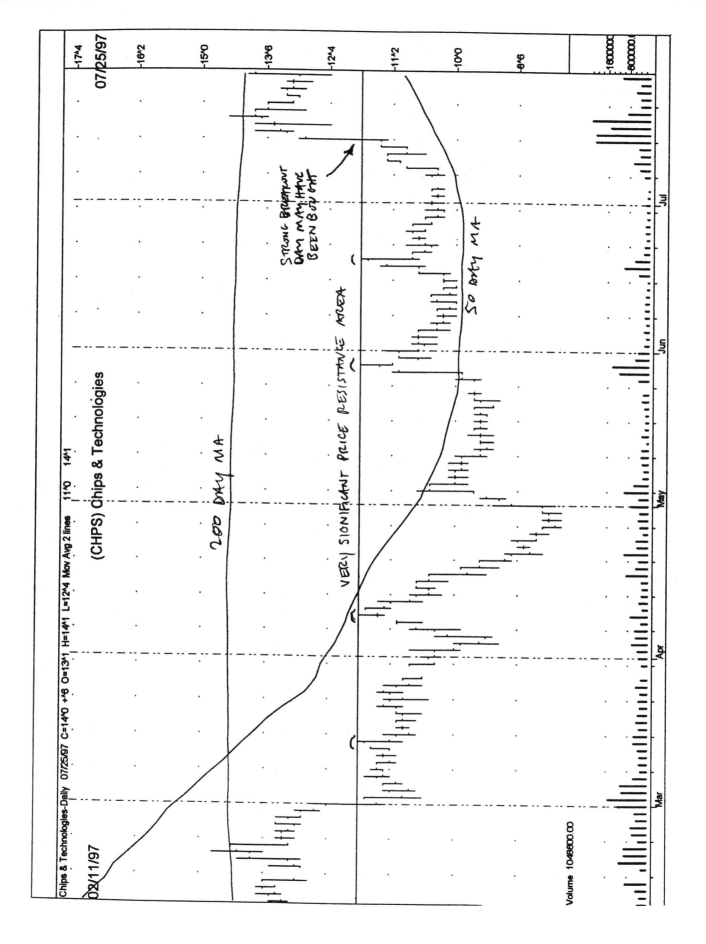

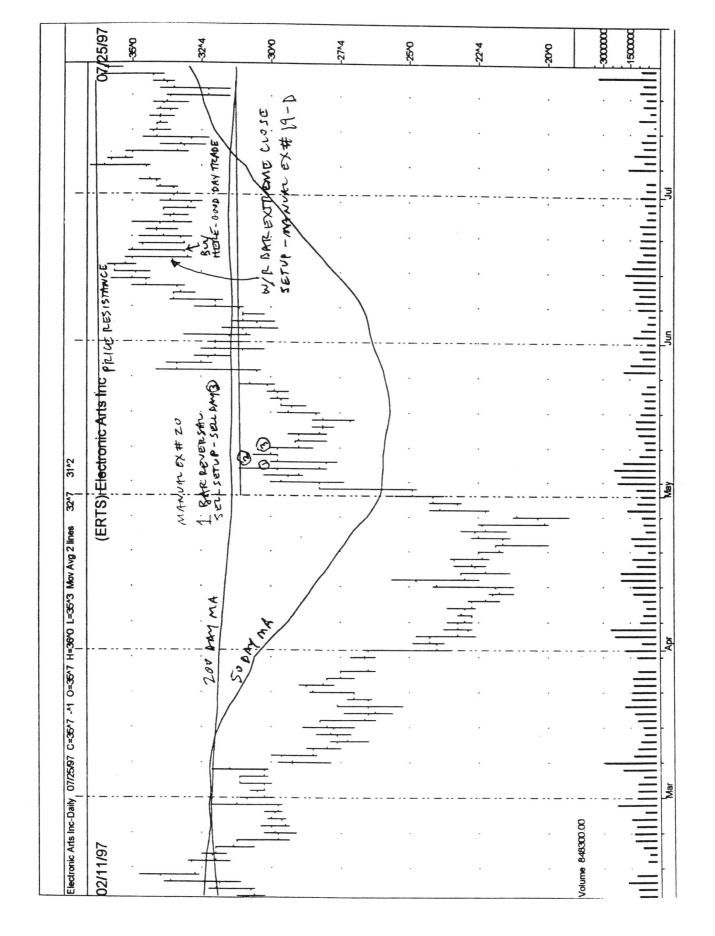

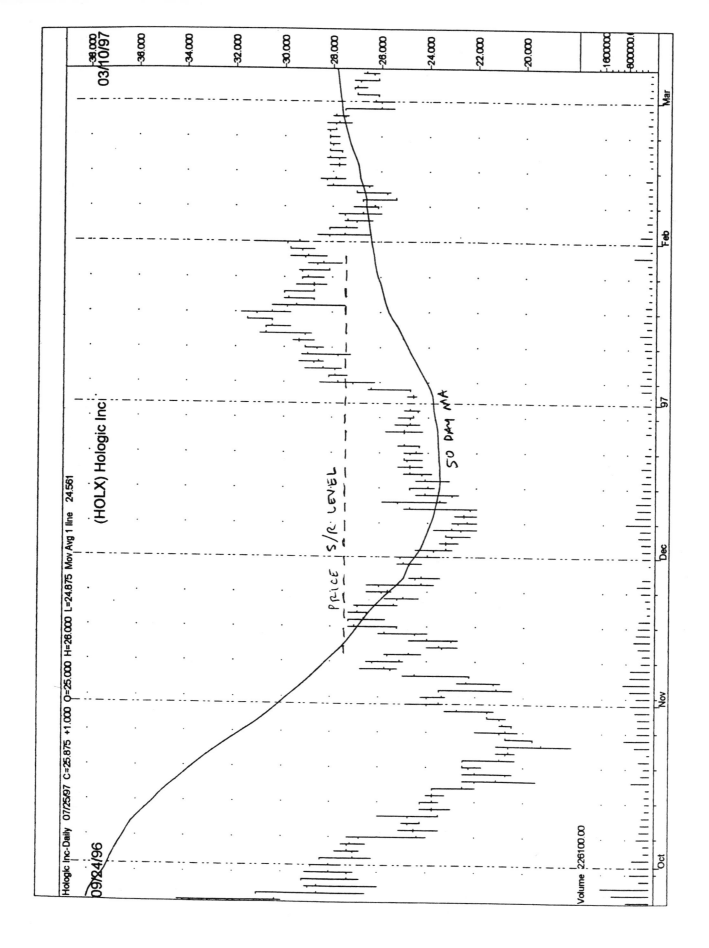

Ascend Communications-Daily 07/25/97 C=48^7 -1^0 O=50^0 H=50^1 L=48^5 Mov Avg 2 lines 47^5 57^1
02/11/97
(ASND) Ascend Communications
NOTICE THAT STOCKS HAVE THEIR OWN PERSONALITY.
YOU'LL OFTEN SEE A SETUP THAT WORKS WELL AND OCCURS OFTEN,
IN THIS CASE IT IS THE 1 & 2 DAY REVERSAL SETUPS
MANUAL EX # 20 & 20A
200 DAY MA
50 DAY MA
SELL WAS NEGATED BECAUSE DAY GAPPED DOWN TOO FAR ON THE OPEN
BUY
PRICE S/R LINE
Volume 4252600.00
65^0
62^4
60^0
57^4
55^0
52^4
50^0
47^4
45^0
42^4
40^0
37^4
2000000
1000000
Mar
Apr
May
Jun
Jul

Hologic Inc-Daily 07/25/97 C=25.875 +1.000 O=25.000 H=26.000 L=24.875 Mov Avg 1 line 24.561

(HOLX) Hologic Inci

PRICE S/R LEVEL

50 DAY MA

09/24/96

03/10/97

38.000
36.000
34.000
32.000
30.000
28.000
26.000
24.000
22.000
20.000

Volume 226100.00

1600000.0
800000.0

Oct   Nov   Dec   97   Feb   Mar

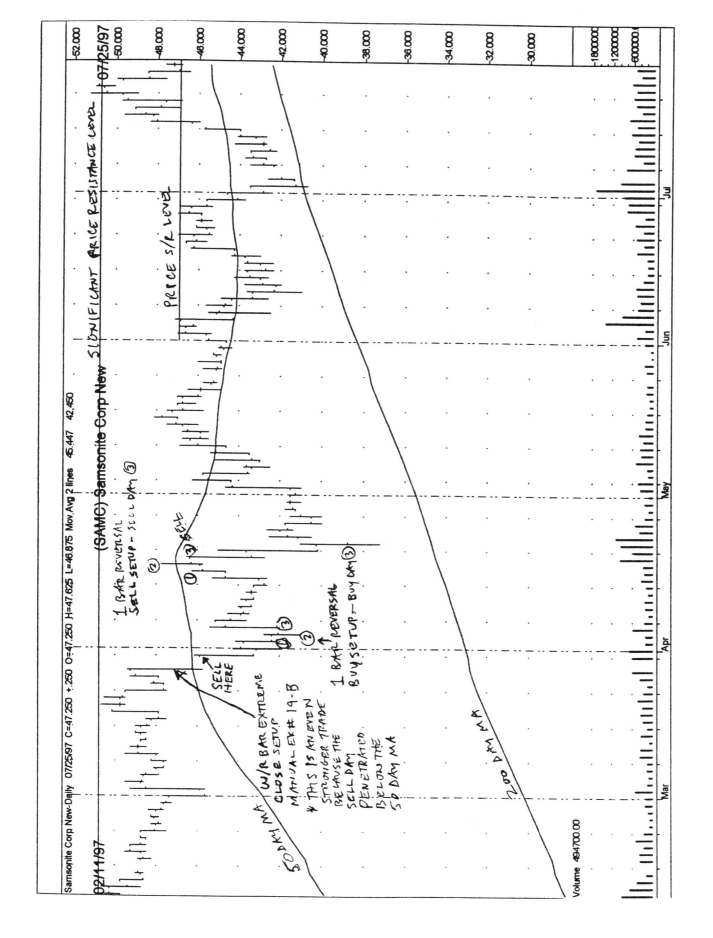

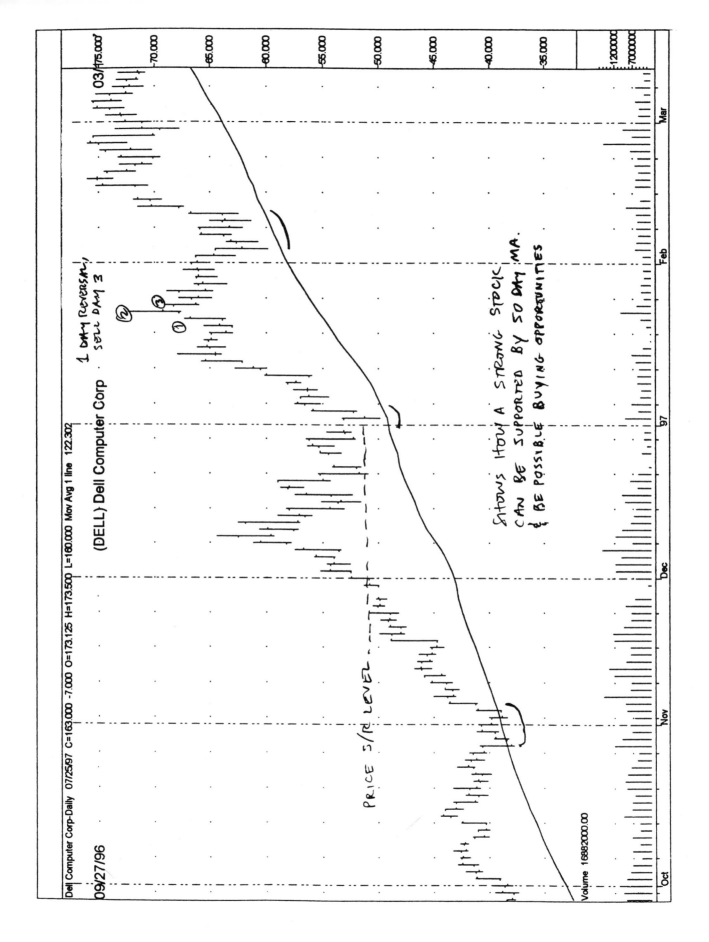

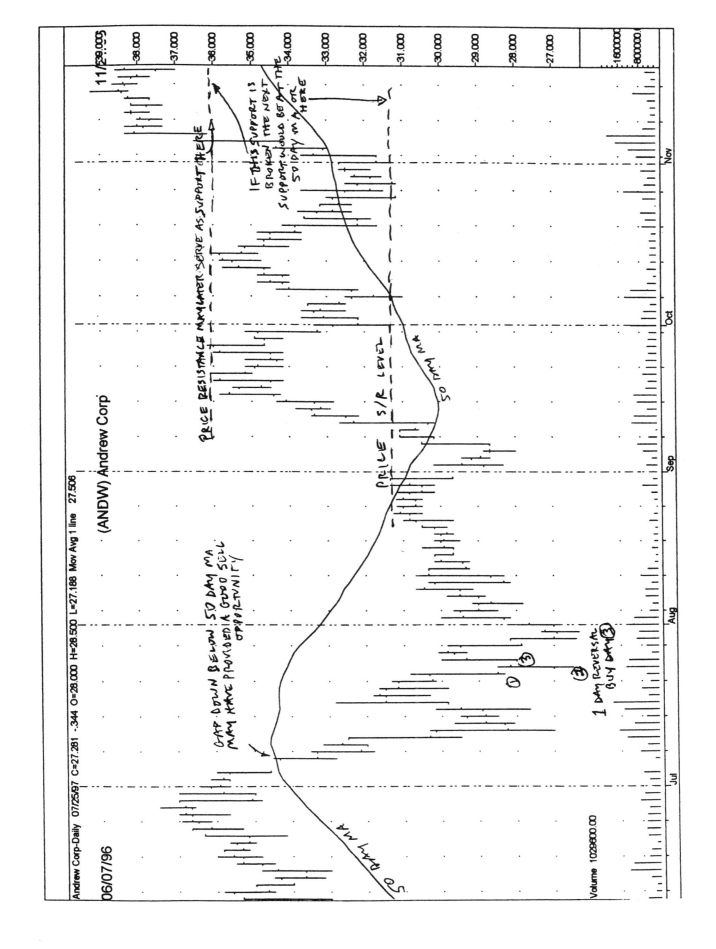

WORKSHEET

For nightly analysis

* Including worksheet <u>KEY</u> for "Day trades" and "Swing trades"

Use the blank worksheet to write in stock symbols which fit under each category as described by the worksheet keys. The worksheet also has an area in the lower right hand corner to list stocks that have news or upcoming earnings. Space is also provided for stocks that you want to add to your ticker and stocks that you want to create a hedge ("box") in the next day.

* Photocopy the blank worksheet and use it to help with market analysis for the next day

DAY TRADES

* KEY for the "Day trades" section of the nightly worksheet

1) WIDE RANGE BAR W/ EXTREME CLOSE

This is a daily bar whose distance from high to low is greater than average for a particular stock. It also should have a close at or near either the high or low of the day. The open should typically be near the other end of the bar. This setup is best when the close has penetrated a support or resistance level or moved out of a sloppy trading range. It also works well after a strong run up or down for several days in a row.

broke out of sloppy
trading range

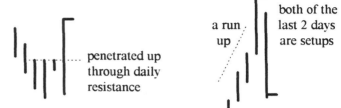
penetrated up
through daily
resistance

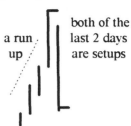
a run
up
both of the
last 2 days
are setups

2) POSSIBLE "REVERSAL" SETUPS (& Delayed Reversals)

This is a 2-3 bar setup where the most recent bar is a reversal type bar. This creates the possibility for a trade on the 3rd or 4th bar completing the reversal pattern.

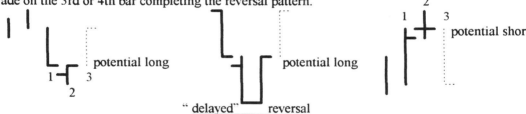

1 3
2
potential long

"delayed" reversal
potential long

2
1 3
potential short

3) NEW HIGHS / LOWS (recent & long term)

This is a day where a stock closes very near or at an all time high, a 52 week high, or a more recent high (6 to 8 week) especially. out of daily consolidation. Also watch for Cup-With-Handle.

4) MISC.

This lists stocks that you may want to keep an eye on based on one or more of the following:

1) A "wedge" 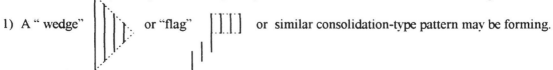 or "flag" or similar consolidation-type pattern may be forming.

2) A significant <u>Support or Resistance</u> price level has been broken, or the stock appears <u>ready to break</u> out of an S/R level...or conversely, an S/R level that <u>appears it will hold</u>.
3) A stock has had a <u>strong run up or down for several days</u> (usually including some W/R bars).
4) <u>50 or 200 day M.A.</u> is holding price...or price has penetrated it.
5) <u>Trend Channel</u> providing S/R or possible trade setup.
6) A significant spike up in <u>volume</u>, or a strong <u>gap</u> (up or down) from the previous day. or recent increased <u>volatility</u> (a larger daily range from high to low for several days).

SWING TRADES
(trade setups for 2 to 5 day holds)

*KEY for the "Swing trade" section of the nightly worksheet

1) <u>TREND CHANNELS</u>

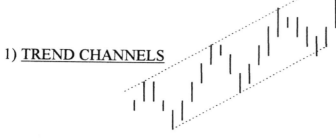

2) <u>1-2 MONTH BREAKOUTS</u>

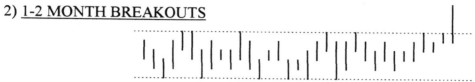

3) <u>CUP W/ HANDLE</u>

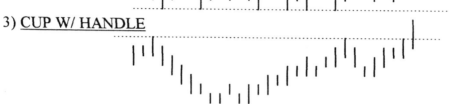

4) <u>50 & 200 DAY M.A.</u>

be aware of stocks bouncing off their 50 day or 200 day moving averages. or a strong penetration of one of the averages - if you have a trade pattern setup, this may help confirm or avoid the trade

5) <u>FAX SERVICES</u>

2 of the best services around are:

1) THE PRISTINE DAY TRADER - internet address: www.pristine.com
2) TRADERS FAXLINE - call Mark at 561-743-6115

6) <u>MISC.</u>

DAY TRADES

1) W/R DAY, EXTREME CLOSE

2) REVERSAL SETUPS

3) NEW HI / LO's (recent & long term)

4) MISC.

SWING TRADES

1) TREND CHANNELS

2) 1-2 MONTH BREAKOUTS

3) CUP W/ HANDLE

4) 50 & 200 DAY M.A.

6) FAX SERVICE(S)

7) MISC.

earnings	news	add ticker	box

EXTRA TIPS AND TRADING IDEAS

This is simply a collection of a few other price pattern setups to watch for. Also, some additional tips about day trading are described to bolster your ability to find other trading opportunities to exploit.

1) This is a 5 minute bar chart pattern that plays out within the first hour of trading and works especially well to the short side if the market index begins a strong, fast, morning sell-off. Also, if the market index gaps up strongly on the open and then begins a strong sell-off, this pattern can work even better. This setup is not as solid as a consolidation / breakout trade, but it may be considered. Look to the daily chart to make sure the stock is not in congestion and that there are no nearby price support levels that may halt the downward move.

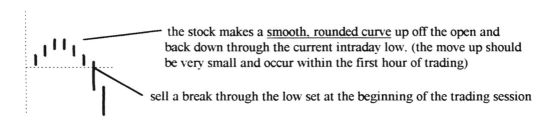

the stock makes a smooth, rounded curve up off the open and back down through the current intraday low. (the move up should be very small and occur within the first hour of trading)

sell a break through the low set at the beginning of the trading session

2) This is a 5 minute bar consolidation at the high of today that is also the high of yesterday. Although shown earlier on some chart examples, I am emphasizing this setup because of its strength. The sell setup is consolidation at the low of today that is also the low of yesterday. Here is an example of a buy setup:

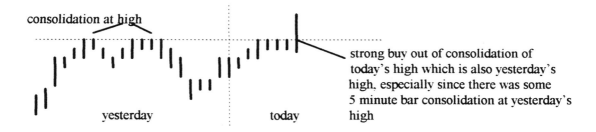

consolidation at high

yesterday

today

strong buy out of consolidation of today's high which is also yesterday's high, especially since there was some 5 minute bar consolidation at yesterday's high

3) A daily reversal bar at a recent support or resistance price level signals an even stronger setup of the reversal bar patterns described in the 1 to 3 daily bar setups.

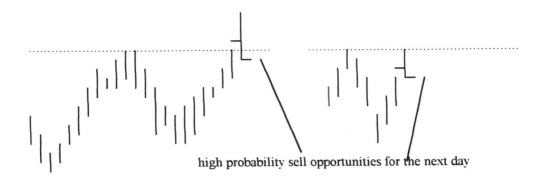

high probability sell opportunities for the next day

The above diagram was a daily reversal sell bar off of prior price resistance. The converse of the diagram would be true for a daily reversal buy setup that bounced off of a prior price support level.

4) If a stock has had a strong, quick run up on the daily chart (usually with some wide range days), it then may have several smaller range days that have successively lower lows with closes at or near their lows. When you see this be ready for a strong sell-off day.

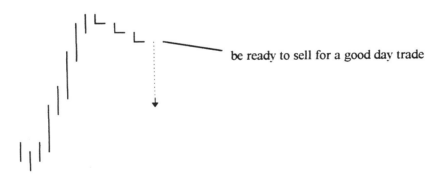

be ready to sell for a good day trade

6) Time of day - The best times of the day to trade are between 8:30 a.m. to 11:00 a.m. and 1:30 p.m. to 3:00 p.m. central standard time. This is when you have more volume and follow-through for the price setups in this manual. Trading primarily during these times enhances the odds of a successful trade. The middle of the day is often illiquid and the trade setups tend to not follow through as well.

7) <u>Round price numbers</u> - This refers to whole numbers like 33, 42, 17, etc. Price sometimes has a tendency to stall at round numbers. If you have consolidation at a round number that then breaks out beyond that price, you tend to see more follow-through. Of more importance are the tens such as 20, 40, 70 etc. Even more significant round numbers to be aware of are 50 and 100. These numbers tend to halt price, or if penetrated, price tends to follow through in the direction of the penetration. This is an added nuance to help with your day trading entry and exit decisions.

8) <u>Price targets</u> - Price targets are prices where you may want to go ahead and take profits as opposed to using the "wiggle". An example was shown in the 1 to 3 daily bar setups covering the reversal bar pattern. In the buy setup, if price reached the high of the first day of the setup then you might want to take your profits. Another example is if you have a good profit in a stock, and it has reached a daily support or resistance area. You may choose to "cut" out of the stock since it may not surpass the support or resistance price level. A third example is when you get a <u>strong, fast price "spike"</u> out of consolidation on the 5 minute bar chart that moves 3/4 point or more. This is especially true if this takes place during the middle of the day. Often price will retrace more than the standard wiggle and stop you out for only a small profit or at break-even. Consider taking profit when a spike has stalled after a breakout. NOTE: This is not an excuse to avoid using the wiggle. This refers only to price spikes of roughly 1 point or more that take place within 5 to 10 minutes after the breakout. In most trades it is best to use the wiggle and be quick to take a loss and slow to take a profit.

9) <u>Relative strength</u> - If the overall market sells off strongly intraday, look for stocks that did not sell off with the market. They have strong "relative strength" when compared to the market. If the market begins to rally, these will be good buy candidates, look for a price pattern setup before entering. They will usually provide a good move up. The same is true if the market is moving up strongly and a stock stays at its low for the day. If the market begins to sell off, that stock has even higher odds of success as a short candidate. Make sure to enter any of these trades on a price pattern setup using the 5 minute bar chart.

10) <u>Bad price fills / Mistakes</u> - If you accidentally get filled at a price beyond what you wanted, or you immediately realize that you made a trade that wasn't based on a good setup (a mistake) then immediately exit the position at the best price that you can get. It is better to take the small loss on a trade that does not have the odds of success behind it. If you wait and hope, it will usually cost you a bigger loss. Solve the problem by exiting the trade and then move on.

11) Paper trading - If you are just beginning to trade, or if you are having a confidence problem with your trading, don't risk real money. Take time to trade and manage your positions as if you were trading, but don't actually trade your account. "Paper trading" will provide the learning ground and give you confidence in the trading methodology as well as confidence in your trading decisions. If you are a beginning trader I recommend at least 3 to 4 weeks of paper trading. This helps you learn the method, gain confidence in its success, and learn the personalities of each individual stock that you follow on your ticker.

12) "Trader-friendly" stocks - Remember that each individual stock cycles in and out of times when it can be traded successfully. It may trade well with this methodology for 2 weeks and then start to behave more erratically, usually going into a price congestion period. Be aware of when this begins to happen, and avoid that stock until it rotates back into a "trader-friendly" mode.

13) News and reports - Anytime a significant report comes out during the day that can affect the stock market, it is best to stand aside and let the dust settle after the initial burst of trading activity. It is hard to make money off of reports and company news. Let the market digest the new information and choose a direction, then look for price pattern setups to hop aboard for a safer ride.

PRICE FRACTIONS SHOWING DOLLAR AMOUNT
(Based on 1000 share trades)

FRACTION	$$$	FRACTION	$$$
1/64	15.625	33/64	515.625
3/64	46.875	35/64	546.875
1/16	**62.50**	**9/16**	**562.50**
5/64	78.125	37/64	578.125
7/64	109.375	39/64	609.375
1/8	**125.00**	**5/8**	**625.00**
9/64	140.625	41/64	640.625
11/64	171.875	43/64	671.875
3/16	**187.50**	**11/16**	**687.50**
13/64	203.125	45/64	703.125
15/64	234.375	47/64	734.375
1/4	**250.00**	**3/4**	**750.00**
17/64	265.625	49/64	765.625
19/64	296.875	51/64	796.875
5/16	**312.50**	**13/16**	**812.50**
21/64	328.125	53/64	828.125
23/64	359.375	55/64	859.375
3/8	**375.00**	**7/8**	**875.00**
25/64	390.625	57/64	890.625
27/64	421.875	59/64	921.875
7/16	**437.50**	**15/16**	**937.50**
29/64	453.125	61/64	953.125
31/64	484.375	63/64	984.375
1/2	**500.00**	**1**	**1000.00**

TRADE SHEET

Trader: _____ Date: _/_/_

	Stock	In	Out	Buy	Sell	G/L	Cum G/L
1	STOCK SYMBOL	ENTRY TIME	EXIT TIME	BUY PRICE	SELL PRICE	GAIN/LOSS	CUMULATIVE GAIN/LOSS
2							
3							
4							
5							
6							
7							
8							
9							
10							
11							
12							
13							
14							
15							
16							
17							
18							
19							
20							
21							
22							
23							
24							
25							
26							
27							
28							
29							
30							
31							
32							
33							
34							
35							

TRADE SHEET

Trader: _____   **Date:** __/__/__

	Stock	In	Out	Buy	Sell	G/L	Cum G/L
1							
2							
3							
4							
5							
6							
7							
8							
9							
10							
11							
12							
13							
14							
15							
16							
17							
18							
19							
20							
21							
22							
23							
24							
25							
26							
27							
28							
29							
30							
31							
32							
33							
34							
35							

THE 10 COMMANDMENTS OF TRADING

1) NEVER LOSE MORE THAT $1000 NET PER DAY (GO HOME)

2) LAYER YOUR TRADES BEGINNING WITH THE FIRST ONE (I.E. MAKE SURE EACH TRADE HAS AN OPEN PROFIT BEFORE YOU ENTER ANOTHER TRADE)

3) TAKE 10 TRADES OR LESS EACH DAY - UNLESS YOUR CUMULATIVE P/L IS INCREASING

4) "CHERRY PICK" ONLY THE BEST TRADES

5) DO NOT EXECUTE A TRADE IN THE FIRST 10 MINUTES OF TRADING

6) DO NOT RISK MORE THAN 1/4 POINT LOSS PER TRADE

7) ONCE YOU HAVE A GOOD PROFIT ON THE DAY, BOOK SOME $$$$
   EX. IF YOU HAVE $1500 NET PROFIT – POCKET $1000 AND USE $500 FOR MORE TRADES & COMMISSIONS

8) IF YOUR WELL PICKED TRADES ARE NOT CLEARING, OR YOU HAVE 3-4 LOSSES IN A ROW, STOP TRADING AND REASSESS IF YOU SHOULD BE IN THE MARKET

9) GIVE A GOOD TRADE THE "WIGGLE"

10) TRADING IS 90% MENTAL DISCIPLINE

IF YOU CANNOT ADHERE TO THESE RULES, YOU WILL LOSE MONEY, AND YOU WILL FAIL!!!

SCALPING MODULE

A SUPPLEMENT

TO

STOCK PATTERNS
FOR
DAY TRADING
AND
SWING TRADING

Barry Rudd

SCALPING METHODOLOGY

As a day trader, scalping simply means you are looking for a quick, small profit in a stock. Usually, you are attempting to make 1/8 point profit (and sometimes more) within a few seconds or a minute or two. Therefore, you want a momentum surge in a stock's price that you can hop on board for a quick and profitable ride. During the day most price movement in a stock is random noise. The majority of moves do not provide enough follow-through in one direction to be profitably traded. So, how do you isolate and predict the strong "price spikes" from the regular ebb and flow of price? The answer lies in intraday price "compression". This can easily be seen on a 5 minute bar chart graph as it unfolds during the trading session. When a stock begins to trade in a very tight range (called consolidation) at the day's current high or low, a potential trade "setup" may be unfolding. To further screen these price pattern setups, two other criteria are applied to filter out only the highest probability trades. First: The consolidation on the 5 minute chart must be <u>hugging</u> up against the current high of the day for a long trade, or <u>hugging</u> down against the current low of the day for a short trade. Second: The consolidation should last for at least 20 - 30 minutes and preferably longer (the longer, the better). This compression builds up like a pressure cooker, and when the stock breaks to a new high or low, you usually get a strong, quick follow-through move in price, i.e. a "price spike". By watching these trades set up during the day you are ready to be one of the first traders to enter the stock at the best price and at the very beginning of a highly reliable momentum surge.

Once you are filled, you immediately bid or offer out for a profit while the momentum is still continuing. Often these trades will move far enough where you can get 1/4 or 3/8 point...and even more. The key to exiting is not to be too greedy or wait too long, because once the momentum begins to slow or stops, your bid or offer is less likely to be filled. Also, if the trade does not follow through like you expected, be ready to buy or sell at break-even if that price is available to you. If momentum has stopped and you haven't been filled on your bid or offer, exit the trade. It is better to take a "flat" than wait for the stock to reverse and hand you a 1/8 point loss or worse. When commissions are factored in, you realize that to be profitable you must risk no more than a 1/8 point loss on any given trade and be ready to exit flat if you are wrong. Also, you must have a high percentage of winning to losing trades to be net profitable. That is why you must rely upon the trade setups in this module.

You must time your entries at the price just prior to the breakout if a breakout move seems imminent as you monitor the activity on the "market maker" and "time and sales" screens. You may also wish to enter one price level later, the actual breakout price. If you do not get your price then pass up the trade. There will be other good setups later.

A good characteristic of the "compression / price spike" is that opportunities of profits beyond 1/8 point present themselves more frequently than with other scalping methods. Sometimes the stock will move so quickly after you enter, that by the time it takes you to put out your bid or offer you are already looking at a 3/8 point move and probable 3/8 point profit. These "windfall" scalps, although infrequent, can sometimes yield even a 1+ point profit with just one trade.

Since you need to keep your maximum loss per trade to 1/8 point you must trade only stocks that typically have a 1/8 point bid / ask spread. This way if you are wrong and the trade immediately goes against you, only 1/8 point is lost. Usually 1000 shares are traded. If you want to trade some 1/4 point spread stocks that tend to have very strong moves out of the setups presented in this manual, then you can drop the number of shares you trade to 500 and look for at least a 1/4 point profit. Either way you risk no more than $125 per trade with the expectation of at least a $125 profit before commissions.

If you buy a stock using a trade setup, you then offer out that stock usually on Selectnet. You may also offer out using Instinet or one of the other E.C.N.'s through your brokerage firm. Conversely, if you short a stock then you bid out into the momentum for a profit.

Don't necessarily limit yourself to 1/8 point increments. 1/16 point increments can be used to increase the profit of a trade or decrease the loss if you are wrong. Every 1/16 point makes a $62.50 difference. Over time these can add up to more profits.

The intraday section in this module covers the main setups that you will be trading based on the 5 minute bar chart. It is very similar to the corresponding section from the "Stock Patterns" manual but is the core of your scalp trading setups. *Therefore it is included in this scalping module with some changes tailored to scalping versus intraday trend trading.* Remember, never risk any more than $125 per trade with any setup when scalping. This includes trades based on the 5 minute bar chart setups and on the daily bar chart setups covered in the "Stock Patterns" manual. Those "1 to 3 daily bar setups" and the "longer term daily bar setups" can also be scalped early in the trading session. You may wish to decrease your lot size from 1000 shares to 500 to minimize risk on those trades due to early morning volatility.

The daily bar chart is often referenced even when using the 5 minute bar chart for your primary setups and trade entries. This is because it is important to be aware of the daily bar chart's price support and resistance areas even when scalping. If you have a buy setup on the 5 minute chart but also see nearby price resistance just above on the daily chart, then the strength of the price spike may be lessened (vice versa with daily bar chart support on the sell setups). On the other hand if a buy setup on the 5 minute chart is hugging the same price as the resistance level on a daily chart (or is above daily resistance) then there is more room for the stock to move up on a breakout with a strong price spike. The converse is true with support levels when shorting a stock. The "Stock Patterns" manual covers the "market maker" and "time and sales" screen with examples. This will help you pick the appropriate stocks you'll track on your "ticker" for scalping.

The 10 commandments of trading for scalpers is different from the "Stock Patterns" manual and gives you a roadmap to help you manage your trading. With scalping, mental discipline will be the biggest factor in your success or failure. Finally, since the 5 minute bar chart setups are the core of this scalping method, actual chart examples are provided at the end of this module. You can also refer back to the 5 minute bar chart examples in the "Stock Patterns" manual at the end of the "intraday setups" section for more nuances as to how these patterns set up and play out in actual trading.

You will see some overlap and duplication of this scalping module with the main "Stock Patterns" manual. This is because **the trade setups and entries are exactly the same**. The primary difference is how you subsequently manage your exit from the trade. While the "Stock Patterns" manual is based on intraday trend trading, the scalping module is based on exiting quickly with smaller, high-probability profits derived from the price spikes seen primarily on the 5 minute bar chart setups. The primary manual and scalping module are designed to dovetail with each other to enhance your trading options while maintaining the same trade entry methodology.

You therefore are provided two different day trading approaches: The "Stock Pattern" manual's intraday trend trading as well as the scalping approach which is presented in this module. This is important because you will find either one style or the other tends to fit your personality as a trader. Choose what works best for you and stick with it. At the same time, each style lends itself to two different market conditions. If you are able to determine early in a trading session whether you are in an intraday trending market, or rather in a choppy market, you can then trade the appropriate style that best fits current market conditions. Knowledge of both styles gives you an edge. Resist the temptation to create a hybrid of the two approaches; it is best to trade either one or the other. Remember, don't impose your will on the market. Instead, react to what the market is telling you. A consistent methodology yields consistent results which equals $$$$ in your account.

WHY USE PRICE BAR CHARTS TO SCALP

Price bar charts paint a graphic picture of a stock's price movements both during the day with the 5 minute bars, and longer term with the daily bars. The picture unfolds showing short and long term supply and demand and how it has moved the stock's price. This helps pinpoint specific areas of buying or selling pressure as they develop. The bar charts alert you to this "at a glance" when the bars trade into a tight range that hugs up or down against a certain price (usually the day's current high or low). This consolidation creates a price "compression" point where pressure builds and is finally released when the price level that held the stock is penetrated. Usually this penetration is a strong and quick "price spike" that offers great scalping potential of 1/8 point or more. By monitoring different stock charts throughout the day, a trader can quickly identify these scalping pattern setups. Since the trader knows which stocks are currently setting up for a price spike, he or she has the edge of catching a strong price move as it <u>begins</u> and then bidding or offering out into the momentum as other traders rush in to participate in the price move. The advantages of using a daily bar chart in conjunction with the 5 minute bar chart were covered at the end of the prior section on methodology. Using the 5 minute bar chart gives you an edge over other market participants in 3 ways:

- It allows you to follow more than just a very few stocks which must be micro-managed. With more stocks on your ticker, more scalping opportunities are uncovered and therefore more potential profits are available.

- The specific price bar setups in the "Stock Patterns" manual and in the scalping module make sure you are entering the stock at the <u>beginning</u> of the momentum surge. This leads to a higher success rate per trade and a larger average profit per trade.

- Since these price pattern setups reflect compression built up against the day's current high or low, the breakout is a very high-odds trade. The success rate of a price spike out of these setups far exceeds the random movements ("noise") back and forth in price throughout most of the day.

Without charts you are only looking at a snapshot of price in time. So much more can be seen with charts to give you an edge. Trading without charts is like flying blind, even when scalping!

TERMS AND DEFINITIONS

* Some terms overlap with the "Stock Patterns" manual in this scalping module, but also some additional definitions are provided related to scalping.

DAY TRADE - Refers to entering and exiting a stock on the same day, typically using 1000 shares.

DAILY BAR CHART - A daily bar shows the open, high, low, and close of a day's trading activity for a stock.

INTRADAY BAR CHART - An intraday bar chart shows a stock's price movement during the day, usually with 5 minute bars.

SUPPORT & RESISTANCE - (also referred to as "S/R") Price support and resistance are areas on a chart that have halted past price movement. A support area tends to halt downward price action, and resistance often halts upward price movement. You can visually see these on both daily and intraday bar charts. It may help to draw a horizontal line through these areas. The significance of support and resistance is to determine if a potential trade setup has enough room to give you a reasonable profit before the stock stalls at one of these S/R areas. Also, a penetration up through a resistance area may open the door for follow-through in the stock's upward movement. Conversely, a penetration down through a support area may then enable the stock to more easily continue its downward movement.

CONSOLIDATION (daily and intraday) - Is when the stock trades in a tight, well defined price range for more than a few price bars. Consolidation can be seen on both the intraday and daily time frames simply by looking at the chart. On an intraday basis, consolidation at the high of the day or at the low of the day can be a potential setup to enter a trade on the breakout to new highs or lows. Price "congestion" is somewhat different and applies primarily to the daily chart. Usually it is best not to trade a stock while it is congested (i.e., has a lot of daily bars clustered together side by side without a well defined support or resistance area). This is characteristic of choppy price movement. Wait for the stock to break out of a congestion area and begin moving before you trade it

PRICE "CONGESTION" - This is when a stock trades in a sideways, choppy manner without a definite direction or trend. It can easily be seen on a daily chart. Avoid trading stocks while they are in this mode. Wait for the price to move out of the congestion area or until it has a good consolidation type breakout setup as described in the price setup patterns of this manual.

BREAKOUT - Consider a stock that has consolidated against a price level for several bars (especially on the 5 minute chart). The point where it breaks beyond that price level is called the "breakout" and often is the beginning of a short to intermediate term move in the direction of the breakout.

<u>FILL-PRICE</u> - When you put an order out to buy or sell a stock, the actual price at which it is executed is called the "fill-price".

<u>STOP-LOSS</u> - This is your mental exit price from a trade that you have entered. It is initially 1/8 point from your actual "fill-price" when you have taken a long or short position in a stock. If the stock moves against you, you exit the trade and are said to be "stopped out" for a loss. Strictly adhere to your stop-loss. It is an integral part of money management.

<u>SCALPING</u> - Scalping is the style of trading based on taking small, quick profits. If a stock has a momentum surge in price, the trader quickly buys or sells in the direction of the price movement. He or she then puts out a bid or offer anywhere from 1/16 to 1/4 point (and sometimes more) from the fill price before the momentum surge slows. Hopefully their bid or offer is taken and a quick profit made on the 1000 share trade. A scalp trade will typically last from just a few seconds to several minutes. To make a decent profit scalping requires a high success rate per trade and strict money management.

<u>FLAT</u> - Exiting a trade at break-even (less commissions and fees).

<u>PRICE SPIKE</u> - A strong, quick move up or down in price, usually occurring out of consolidation on the price bar chart.

<u>BIDDING</u> - If a trader is bidding, he or she is trying to buy a stock at a specific price which he or she chooses. Market makers and/or other market participants can then see the trader's bid to buy a specified number of shares. A bid is usually used to exit a short trade while the stock's momentum is still continuing down.

<u>OFFERING</u> - If a trader is offering, he or she is trying to sell a stock at a specific price which he or she chooses. Market makers and/or other market participants can then see the trader's offer to sell a specified number of shares. An offer is usually used to exit a long trade while the stock's momentum is still continuing up.

INTRADAY TRADING PATTERNS
(for day trading scalps)

INTRODUCTION:

This section covers the day trade setups using 5 minute bar charts. They provide the best scalping potential from "compression" followed by "price spikes". You will almost always be buying and selling breakouts of the current day's high or low based primarily on bar chart pattern setups. Momentum of price movement will be the key to timing the entry. Momentum can be seen with action on the market maker screen and time of sale screen. Recognizing the best setup pattern is the key to entering the highest probability trade. We will present the most consistent trade setups and where to enter long or short with diagrams. Other secondary trades which may also be taken under certain circumstances will be graphically analyzed and explained. Remember, although these rules are not set in stone, they provide the foundation of a strong, high probability methodology for choosing profitable trades. Vertical dotted lines represent the start of the day, horizontal dotted lines show support and resistance areas as well as consolidation boundaries.

* Most examples show buy setups. Sell setups are the same, just inverted.

HIGH PROBABILITY TRADES:

The first trade is an intraday pattern of a 5 minute bar chart that is the basic "dip and rally" setup for a buy breakout.

1)

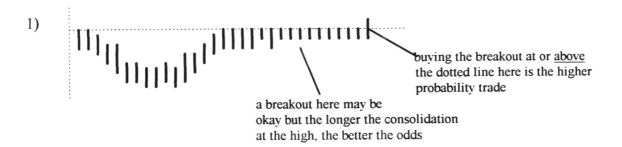

buying the breakout at or above the dotted line here is the higher probability trade

a breakout here may be okay but the longer the consolidation at the high, the better the odds

The consolidation at the high of the day is the key to the success of this setup, as it is with other pattern variations. The longer and tighter the consolidation, the better. This is a setup that develops through the day. Another more obvious pattern looks like this:

2)

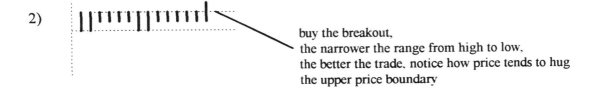

buy the breakout, the narrower the range from high to low, the better the trade. notice how price tends to hug the upper price boundary

Another intraday consolidation pattern that you may see looks a bit different but it can also be a powerful setup:

3)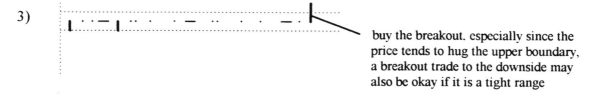

buy the breakout, especially since the price tends to hug the upper boundary, a breakout trade to the downside may also be okay if it is a tight range

In the above setup #3, an active stock can show a deceptively illiquid intraday bar chart. The key to this chart pattern is to make sure the stock averages good volume on a daily basis (i.e. 100k shares +), and that the <u>daily</u> bar chart shows good room for movement to the upside with nearby price resistance. You can also keep tabs on its volume in the market maker screen.

The next chart is another common example leading to consolidation and a good breakout trade:

4)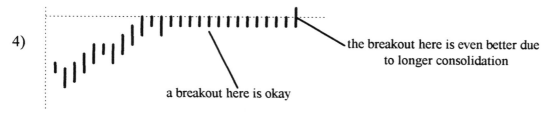

the breakout here is even better due to longer consolidation

a breakout here is okay

Early morning consolidation (similar to pattern #2) can be an integral part of entering trades at the start of the trading day (although it is best to wait 10 minutes before you enter a trade). This way you can catch the first and best breakout. If you are following a particular stock with the expectation of a good move on the day (or simply stumble across one with the following pattern), it may be a strong trade candidate. This is especially true if your market maker screen is moving and showing momentum coming into the breakout. The pattern consists of just a few bars on the morning and a range of only a 1/8 to 1/4.

5) buy the breakout

The point here is to catch the earliest breakout and best price...otherwise pass up the trade. Never chase a stock.

Once a breakout takes place, the stock normally spikes out of the consolidation to begin a strong move. If you miss the initial breakout, other consolidation opportunities may setup in the stock as the day progresses. For example:

6)

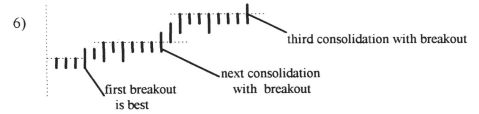

third consolidation with breakout

next consolidation with breakout

first breakout is best

Obviously the first breakout is the best to take. The question arises as to whether you should take the second, third, fourth, etc... breakout. If you missed the earlier breakout(s), how do you know whether or not to take the next one? The best way is to know how long the overall market has been moving in a direction, and if it is losing steam. Also, consider the average daily range of the stock as well as the strength (momentum) coming into the breakout. If the stock often trades a 2 to 3 point daily range, then the subsequent breakouts may still have scalping potential if the range on the day is, for example, only 1 and 1/8 points at that time. Looking at the daily historical chart will show whether the price is breaking out of a daily consolidation area and if daily support or resistance has been broken. This can often lead to a large magnitude move and a stronger initial price spike, even if the last few daily bars have been in a narrow price range. Again, the longer the consolidation on the 5 minute bar chart, the better the trade.

Trade setup #7 depicts 2 good trade entry points following extended consolidation. Both of them may be worth taking. The second breakout to the downside could also be traded

7)

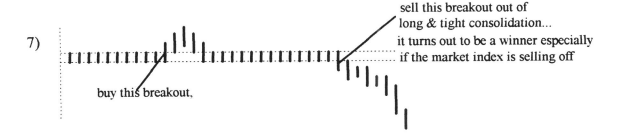

sell this breakout out of long & tight consolidation...
it turns out to be a winner especially if the market index is selling off

buy this breakout,

8)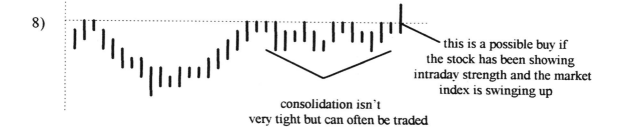

this is a possible buy if
the stock has been showing
intraday strength and the market
index is swinging up

consolidation isn't
very tight but can often be traded

"Wedging" consolidation on the 5 minute chart, especially if it develops over the first 1 to 2 hours of trading, can precipitate strong breakout moves. This pattern usually sets up for a trade on the long side. Consolidation at the high of the day must be present and hugging the upper price boundary as the wedge pattern unfolds. Here is the buy setup:

9)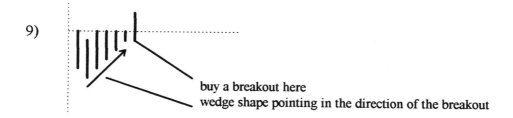

buy a breakout here
wedge shape pointing in the direction of the breakout

So far we've looked at the best and preferred trade setups where you should trade the breakout of the current high or low of the day out of strong consolidation...the longer the consolidation, the better. Remember, you are looking for a strong price spike for maximum scalping potential. There are also a few setups that are more aggressive and may be tradable.

<u>LOWER PROBABILITY TRADES</u>:

These are secondary and somewhat lower probability patterns. But when paired with other analysis, such as momentum from the market maker screen, they may be traded successfully.

10)

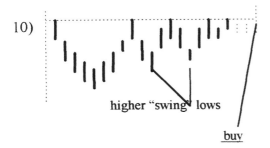

this pattern may well be showing price strength to the upside with successively higher swings down in price as it goes back up to test the <u>same</u> high price, wait for some consolidation before buying a breakout to the upside

higher "swing" lows

<u>buy</u>

11)

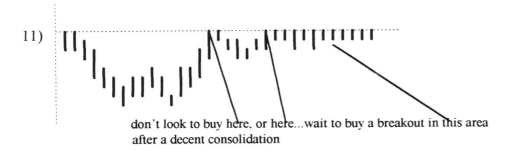

don't look to buy here, or here...wait to buy a breakout in this area after a decent consolidation

The "FLASHBACK" is another morning trade based on a quick reversal in direction of a stock's price. It quickly fakes one direction, then reverses back the other way to break the current high or low of the day. Look for the market index to be moving in the same direction the trade is taken for it to be worthwhile. Here is how it sets up for a buy trade:

12)

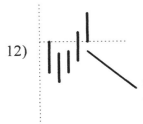

buy a breakout of today's high if it happens within the first 10 - 20 minutes of trading and the distance from the low up to the breakout point is 1/2 point or less ...also the overall market must be moving up <u>convincingly</u> (be careful with this one!!)

13)

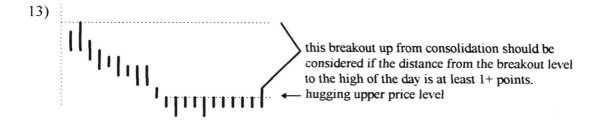

this breakout up from consolidation should be
considered if the distance from the breakout level
to the high of the day is at least 1+ points.
← hugging upper price level

This could be considered if the overall <u>market index begins moving up strongly</u> and there is enough distance to the high from the breakout to make a decent profit. In order for the trade to yield you money there should be at least 1 + points from the breakout point to the high of the day. These trades can be good on a day when the market runs down in the morning and then makes a smooth, rounding bottom that subsequently swings back up.

These examples are often strong trade setups that may be taken for a reasonable percentage of success. The rationale is to get in early on a strong move that will allow a quick and decent scalping profit.

<u>LOWEST PROBABILITY TRADES</u>: Be very careful with these patterns

Here are some similar and seemingly desirable price patterns that should <u>usually</u> not be traded unless there is another convincing reason to enter. The first is a "dip and rally" consolidation that is not quite at the high of the day:

14)

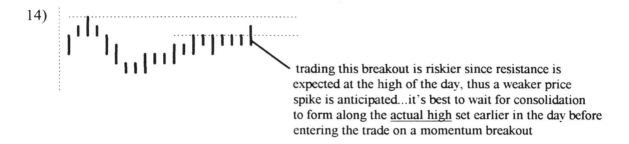

trading this breakout is riskier since resistance is expected at the high of the day, thus a weaker price spike is anticipated...it's best to wait for consolidation to form along the <u>actual high</u> set earlier in the day before entering the trade on a momentum breakout

These other patterns are all further examples of price action that <u>probably</u> should not be traded, even though they may look enticing:

15)

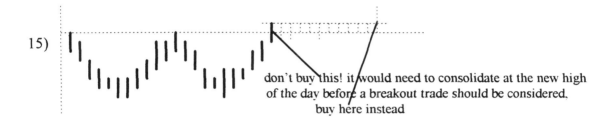

don't buy this! it would need to consolidate at the new high of the day before a breakout trade should be considered, buy here instead

16)

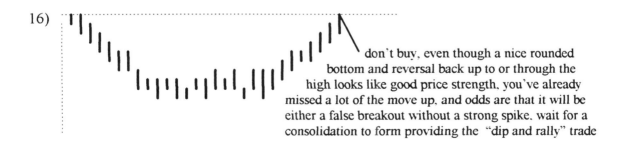

don't buy, even though a nice rounded bottom and reversal back up to or through the high looks like good price strength, you've already missed a lot of the move up, and odds are that it will be either a false breakout without a strong spike, wait for a consolidation to form providing the "dip and rally" trade

17)

don't buy or sell a breakout of the high or low, even though you have definite support and resistance areas, this is <u>not</u> consolidation

18)

great consolidation but it's not at the <u>high</u> or <u>low</u> of the day,
odds are that a breakout trade will not move far enough to give you
a profit

SUMMARY

These have been a few graphic <u>intraday</u> price patterns to give you a feel for what to look
for. They cover the best setups and higher risk trades, as well as what typically not to
trade. Obviously these are drawn as textbook examples. Actual stock charts, as they
unfold during the day, will vary somewhat.

<u>CONCLUSION</u>: What about yesterday's intraday price chart?

Finally, there are occasions to consider yesterday's intraday price chart, especially as it
finished the last hour or two of the day. Here you are looking for stocks that traded in a
tight consolidation pattern into yesterday's close at or near the high or low of that day.
Today, if the stock opens in the same consolidation price range, you are looking at the
possibility of an even more powerful breakout trade. Here is how it should look:

yesterday   today

This presents a great breakout trade of <u>today's current high or low</u>. Refer to the daily bar
price chart for analysis to get a better idea of whether a breakout to the upside or to the
downside is the best trade to take. This price pattern also enhances the success of trades
in the "Stock Patterns" manual section covering <u>daily</u> setups (w/r bars w/extreme close,
and reversal bars). These daily setups are traded early in the market session and may also
be scalped effectively. Refer to the "1 to 3 daily bar setups" and "longer term setups"
from the "Stock Patterns" manual for these day trade scalp patterns.

THE 10 COMMANDMENTS OF TRADING
(FOR SCALPING)

1) NEVER LOSE MORE THAT $650 NET PER DAY (GO HOME)

2) ONLY OPEN 1 TRADE AT A TIME. CLOSE IT OUT BEFORE YOU ENTER ANOTHER TRADE

3) CONTINUE TRADING ONLY IF YOUR CUMULATIVE P/L IS TRENDING UPWARD

4) "CHERRY PICK" ONLY THE BEST TRADES

5) DO NOT EXECUTE A TRADE IN THE FIRST 10 MINUTES OF TRADING

6) DO NOT RISK MORE THAN 1/8 POINT LOSS PER TRADE - AND-REMEMBER, A FLAT TRADE IS YOUR BEST FRIEND IF THE ALTERNATIVE IS A LOSS

7) ONCE YOU HAVE A GOOD PROFIT ON THE DAY, BOOK SOME $$$$
EX. IF YOU HAVE $1000 NET PROFIT -- POCKET $700 AND USE $300 FOR MORE TRADES & COMMISSIONS

8) IF YOUR WELL PICKED TRADES ARE NOT CLEARING, OR YOU HAVE 3-4 FLATS / LOSSES IN A ROW, STOP TRADING AND REASSESS IF YOU SHOULD BE IN THE MARKET

9) BE QUICK TO TAKE A PROFIT WHILE MOMENTUM IS STILL MOVING IN YOUR FAVOR

10) TRADING IS 90% MENTAL DISCIPLINE

IF YOU CANNOT ADHERE TO THESE RULES, YOU WILL LOSE MONEY, AND YOU WILL FAIL!!!

5 MINUTE BAR CHART EXAMPLES

The following pages show actual examples of what the 5 minute bar charts tend to look like in actual trading. Most pages have 2 stock charts with each chart providing 4 days of trading activity. Knowing the intraday price action of a stock for 1 or more prior days helps give you a better feel for that stock's personality at a glance. These intraday chart examples are marked to show consolidation at the high or low of the day and the breakout point. You will be able to see how the setups from the 5 minute intraday bar chart section play out. This is the core of your scalping strategy. Although I've marked most of the successful trades with a decent price spike, you will also see some places where trades would not have worked out and probably provided you with a flat or a loss. You will find in actual trading that many of these "fakeouts" can be eliminated by trading in the direction of the current intraday market indexes and/or by realizing early in a trading day that the market is choppy and not worth trading. Also, being aware of the daily bar chart characteristics (described earlier) helps to filter out only the best trade candidates. Only trade entry points are marked, but what about the exit points? Since you are scalping, you are immediately bidding or offering out into the momentum. Usually you bid or offer for a 1/8 point profit. Sometimes the price moves so quickly that you will look for a 1/4 to 3/8 point profit or more. With some experience you will be able to fine tune your exits to get the greatest available scalping profit. If momentum has stalled and your bid or offer has not been taken, cancel it and buy or sell at market to close out the trade. Not all of the stocks in the following examples are 1/8 or 1/4 point bid / ask spread stocks. I chose them simply because they show what a typical chart will look like. Make sure you trade only stocks which fit the criteria discussed in this module for scalping. These examples will help you translate the "textbook" appearance of the patterns into actual trading.

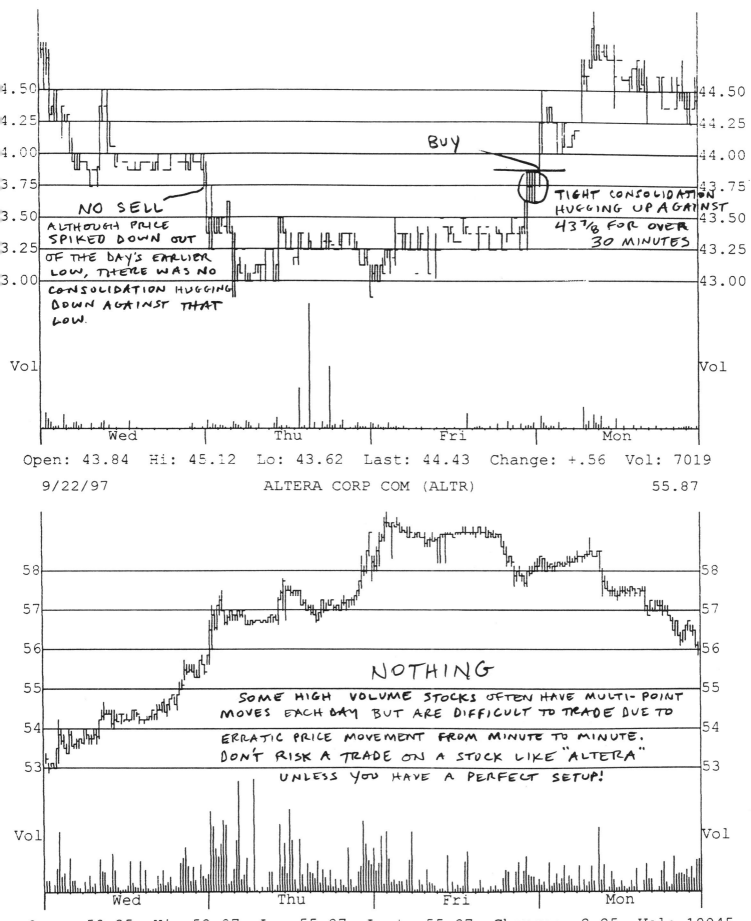

BUY

NO SELL

TIGHT CONSOLIDATION HUGGING UP AGAINST 43⅞ FOR OVER 30 MINUTES

ALTHOUGH PRICE SPIKED DOWN OUT OF THE DAY'S EARLIER LOW, THERE WAS NO CONSOLIDATION HUGGING DOWN AGAINST THAT LOW.

Vol

Open: 43.84 Hi: 45.12 Lo: 43.62 Last: 44.43 Change: +.56 Vol: 7019

9/22/97   ALTERA CORP COM (ALTR)   55.87

NOTHING

SOME HIGH VOLUME STOCKS OFTEN HAVE MULTI-POINT MOVES EACH DAY BUT ARE DIFFICULT TO TRADE DUE TO ERRATIC PRICE MOVEMENT FROM MINUTE TO MINUTE. DON'T RISK A TRADE ON A STOCK LIKE "ALTERA" UNLESS YOU HAVE A PERFECT SETUP!

Vol

Open: 58.25 Hi: 58.87 Lo: 55.87 Last: 55.87 Change: -2.25 Vol: 18045

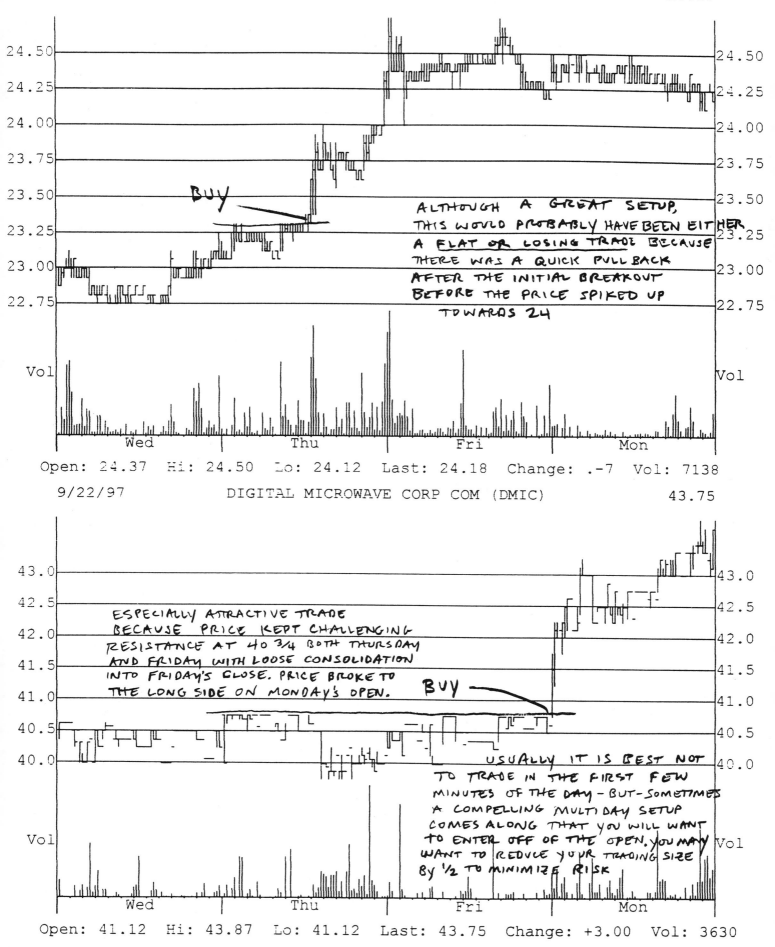

9/22/97 CHIRON CORP COM (CHIR) 24.18

24.50
24.25
24.00
23.75
23.50
23.25
23.00
22.75

BUY

ALTHOUGH A GREAT SETUP,
THIS WOULD PROBABLY HAVE BEEN EITHER
A FLAT OR LOSING TRADE BECAUSE
THERE WAS A QUICK PULL BACK
AFTER THE INITIAL BREAKOUT
BEFORE THE PRICE SPIKED UP
TOWARDS 24

Vol

Wed   Thu   Fri   Mon

Open: 24.37 Hi: 24.50 Lo: 24.12 Last: 24.18 Change: .-7 Vol: 7138

9/22/97 DIGITAL MICROWAVE CORP COM (DMIC) 43.75

43.0
42.5
42.0
41.5
41.0
40.5
40.0

ESPECIALLY ATTRACTIVE TRADE
BECAUSE PRICE KEPT CHALLENGING
RESISTANCE AT 40 3/4 BOTH THURSDAY
AND FRIDAY WITH LOOSE CONSOLIDATION
INTO FRIDAY'S CLOSE. PRICE BROKE TO
THE LONG SIDE ON MONDAY'S OPEN.

BUY

USUALLY IT IS BEST NOT
TO TRADE IN THE FIRST FEW
MINUTES OF THE DAY - BUT - SOMETIMES
A COMPELLING MULTIDAY SETUP
COMES ALONG THAT YOU WILL WANT
TO ENTER OFF OF THE OPEN. YOU MAY
WANT TO REDUCE YOUR TRADING SIZE
BY 1/2 TO MINIMIZE RISK

Vol

Wed   Thu   Fri   Mon

Open: 41.12 Hi: 43.87 Lo: 41.12 Last: 43.75 Change: +3.00 Vol: 3630

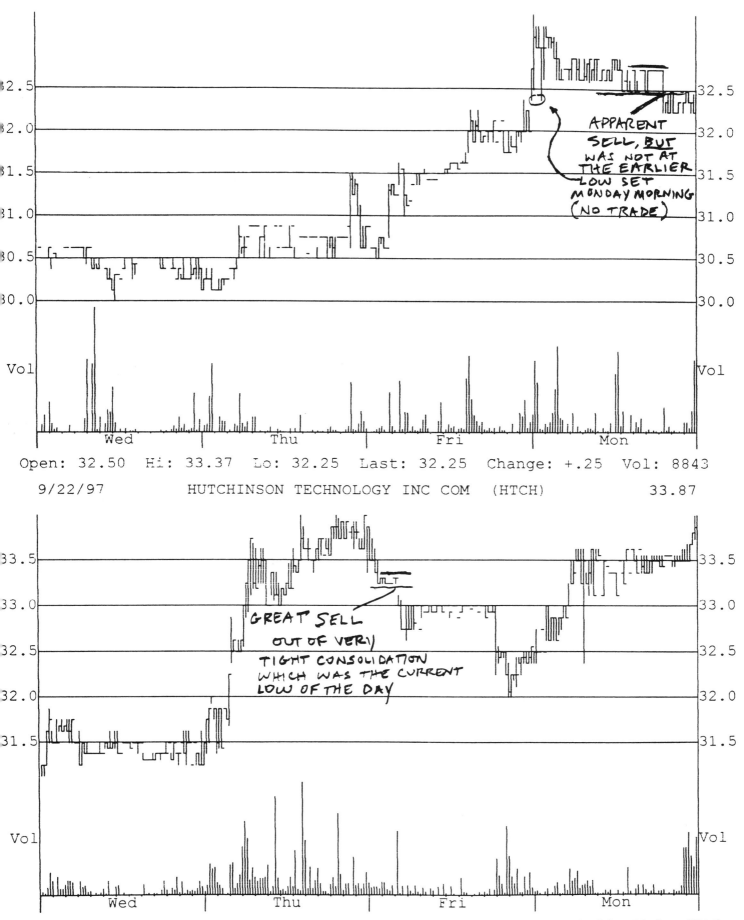

9/22/97   E C I TELECOM LTD COM (ECILF)   32.25

APPARENT SELL, BUT WAS NOT AT THE EARLIER LOW SET MONDAY MORNING (NO TRADE)

Open: 32.50   Hi: 33.37   Lo: 32.25   Last: 32.25   Change: +.25   Vol: 8843

9/22/97   HUTCHINSON TECHNOLOGY INC COM   (HTCH)   33.87

GREAT SELL OUT OF VERY TIGHT CONSOLIDATION WHICH WAS THE CURRENT LOW OF THE DAY

Open: 32.50   Hi: 34.00   Lo: 32.37   Last: 33.87   Change: +1.31   Vol: 4715

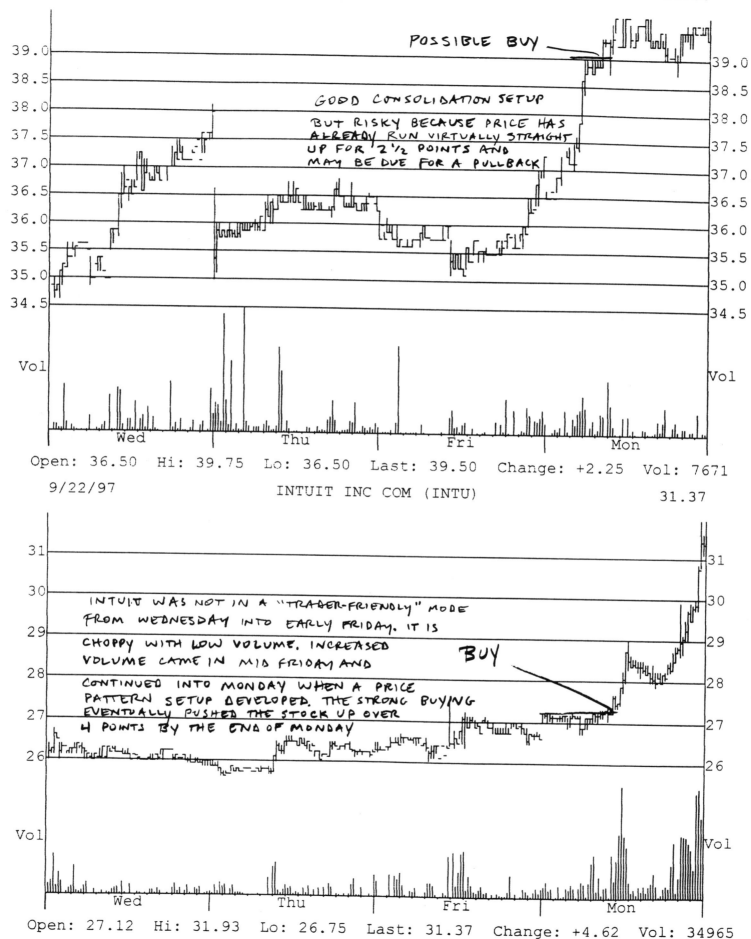

9/22/97   I D E C PHARM CORP COM (IDPH)   39.50

POSSIBLE BUY

39.0

38.5

38.0

GOOD CONSOLIDATION SETUP

BUT RISKY BECAUSE PRICE HAS
ALREADY RUN VIRTUALLY STRAIGHT
UP FOR 2½ POINTS AND
MAY BE DUE FOR A PULLBACK

37.5

37.0

36.5

36.0

35.5

35.0

34.5

Vol

Wed   Thu   Fri   Mon

Open: 36.50 Hi: 39.75 Lo: 36.50 Last: 39.50 Change: +2.25 Vol: 7671

9/22/97   INTUIT INC COM (INTU)   31.37

31

30

INTUIT WAS NOT IN A "TRADER-FRIENDLY" MODE
FROM WEDNESDAY INTO EARLY FRIDAY. IT IS

29

CHOPPY WITH LOW VOLUME. INCREASED
VOLUME CAME IN MID FRIDAY AND

BUY

28

CONTINUED INTO MONDAY WHEN A PRICE
PATTERN SETUP DEVELOPED. THE STRONG BUYING
EVENTUALLY PUSHED THE STOCK UP OVER
4 POINTS BY THE END OF MONDAY

27

26

Vol

Wed   Thu   Fri   Mon

Open: 27.12 Hi: 31.93 Lo: 26.75 Last: 31.37 Change: +4.62 Vol: 34965

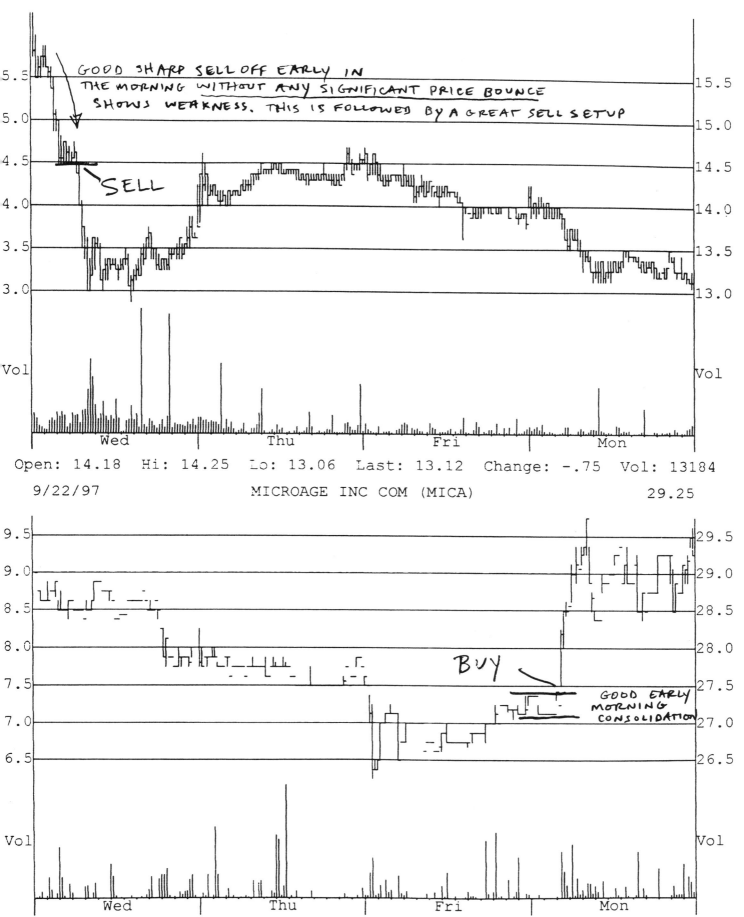

9/22/97   INTERNEURON PHARM INC COM (IPIC)   13.12

GOOD SHARP SELL OFF EARLY IN
THE MORNING WITHOUT ANY SIGNIFICANT PRICE BOUNCE
SHOWS WEAKNESS. THIS IS FOLLOWED BY A GREAT SELL SETUP

SELL

Open: 14.18   Hi: 14.25   Lo: 13.06   Last: 13.12   Change: -.75   Vol: 13184

9/22/97   MICROAGE INC COM (MICA)   29.25

BUY

GOOD EARLY
MORNING
CONSOLIDATION

Open: 27.50   Hi: 29.75   Lo: 27.12   Last: 29.25   Change: +1.93   Vol: 4449

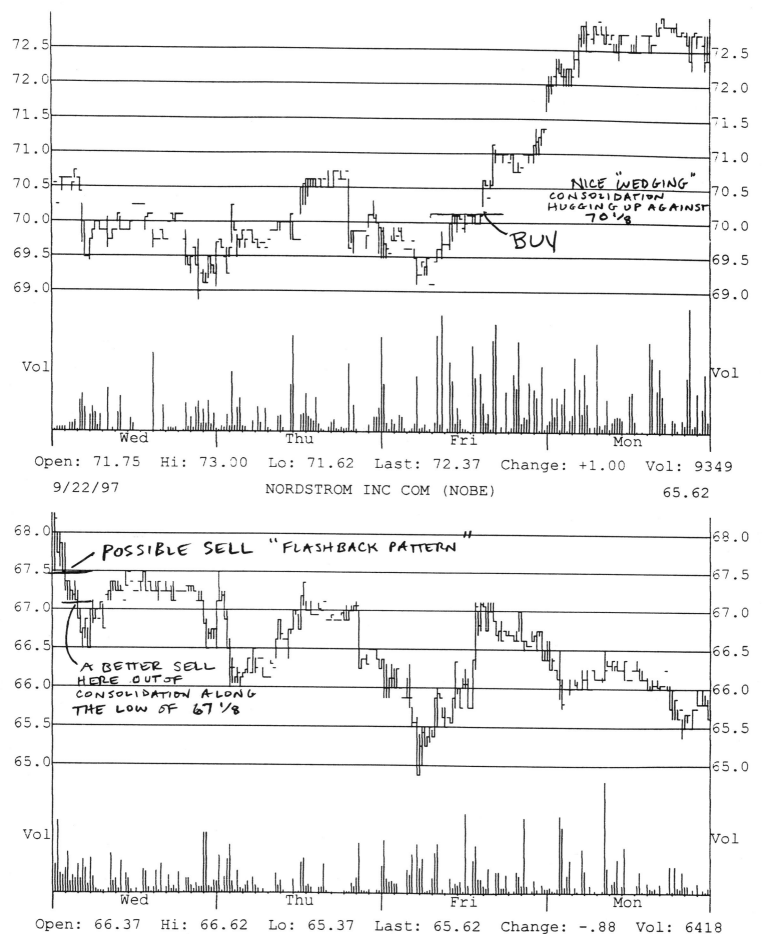

9/22/97   MAXIM INTEGRATED PROD INC COM (MXIM)   72.37

NICE "WEDGING"
CONSOLIDATION
HUGGING UP AGAINST
70 1/8

BUY

Open: 71.75   Hi: 73.00   Lo: 71.62   Last: 72.37   Change: +1.00   Vol: 9349

9/22/97   NORDSTROM INC COM (NOBE)   65.62

POSSIBLE SELL "FLASHBACK PATTERN"

A BETTER SELL
HERE OUT OF
CONSOLIDATION ALONG
THE LOW OF 67 1/8

Open: 66.37   Hi: 66.62   Lo: 65.37   Last: 65.62   Change: -.88   Vol: 6418

186

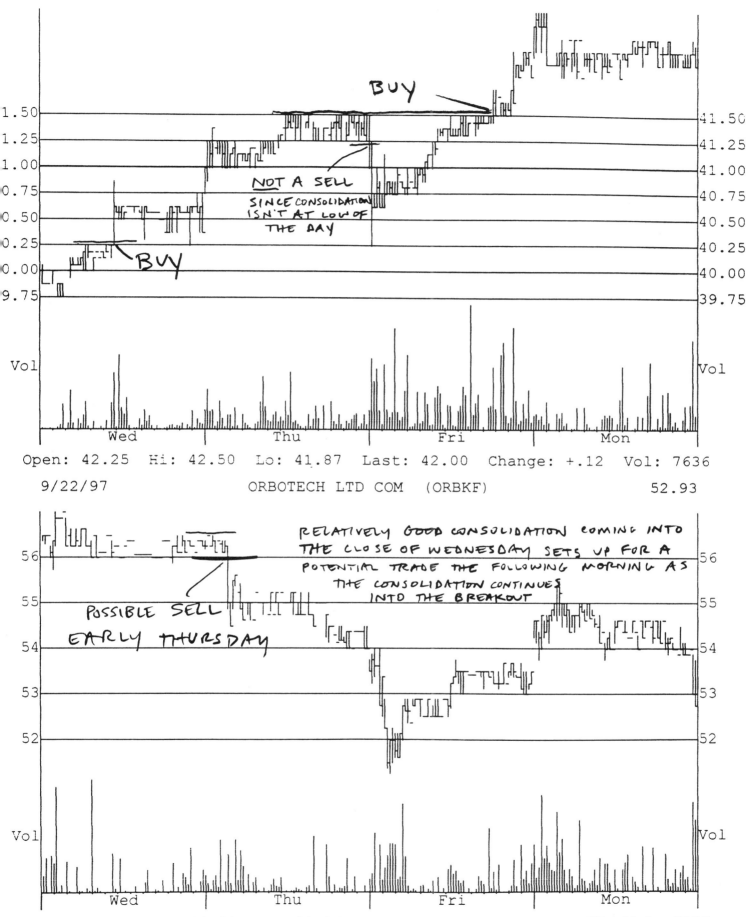

9/22/97 NORTHWEST AIRLINES CORP CL A (NWAC) 42.00

BUY

NOT A SELL
SINCE CONSOLIDATION
ISN'T AT LOW OF
THE DAY

BUY

Vol

Wed   Thu   Fri   Mon

Open: 42.25 Hi: 42.50 Lo: 41.87 Last: 42.00 Change: +.12 Vol: 7636

9/22/97 ORBOTECH LTD COM (ORBKF) 52.93

RELATIVELY GOOD CONSOLIDATION COMING INTO
THE CLOSE OF WEDNESDAY SETS UP FOR A
POTENTIAL TRADE THE FOLLOWING MORNING AS
THE CONSOLIDATION CONTINUES
INTO THE BREAKOUT

POSSIBLE SELL
EARLY THURSDAY

Vol

Wed   Thu   Fri   Mon

Open: 54.25 Hi: 55.50 Lo: 52.75 Last: 52.93 Change: -.57 Vol: 5358

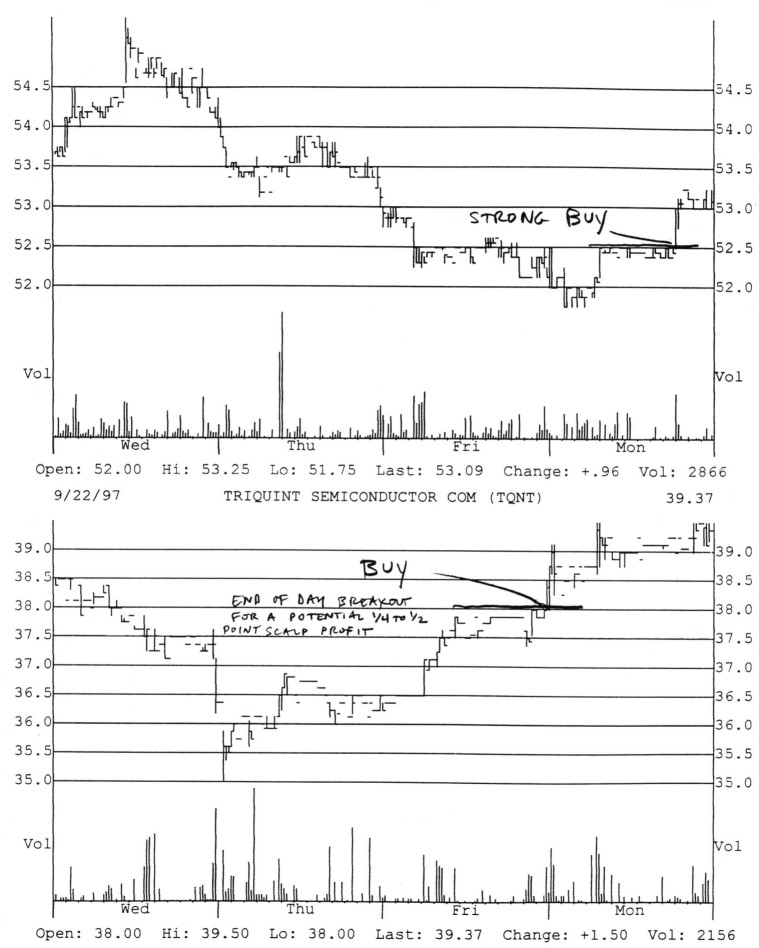

9/22/97   SAFECO CORP COM (SAFC)   53.09

STRONG BUY

Open: 52.00   Hi: 53.25   Lo: 51.75   Last: 53.09   Change: +.96   Vol: 2866

9/22/97   TRIQUINT SEMICONDUCTOR COM (TQNT)   39.37

BUY

END OF DAY BREAKOUT
FOR A POTENTIAL ¼ TO ½
POINT SCALP PROFIT

Open: 38.00   Hi: 39.50   Lo: 38.00   Last: 39.37   Change: +1.50   Vol: 2156

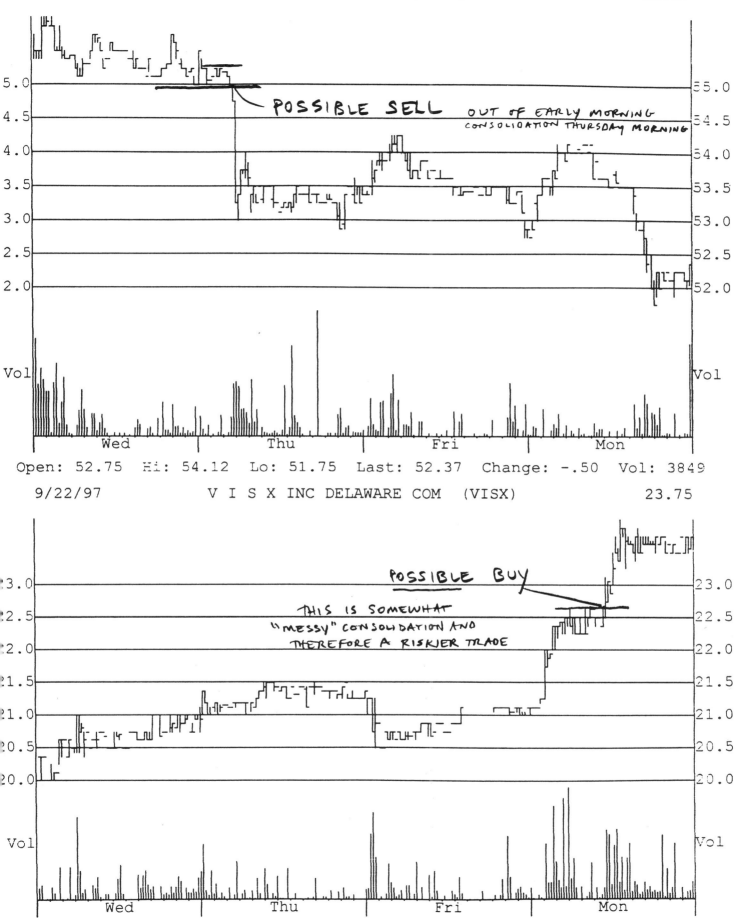

9/22/97 VIASOFT INC COM (VIAS) 52.37

POSSIBLE SELL OUT OF EARLY MORNING
CONSOLIDATION THURSDAY MORNING

Vol

Wed   Thu   Fri   Mon

Open: 52.75   Hi: 54.12   Lo: 51.75   Last: 52.37   Change: -.50   Vol: 3849

9/22/97   V I S X INC DELAWARE COM   (VISX)   23.75

POSSIBLE BUY

THIS IS SOMEWHAT
"MESSY" CONSOLIDATION AND
THEREFORE A RISKIER TRADE

Vol

Wed   Thu   Fri   Mon

Open: 21.00   Hi: 24.00   Lo: 21.00   Last: 23.75   Change: +2.62   Vol: 5545

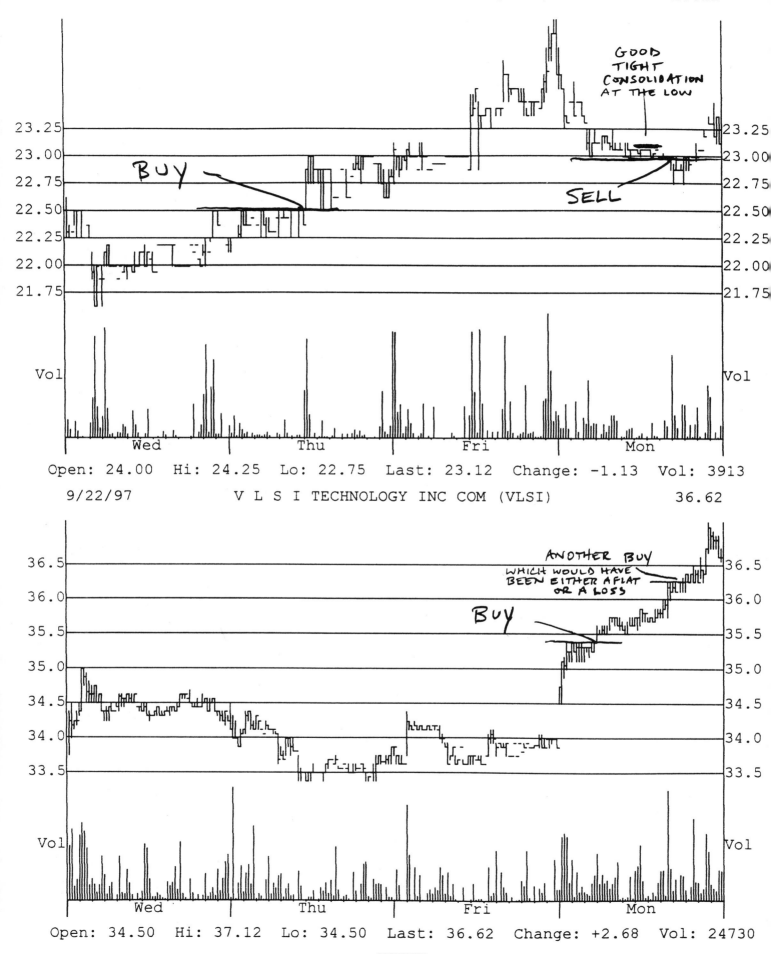

Open: 24.00 Hi: 24.25 Lo: 22.75 Last: 23.12 Change: -1.13 Vol: 3913

Open: 34.50 Hi: 37.12 Lo: 34.50 Last: 36.62 Change: +2.68 Vol: 24730

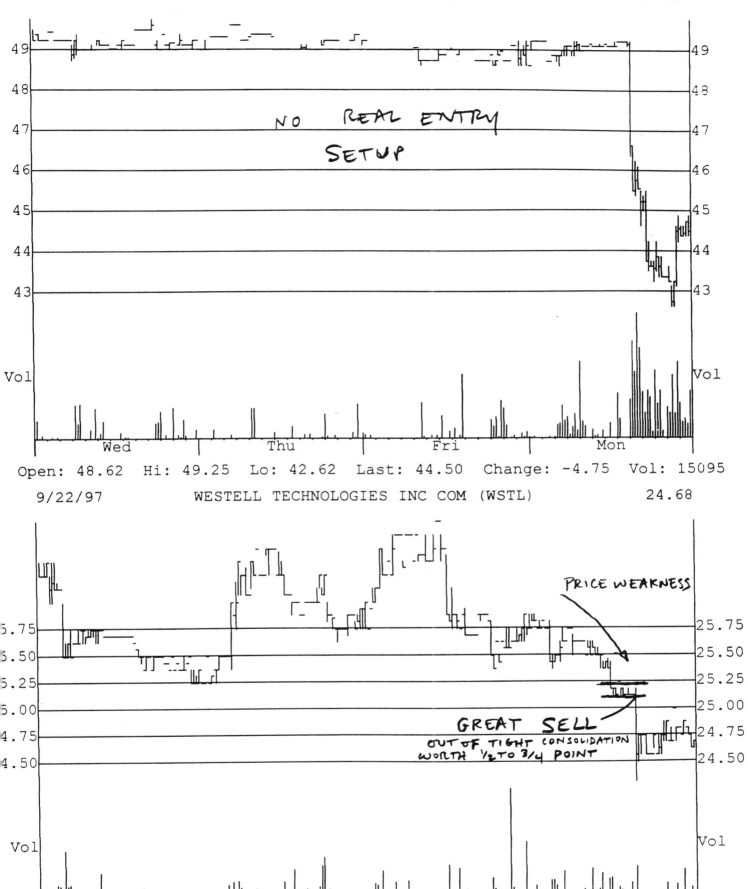

9/22/97   WILLIAMS SONOMA INC COM (WSGC)   44.50

NO REAL ENTRY
SETUP

Open: 48.62 Hi: 49.25 Lo: 42.62 Last: 44.50 Change: -4.75 Vol: 15095

9/22/97   WESTELL TECHNOLOGIES INC COM (WSTL)   24.68

PRICE WEAKNESS

GREAT SELL
OUT OF TIGHT CONSOLIDATION
WORTH 1/2 TO 3/4 POINT

Open: 25.87 Hi: 25.87 Lo: 24.31 Last: 24.68 Change: -1.07 Vol: 3412

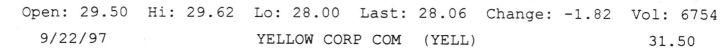

9/22/97   WYMAN GORDON CO COM (WYMN)   28.06

POSSIBLE BUY

POSSIBLE SELL

BOTH TRADES WOULD HAVE PROVIDED
AT LEAST 1/8 POINT SCALPING POTENTIAL

Open: 29.50   Hi: 29.62   Lo: 28.00   Last: 28.06   Change: -1.82   Vol: 6754

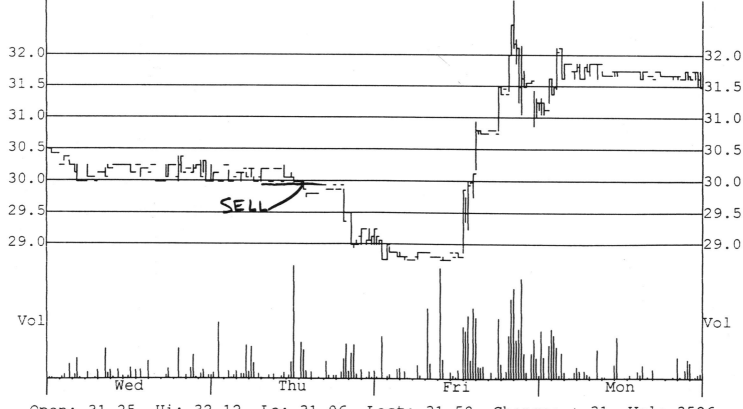

9/22/97   YELLOW CORP COM (YELL)   31.50

SELL

Open: 31.25   Hi: 32.12   Lo: 31.06   Last: 31.50   Change: +.31   Vol: 3596

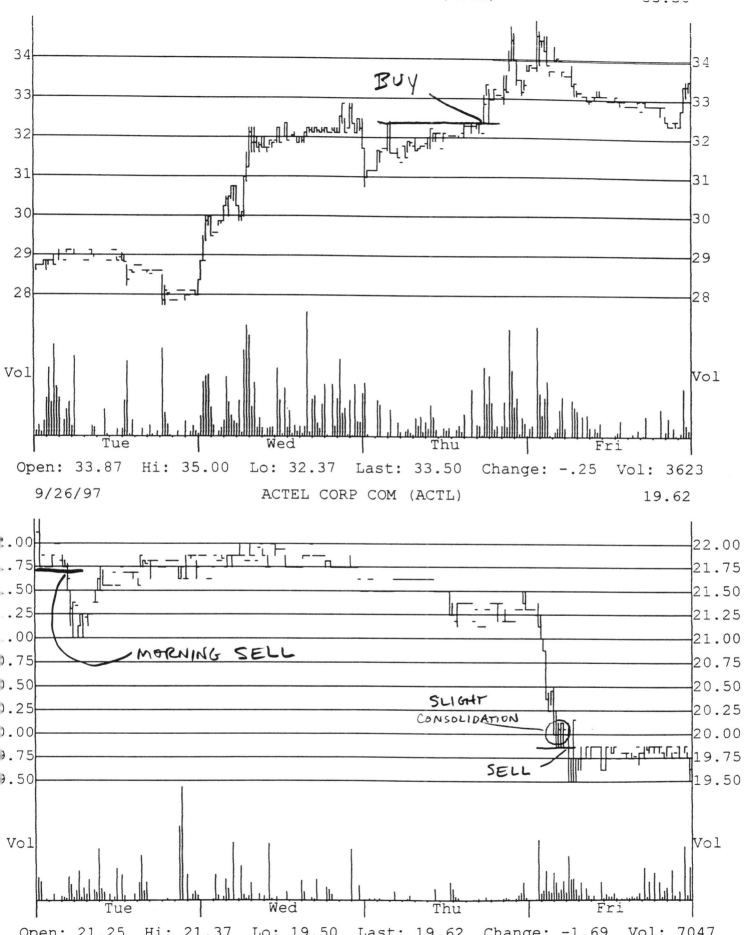

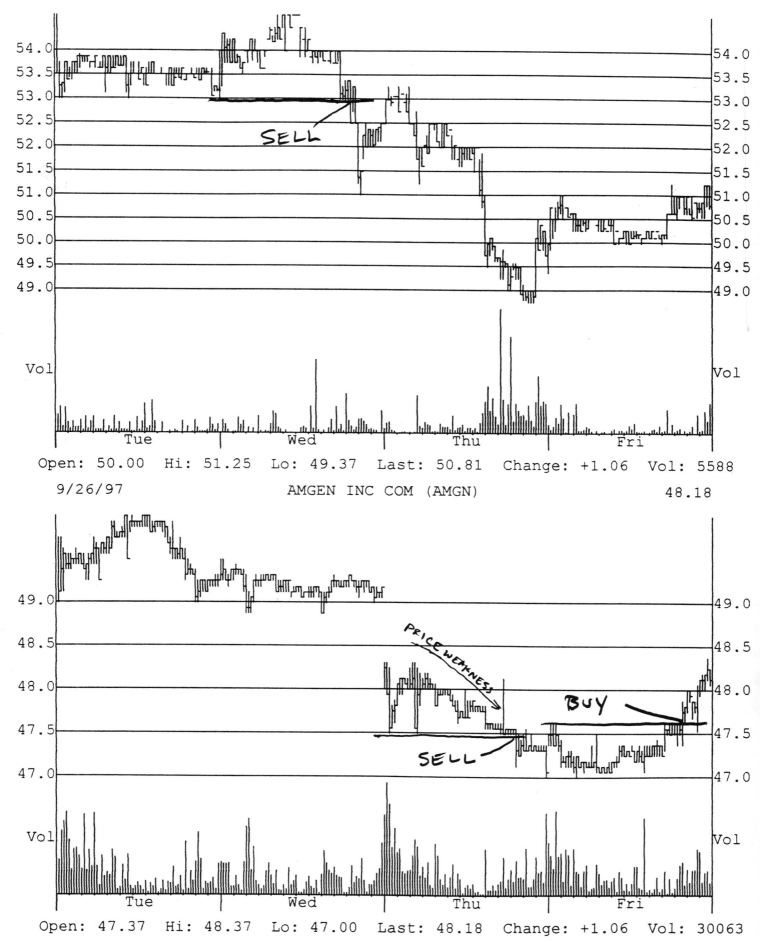

SELL

Open: 50.00 Hi: 51.25 Lo: 49.37 Last: 50.81 Change: +1.06 Vol: 5588

9/26/97   AMGEN INC COM (AMGN)   48.18

PRICE WEAKNESS

BUY

SELL

Open: 47.37 Hi: 48.37 Lo: 47.00 Last: 48.18 Change: +1.06 Vol: 30063

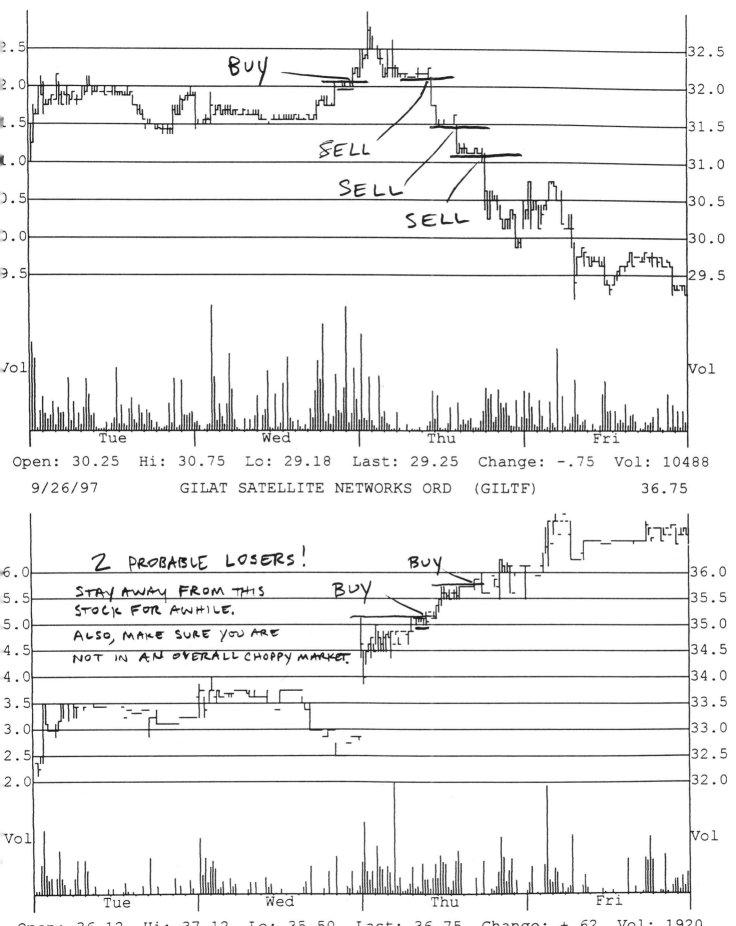

9/26/97   GENZYME CORP COM (GENZ)   29.25

BUY

SELL

SELL

SELL

Vol   Vol

Tue   Wed   Thu   Fri

Open: 30.25 Hi: 30.75 Lo: 29.18 Last: 29.25 Change: -.75 Vol: 10488

9/26/97   GILAT SATELLITE NETWORKS ORD   (GILTF)   36.75

2 PROBABLE LOSERS!

STAY AWAY FROM THIS
STOCK FOR AWHILE.

ALSO, MAKE SURE YOU ARE

NOT IN AN OVERALL CHOPPY MARKET.

BUY

BUY

Vol   Vol

Tue   Wed   Thu   Fri

Open: 36.12 Hi: 37.12 Lo: 35.50 Last: 36.75 Change: +.62 Vol: 1920

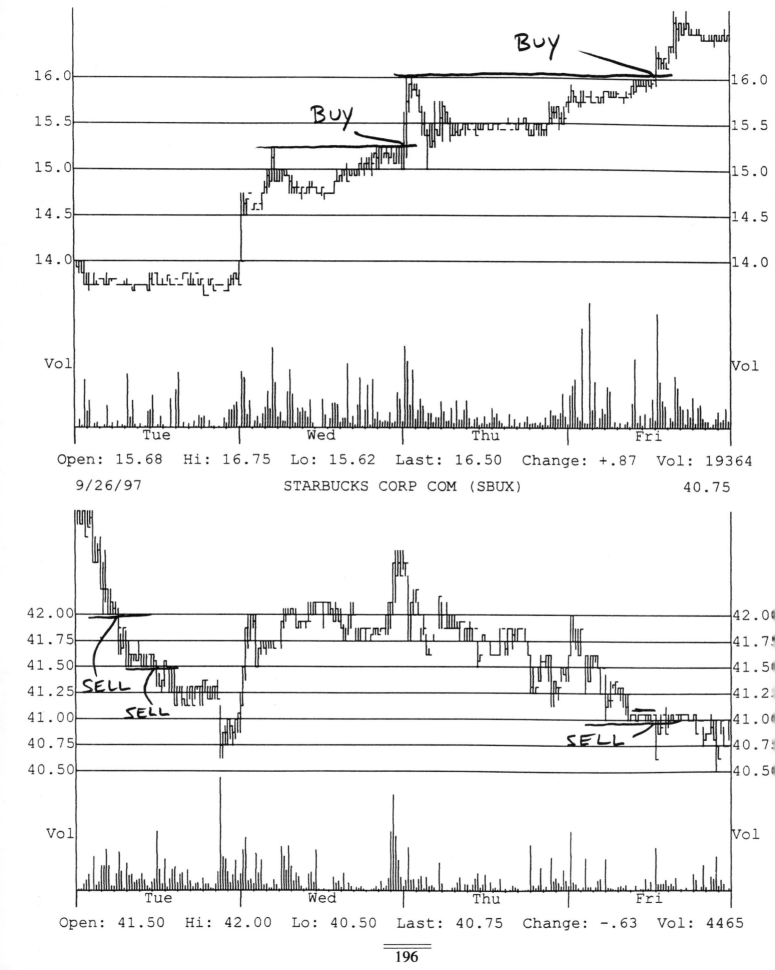

9/26/97   MOBILE TELECOM TECH CORP COM (MTEL)   16.50

BUY

BUY

Open: 15.68 Hi: 16.75 Lo: 15.62 Last: 16.50 Change: +.87 Vol: 19364

9/26/97   STARBUCKS CORP COM (SBUX)   40.75

SELL

SELL

SELL

Open: 41.50 Hi: 42.00 Lo: 40.50 Last: 40.75 Change: -.63 Vol: 4465

196

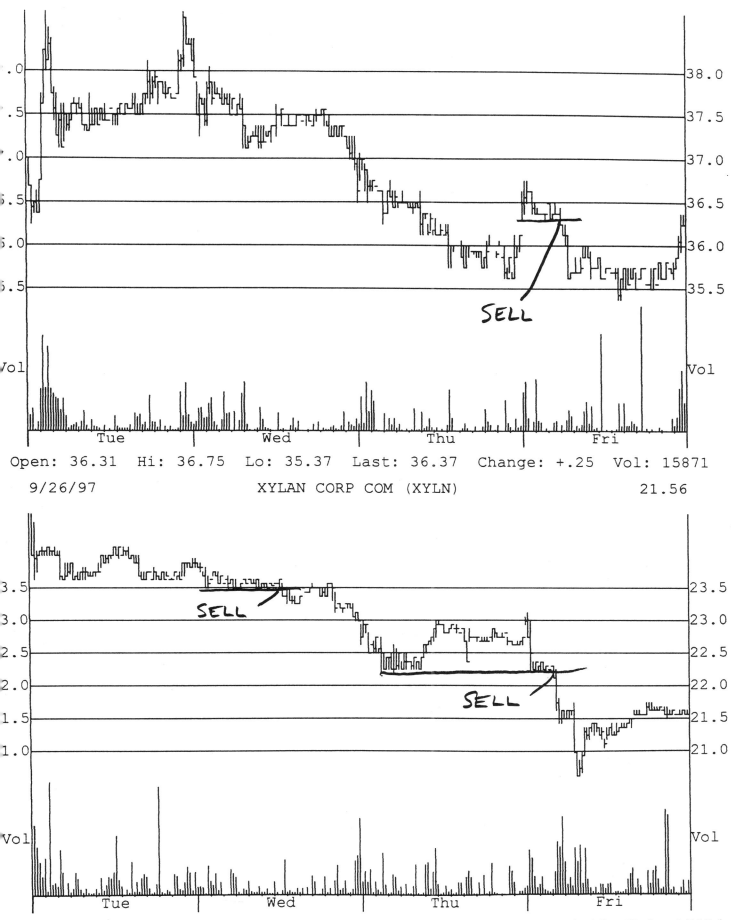

9/26/97   V L S I TECHNOLOGY INC COM (VLSI)   36.37

38.0

37.5

37.0

36.5

36.0

35.5

SELL

Vol   Vol

        Tue   Wed   Thu   Fri

Open: 36.31   Hi: 36.75   Lo: 35.37   Last: 36.37   Change: +.25   Vol: 15871

9/26/97   XYLAN CORP COM (XYLN)   21.56

23.5

SELL

23.0

22.5

22.0   SELL

21.5

21.0

Vol   Vol

        Tue   Wed   Thu   Fri

Open: 23.00   Hi: 23.12   Lo: 20.62   Last: 21.56   Change: -1.19   Vol: 15256

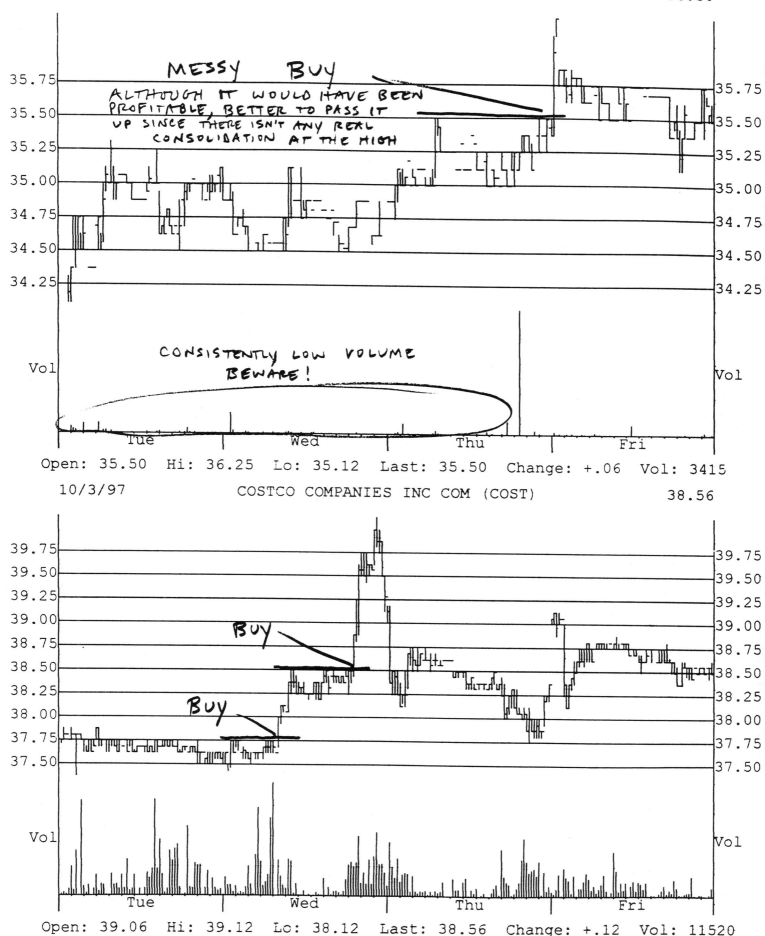

10/3/97   BED BATH & BEYOND INC COM (BBBY)   35.50

35.75

MESSY BUY

ALTHOUGH IT WOULD HAVE BEEN
PROFITABLE, BETTER TO PASS IT
UP SINCE THERE ISN'T ANY REAL
CONSOLIDATION AT THE HIGH

35.50
35.25
35.00
34.75
34.50
34.25

Vol

CONSISTENTLY LOW VOLUME
BEWARE!

Tue   Wed   Thu   Fri

Open: 35.50   Hi: 36.25   Lo: 35.12   Last: 35.50   Change: +.06   Vol: 3415

10/3/97   COSTCO COMPANIES INC COM (COST)   38.56

39.75
39.50
39.25
39.00
38.75
38.50
38.25
38.00
37.75
37.50

Buy

Buy

Vol

Tue   Wed   Thu   Fri

Open: 39.06   Hi: 39.12   Lo: 38.12   Last: 38.56   Change: +.12   Vol: 11520

198

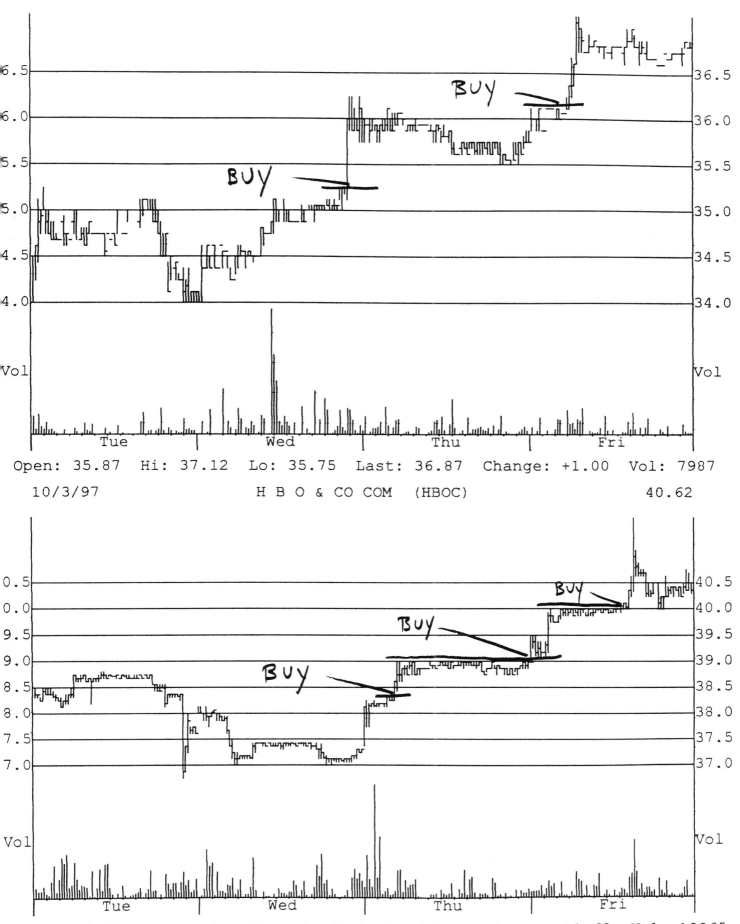

10/3/97   F P A MEDICAL MGMT INC COM (FPAM)   36.87

Open: 35.87 Hi: 37.12 Lo: 35.75 Last: 36.87 Change: +1.00 Vol: 7987

10/3/97   H B O & CO COM (HBOC)   40.62

Open: 39.12 Hi: 41.75 Lo: 39.00 Last: 40.62 Change: +1.62 Vol: 19965

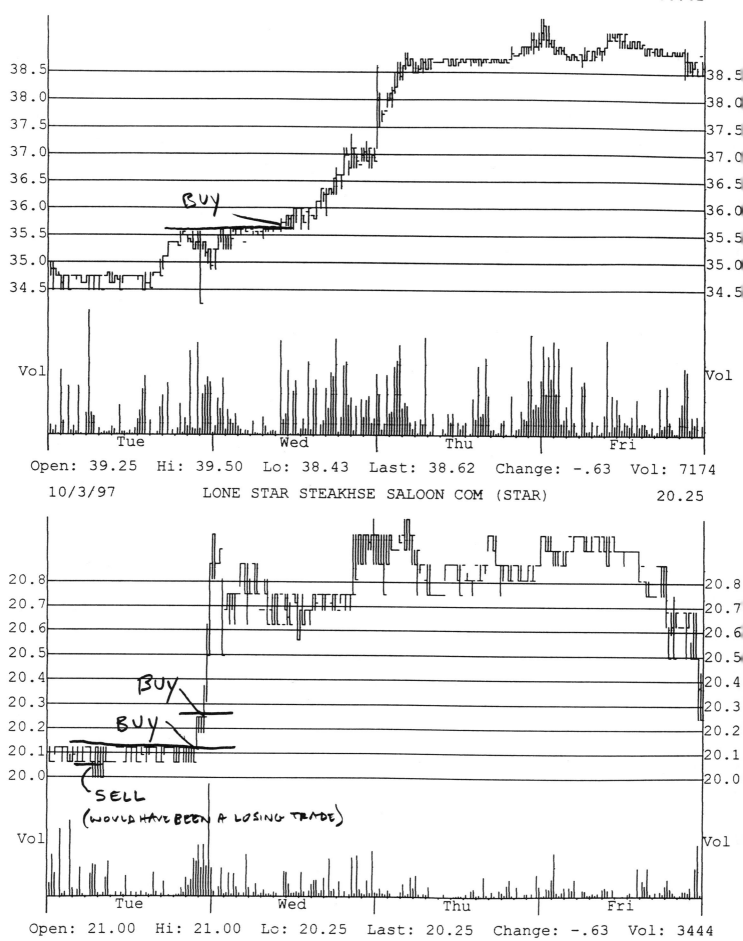

BUY

Open: 39.25 Hi: 39.50 Lo: 38.43 Last: 38.62 Change: -.63 Vol: 7174

BUY

BUY

SELL
(WOULD HAVE BEEN A LOSING TRADE)

Open: 21.00 Hi: 21.00 Lo: 20.25 Last: 20.25 Change: -.63 Vol: 3444

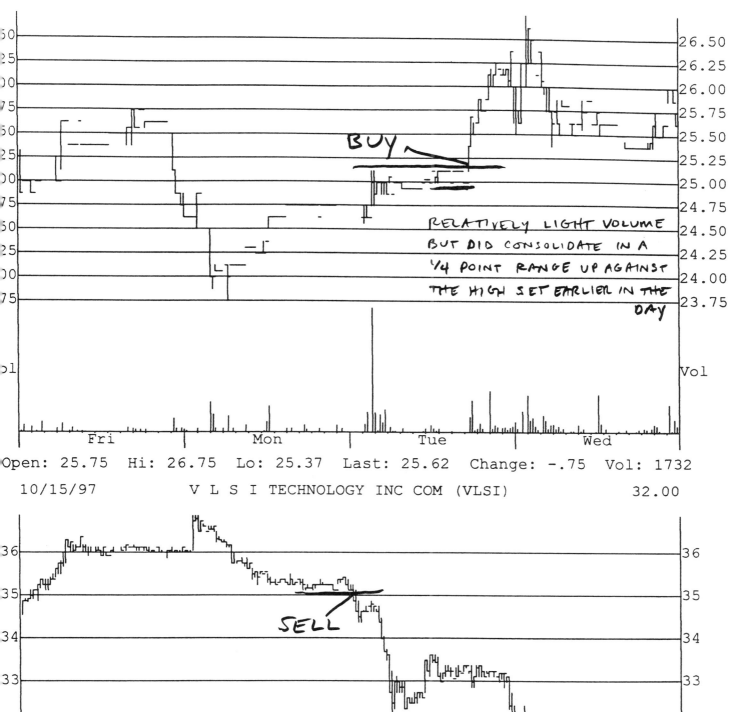

10/15/97   V I S X INC DELAWARE COM (VISX)   25.62

BUY

RELATIVELY LIGHT VOLUME BUT DID CONSOLIDATE IN A 1/4 POINT RANGE UP AGAINST THE HIGH SET EARLIER IN THE DAY

Open: 25.75   Hi: 26.75   Lo: 25.37   Last: 25.62   Change: -.75   Vol: 1732

10/15/97   V L S I TECHNOLOGY INC COM (VLSI)   32.00

SELL

Open: 32.00   Hi: 32.43   Lo: 30.75   Last: 32.00   Change: -.44   Vol: 24089

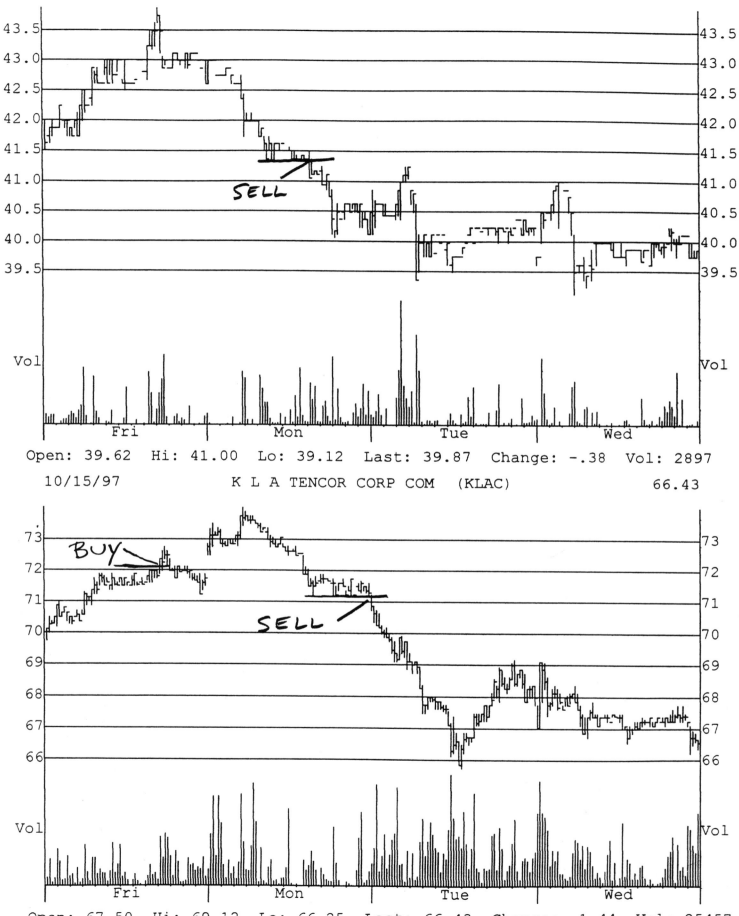

10/15/97   I D E C PHARM CORP COM (IDPH)   39.87

SELL

Open: 39.62   Hi: 41.00   Lo: 39.12   Last: 39.87   Change: -.38   Vol: 2897

10/15/97   K L A TENCOR CORP COM (KLAC)   66.43

BUY

SELL

Open: 67.50   Hi: 69.12   Lo: 66.25   Last: 66.43   Change: -1.44   Vol: 25457

STRONG BUY

GREAT CONSOLIDATION
AND SHOULD BE TRADED EVEN
THOUGH IT IS 1/8 POINT FROM
THE HIGH WHICH WAS MADE
EARLIER IN THE MORNING FRIDAY

Open: 33.12   Hi: 33.25   Lo: 31.43   Last: 31.50   Change: -2.00   Vol: 3174

10/15/97   ELECTROGLAS INC COM (EGLS)   24.93

POSSIBLE
SELL
— BUT —
BREAKOUT NOT AT LOW OF DAY.
IT IS STILL WORTH CONSIDERING BECAUSE OF
LONG, TIGHT TRADING RANGE JUST SLIGHTLY ABOVE THE LOW
OF THE DAY PRIOR TO THE BREAKOUT "SPIKE".

Open: 24.12   Hi: 25.12   Lo: 23.75   Last: 24.93   Change: +.25   Vol: 5464

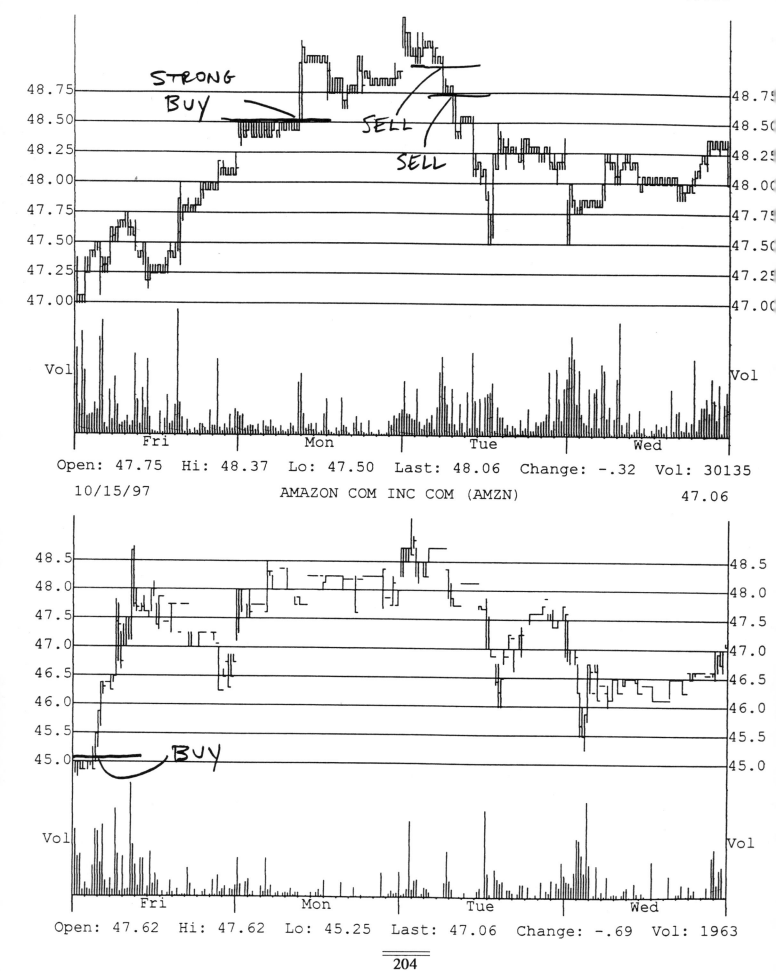

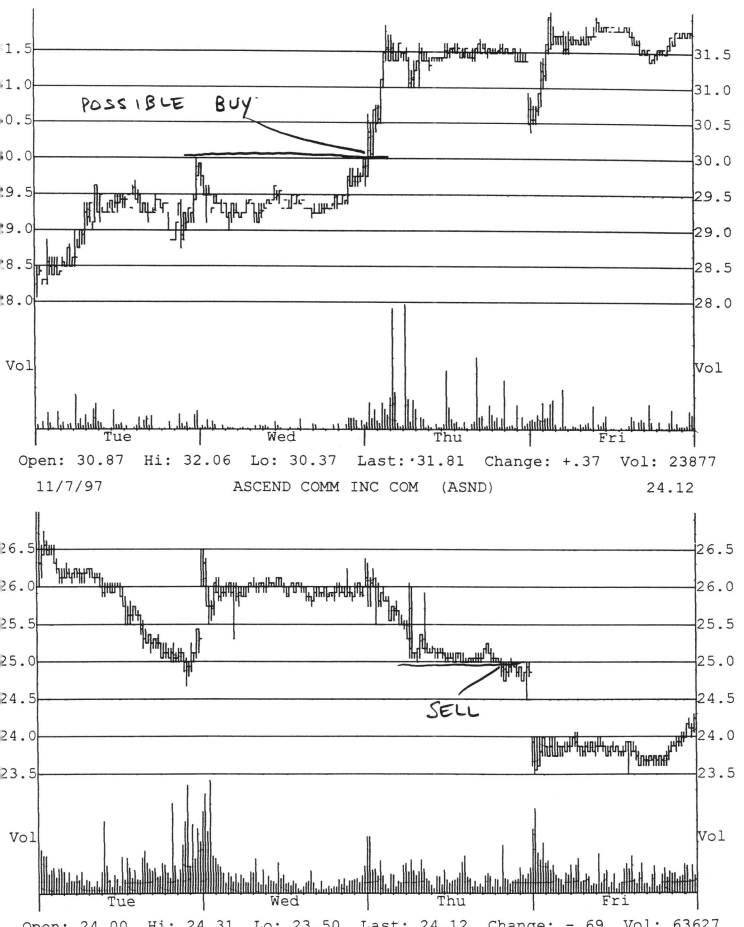

11/7/97   AMERICAN PWR CONVRSN CORP COM   (APCC)   31.81

POSSIBLE BUY

Open: 30.87 Hi: 32.06 Lo: 30.37 Last: ·31.81 Change: +.37 Vol: 23877

11/7/97   ASCEND COMM INC COM   (ASND)   24.12

SELL

Open: 24.00 Hi: 24.31 Lo: 23.50 Last: 24.12 Change: -.69 Vol: 63627

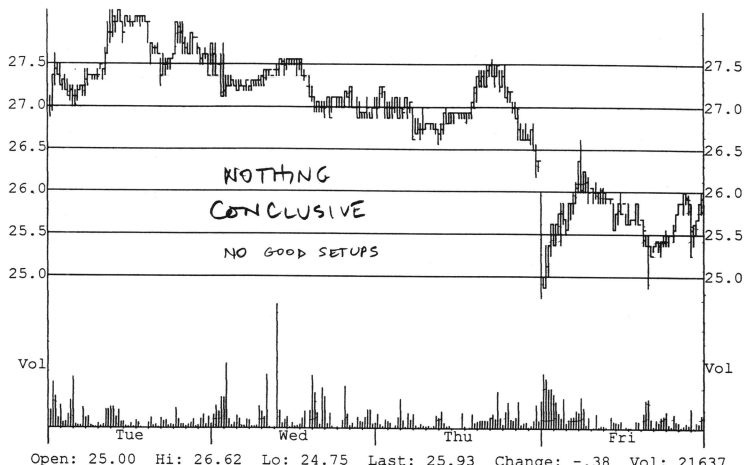

11/7/97   ATMEL CORP COM (ATML)   25.93

NOTHING

CONCLUSIVE

NO GOOD SETUPS

Open: 25.00   Hi: 26.62   Lo: 24.75   Last: 25.93   Change: -.38   Vol: 21637

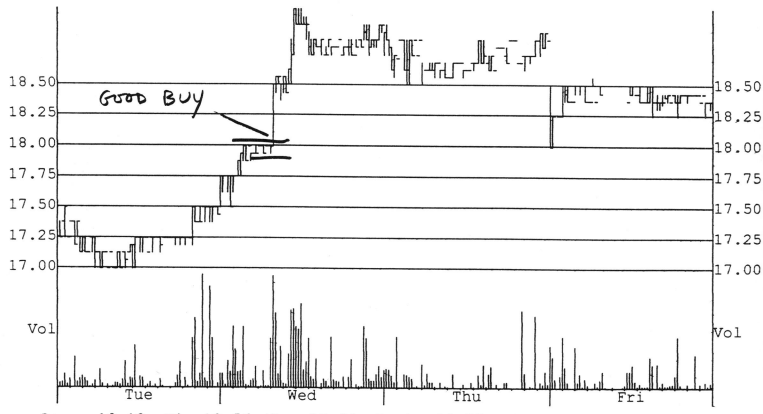

11/7/97   EAGLE HARDWARE&GARDEN INC COM (EAGL)   18.37

GOOD BUY

Open: 18.12   Hi: 18.56   Lo: 18.00   Last: 18.37   Change: -.50   Vol: 1966

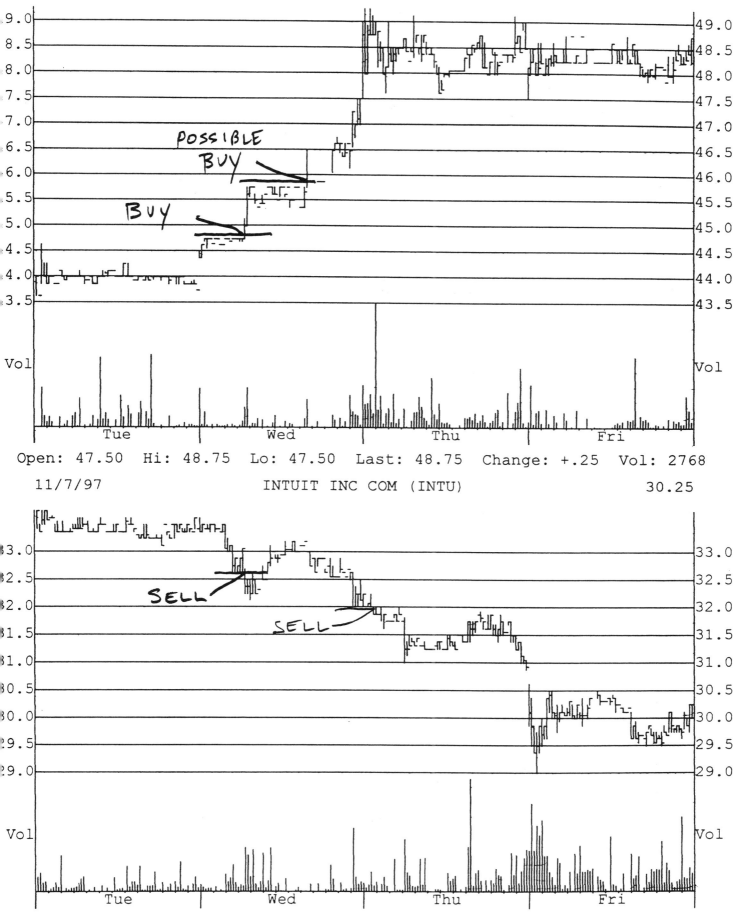

11/7/97   FISERV INC COM (FISV)   48.75

POSSIBLE
BUY

BUY

Open: 47.50 Hi: 48.75 Lo: 47.50 Last: 48.75 Change: +.25 Vol: 2768

11/7/97   INTUIT INC COM (INTU)   30.25

SELL

SELL

Open: 30.62 Hi: 30.62 Lo: 29.00 Last: 30.25 Change: -.63 Vol: 9616

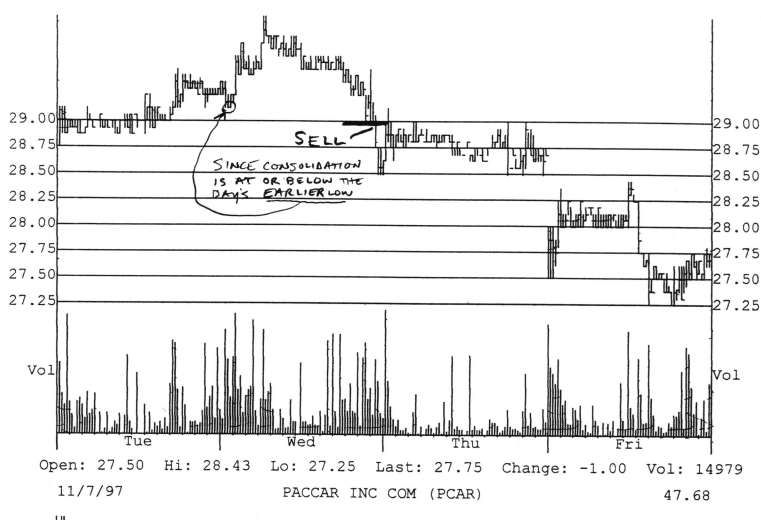

11/7/97   PAIRGAIN TECHNOLOGIES INC COM (PAIR)   27.75

SELL

SINCE CONSOLIDATION
IS AT OR BELOW THE
DAY'S EARLIER LOW

Vol   Vol

Tue   Wed   Thu   Fri

Open: 27.50   Hi: 28.43   Lo: 27.25   Last: 27.75   Change: -1.00   Vol: 14979

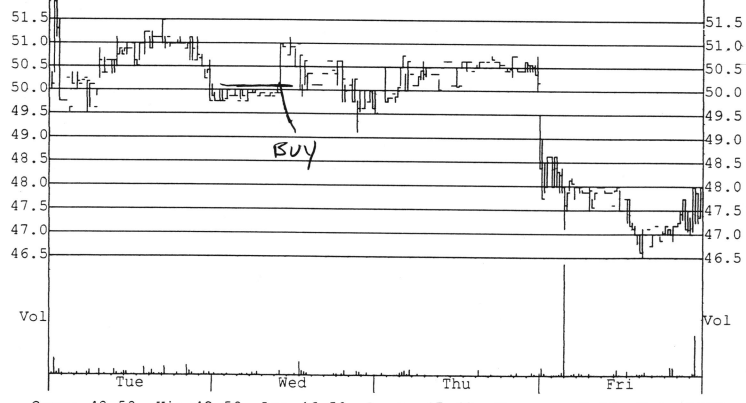

11/7/97   PACCAR INC COM (PCAR)   47.68

BUY

Vol   Vol

Tue   Wed   Thu   Fri

Open: 48.50   Hi: 49.50   Lo: 46.50   Last: 47.68   Change: -2.50   Vol: 7823

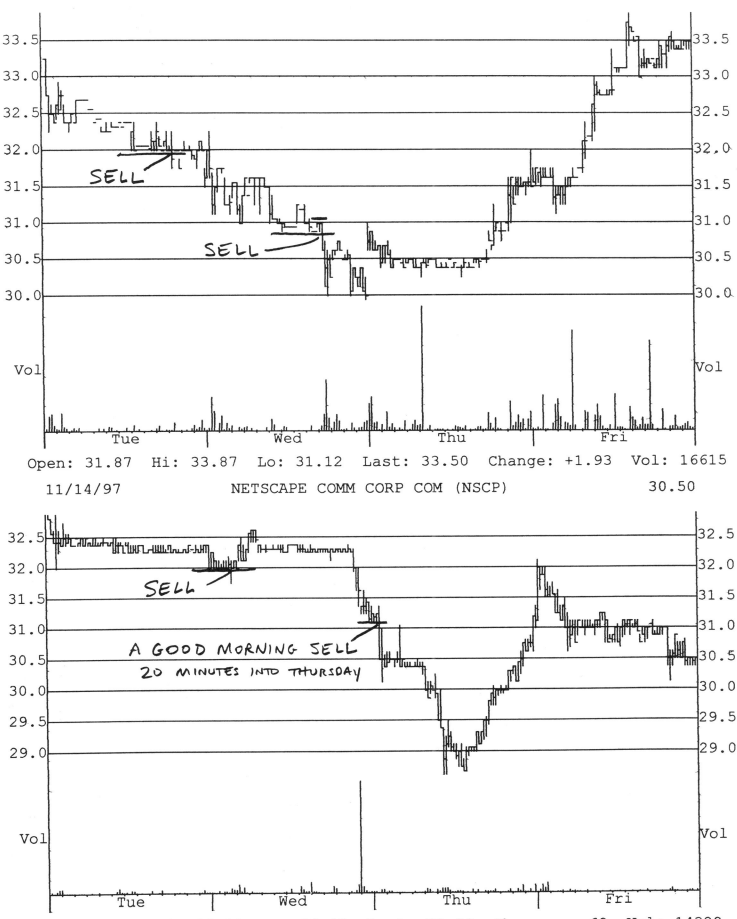

ELECTRONIC ARTS INC COM (ERTS)

11/14/97   ELECTRONIC ARTS INC COM (ERTS)   33.50

SELL

SELL

Open: 31.87   Hi: 33.87   Lo: 31.12   Last: 33.50   Change: +1.93   Vol: 16615

11/14/97   NETSCAPE COMM CORP COM (NSCP)   30.50

SELL

A GOOD MORNING SELL

20 MINUTES INTO THURSDAY

Open: 31.12   Hi: 32.12   Lo: 30.12   Last: 30.50   Change: -.69   Vol: 14329

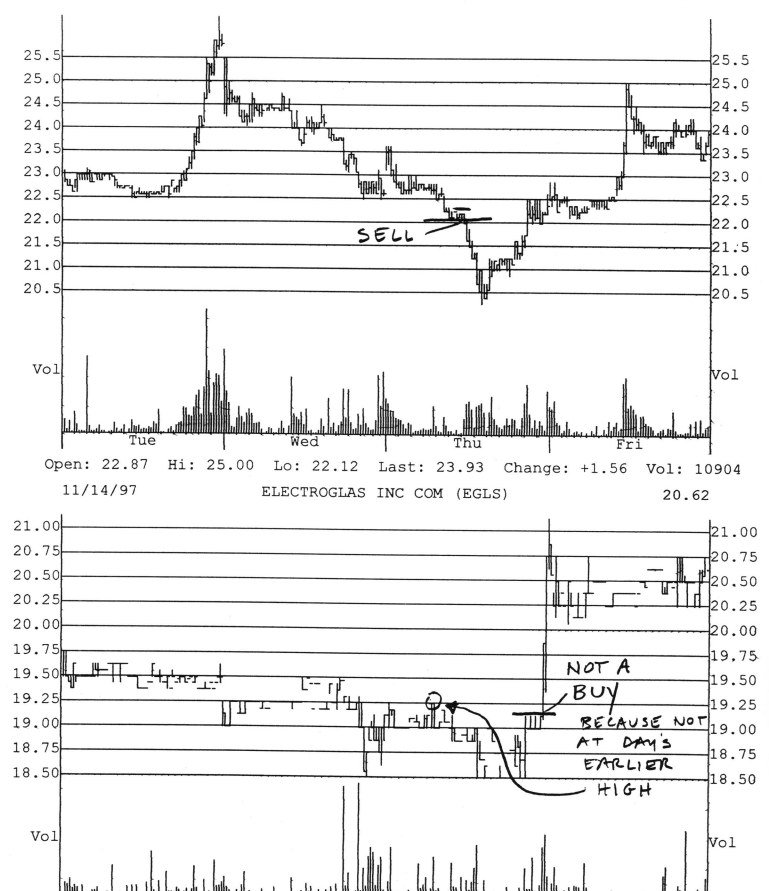

Chart labels:

11/14/97 — C CUBE MICROSYSTEMS INC COM (CUBE) — 23.93

SELL

Tue Wed Thu Fri

Open: 22.87   Hi: 25.00   Lo: 22.12   Last: 23.93   Change: +1.56   Vol: 10904

11/14/97 — ELECTROGLAS INC COM (EGLS) — 20.62

NOT A
BUY
BECAUSE NOT
AT DAY'S
EARLIER
HIGH

Tue Wed Thu Fri

Open: 20.87   Hi: 21.12   Lo: 20.00   Last: 20.62   Change: -.13   Vol: 2321

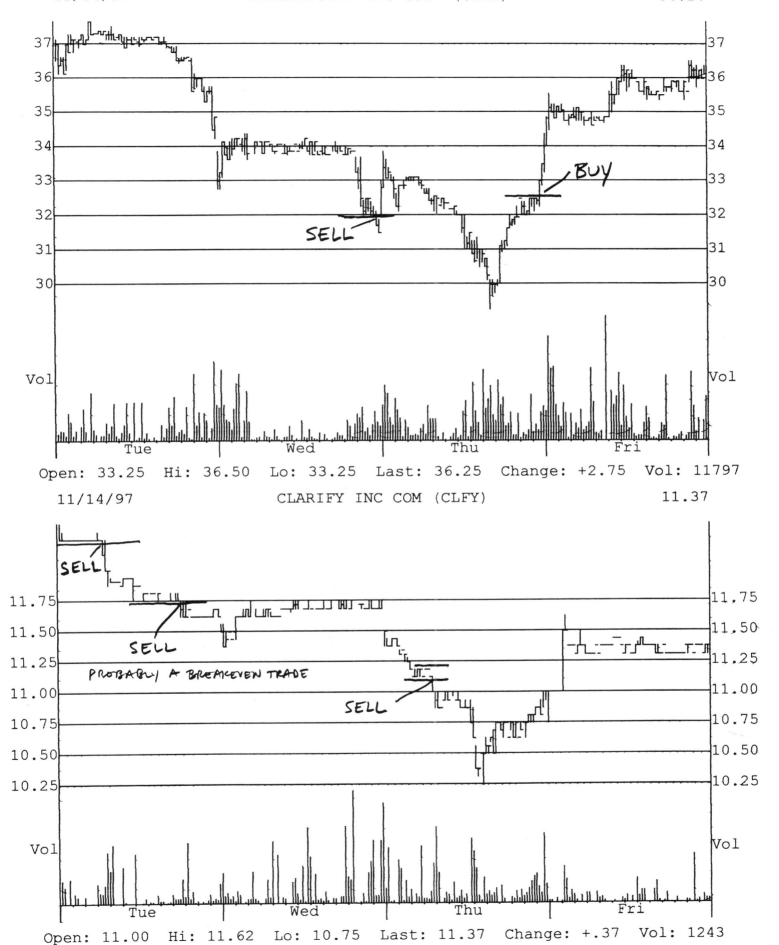

BUY

SELL

Vol

Open: 33.25   Hi: 36.50   Lo: 33.25   Last: 36.25   Change: +2.75   Vol: 11797

11/14/97   CLARIFY INC COM (CLFY)   11.37

SELL

SELL

PROBABLY A BREAKEVEN TRADE

SELL

Vol

Open: 11.00   Hi: 11.62   Lo: 10.75   Last: 11.37   Change: +.37   Vol: 1243

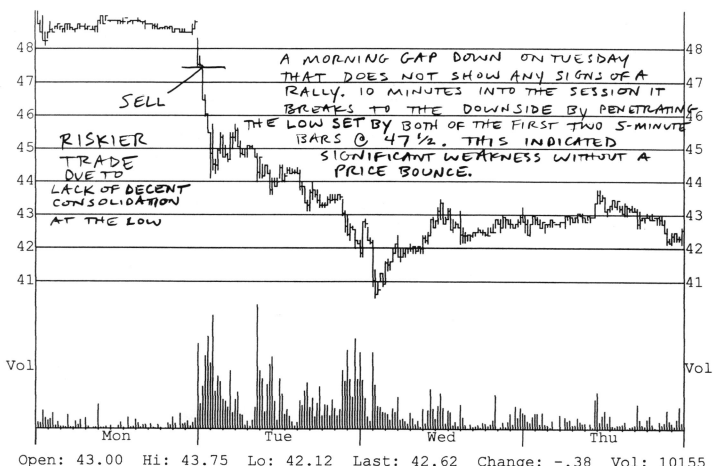

A MORNING GAP DOWN ON TUESDAY THAT DOES NOT SHOW ANY SIGNS OF A RALLY. 10 MINUTES INTO THE SESSION IT BREAKS TO THE DOWNSIDE BY PENETRATING THE LOW SET BY BOTH OF THE FIRST TWO 5-MINUTE BARS @ 47 1/2. THIS INDICATED SIGNIFICANT WEAKNESS WITHOUT A PRICE BOUNCE.

SELL

RISKIER TRADE DUE TO LACK OF DECENT CONSOLIDATION AT THE LOW

Open: 43.00   Hi: 43.75   Lo: 42.12   Last: 42.62   Change: -.38   Vol: 10155

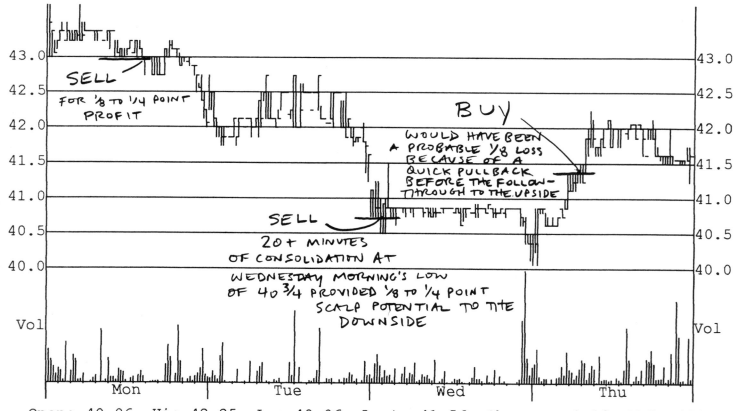

SELL FOR 1/8 TO 1/4 POINT PROFIT

BUY WOULD HAVE BEEN A PROBABLE 1/8 LOSS BECAUSE OF A QUICK PULLBACK BEFORE THE FOLLOW-THROUGH TO THE UPSIDE

SELL 20+ MINUTES OF CONSOLIDATION AT WEDNESDAY MORNING'S LOW OF 40 3/4 PROVIDED 1/8 TO 1/4 POINT SCALP POTENTIAL TO THE DOWNSIDE

Open: 40.06   Hi: 42.25   Lo: 40.06   Last: 41.56   Change: +1.18   Vol: 4954

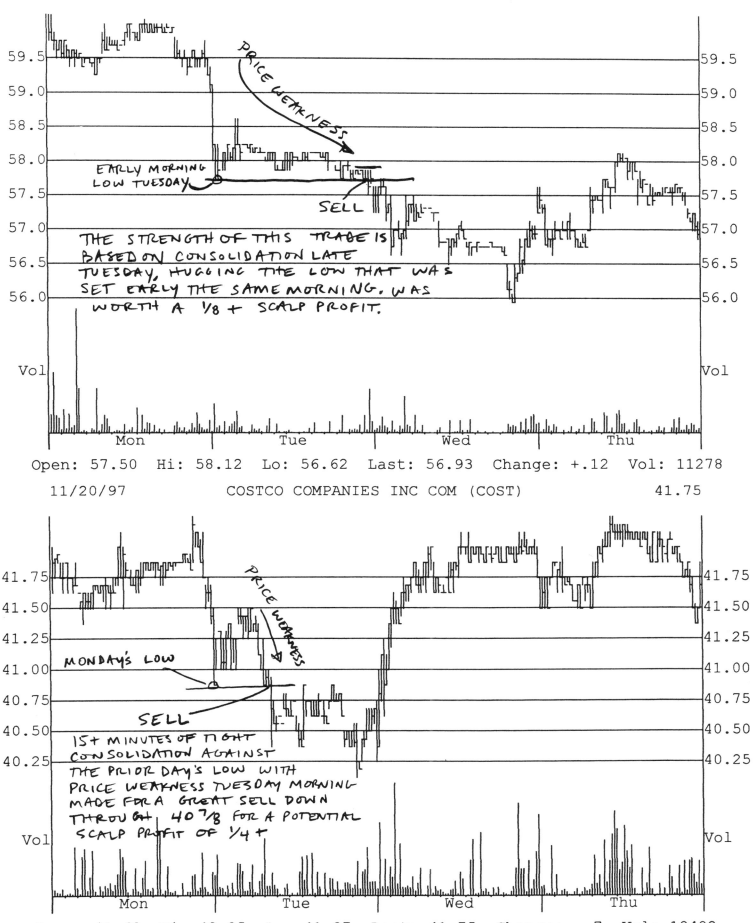

11/20/97   C I E N A CORP COM (CIEN)   56.93

PRICE WEAKNESS

EARLY MORNING
LOW TUESDAY

SELL

THE STRENGTH OF THIS TRADE IS
BASED ON CONSOLIDATION LATE
TUESDAY, HUGGING THE LOW THAT WAS
SET EARLY THE SAME MORNING. WAS
WORTH A 1/8 + SCALP PROFIT.

Vol

Mon   Tue   Wed   Thu

Open: 57.50 Hi: 58.12 Lo: 56.62 Last: 56.93 Change: +.12 Vol: 11278

11/20/97   COSTCO COMPANIES INC COM (COST)   41.75

PRICE WEAKNESS

MONDAY'S LOW

SELL

15+ MINUTES OF TIGHT
CONSOLIDATION AGAINST
THE PRIOR DAY'S LOW WITH
PRICE WEAKNESS TUESDAY MORNING
MADE FOR A GREAT SELL DOWN
THROUGH 40 7/8 FOR A POTENTIAL
SCALP PROFIT OF 1/4 +

Vol

Mon   Tue   Wed   Thu

Open: 41.62 Hi: 42.25 Lo: 41.37 Last: 41.75 Change: .-7 Vol: 18482

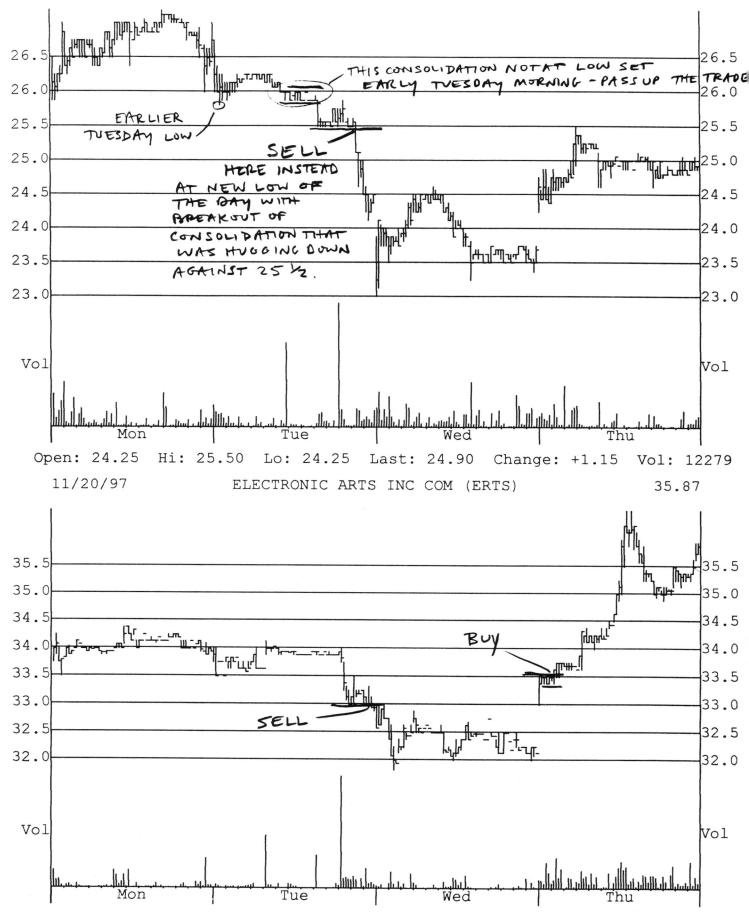

11/20/97   E TRADE GROUP INC COM (EGRP)   24.90

THIS CONSOLIDATION NOT AT LOW SET
EARLY TUESDAY MORNING - PASS UP THE TRADE

EARLIER
TUESDAY LOW

SELL
HERE INSTEAD
AT NEW LOW OF
THE DAY WITH
BREAKOUT OF
CONSOLIDATION THAT
WAS HUGGING DOWN
AGAINST 25 1/2.

Vol   Vol

Mon   Tue   Wed   Thu

Open: 24.25   Hi: 25.50   Lo: 24.25   Last: 24.90   Change: +1.15   Vol: 12279

11/20/97   ELECTRONIC ARTS INC COM (ERTS)   35.87

BUY

SELL

Vol   Vol

Mon   Tue   Wed   Thu

Open: 33.12   Hi: 36.50   Lo: 33.00   Last: 35.87   Change: +3.87   Vol: 25435

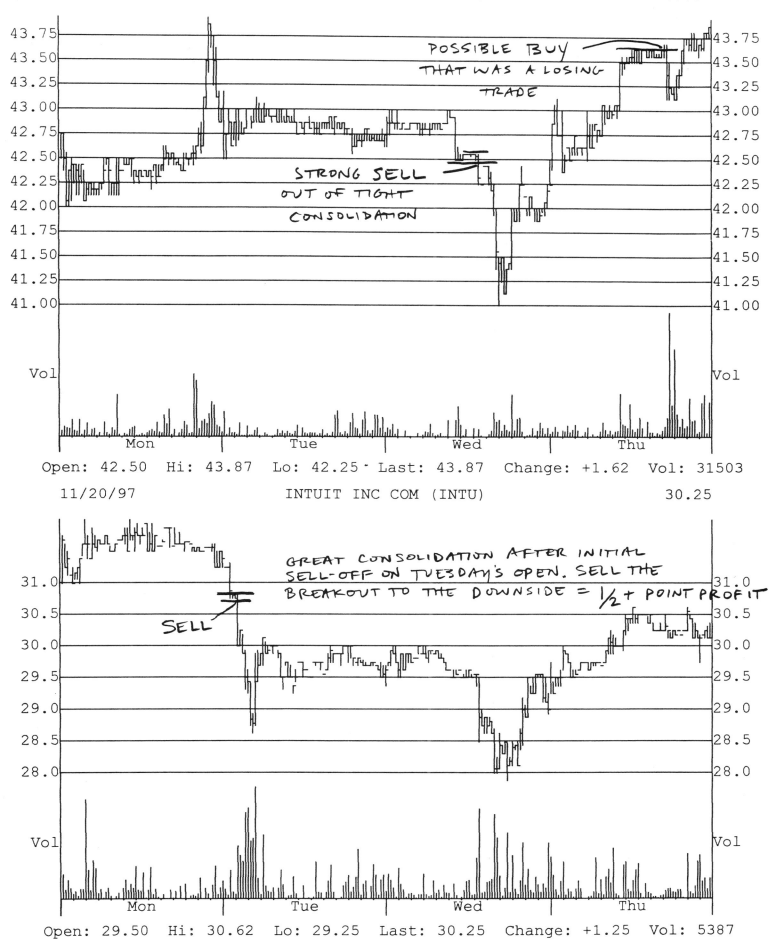

11/20/97   H B O & CO COM (HBOC)   43.87

POSSIBLE BUY
THAT WAS A LOSING
TRADE

STRONG SELL
OUT OF TIGHT
CONSOLIDATION

Vol

Mon   Tue   Wed   Thu

Open: 42.50   Hi: 43.87   Lo: 42.25   Last: 43.87   Change: +1.62   Vol: 31503

11/20/97   INTUIT INC COM (INTU)   30.25

GREAT CONSOLIDATION AFTER INITIAL
SELL-OFF ON TUESDAY'S OPEN. SELL THE
BREAKOUT TO THE DOWNSIDE = 1/2 + POINT PROFIT

SELL

Vol

Mon   Tue   Wed   Thu

Open: 29.50   Hi: 30.62   Lo: 29.25   Last: 30.25   Change: +1.25   Vol: 5387

215

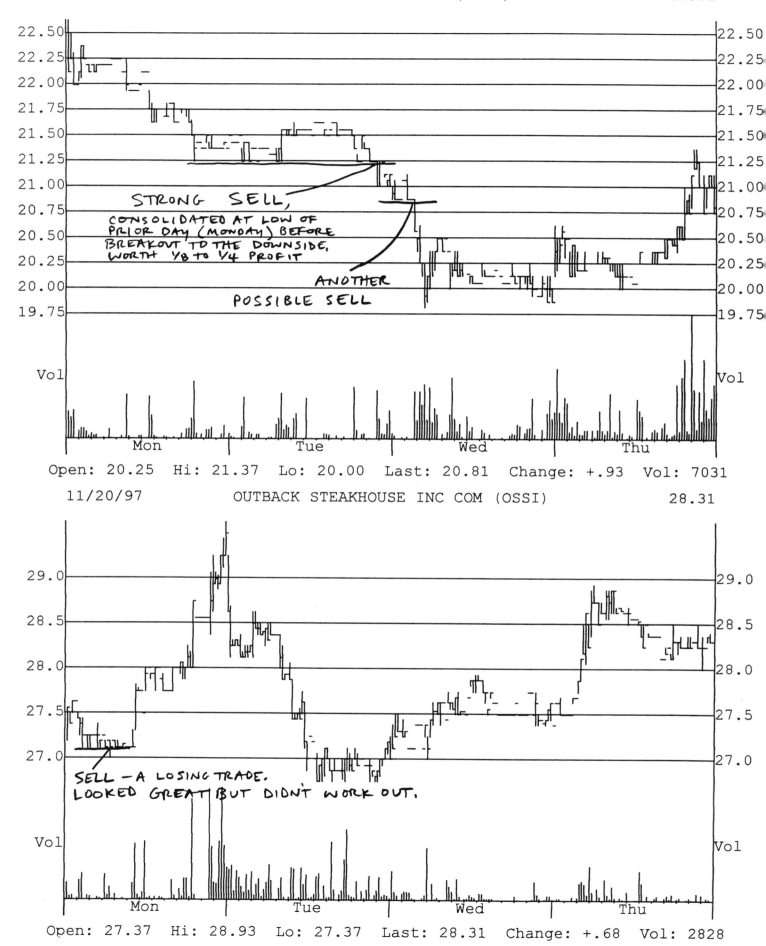

STRONG SELL,
CONSOLIDATED AT LOW OF
PRIOR DAY (MONDAY) BEFORE
BREAKOUT TO THE DOWNSIDE.
WORTH ⅛ TO ¼ PROFIT

ANOTHER

POSSIBLE SELL

Open: 20.25　Hi: 21.37　Lo: 20.00　Last: 20.81　Change: +.93　Vol: 7031

11/20/97　　　OUTBACK STEAKHOUSE INC COM (OSSI)　　　28.31

SELL — A LOSING TRADE.
LOOKED GREAT BUT DIDN'T WORK OUT.

Open: 27.37　Hi: 28.93　Lo: 27.37　Last: 28.31　Change: +.68　Vol: 2828

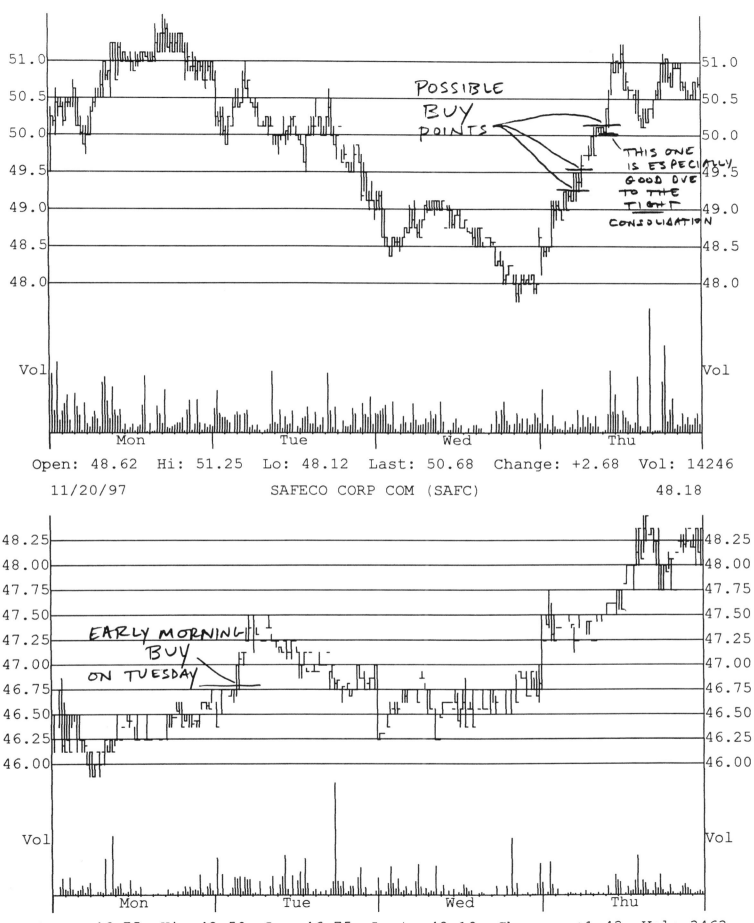

11/20/97   PARAMETRIC TECH CORP COM (PMTC)   50.68

POSSIBLE
BUY
POINTS

THIS ONE
IS ESPECIALLY
GOOD DVE
TO THE
TIGHT
CONSOLIDATION

Open: 48.62   Hi: 51.25   Lo: 48.12   Last: 50.68   Change: +2.68   Vol: 14246

11/20/97   SAFECO CORP COM (SAFC)   48.18

EARLY MORNING
BUY
ON TUESDAY

Open: 46.75   Hi: 48.50   Lo: 46.75   Last: 48.18   Change: +1.43   Vol: 3463

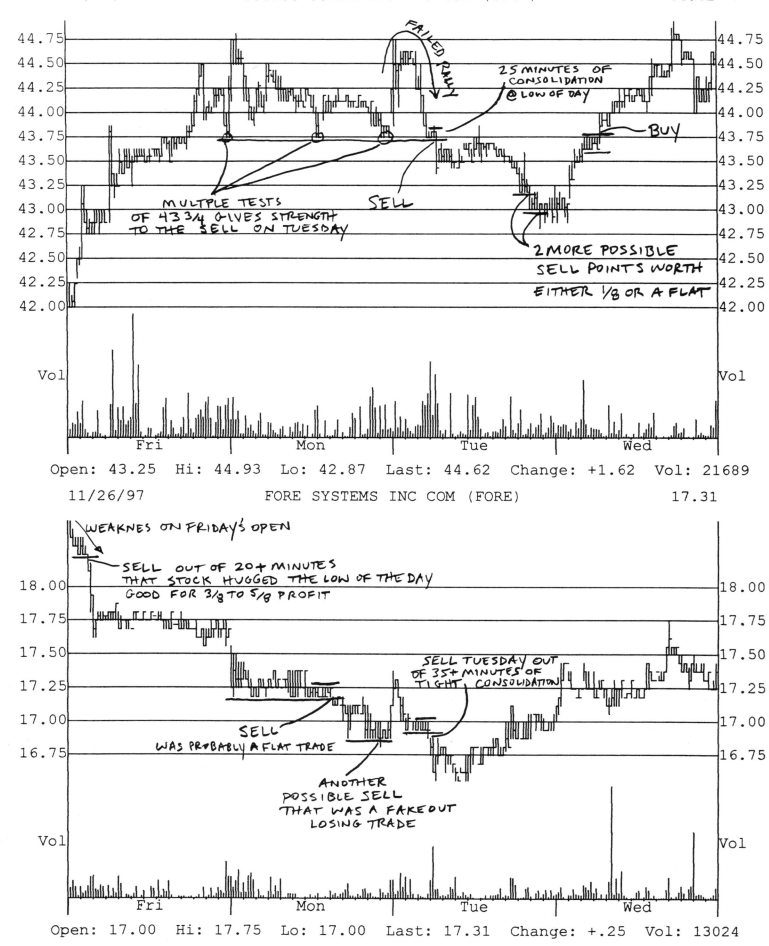

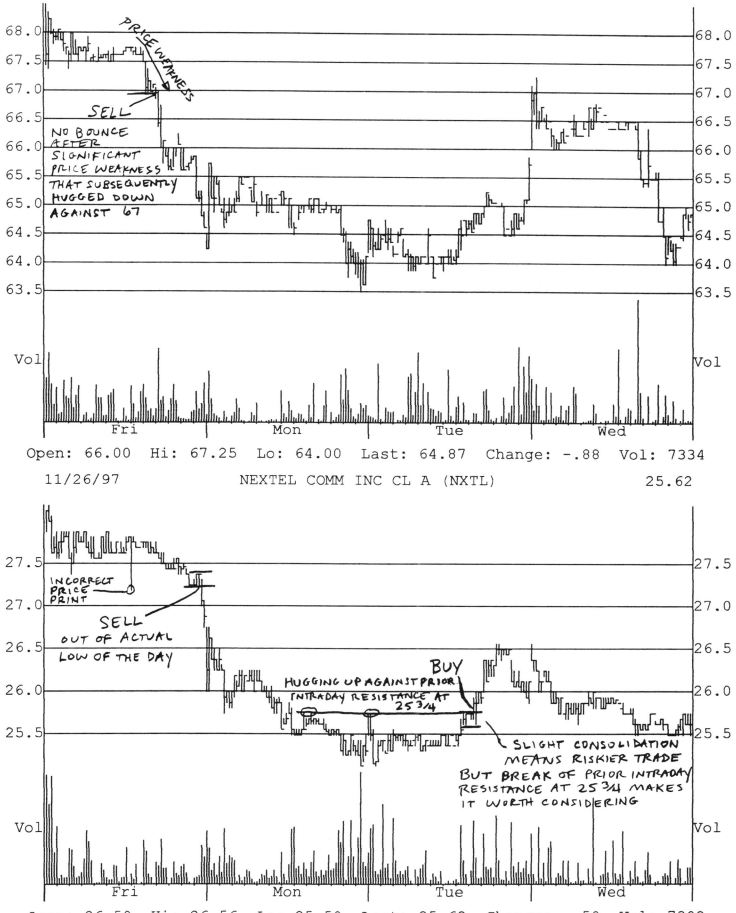

11/26/97   LINEAR TECHNOLOGY CORP COM (LLTC)   64.87

PRICE WEAKNESS

SELL

NO BOUNCE AFTER SIGNIFICANT PRICE WEAKNESS THAT SUBSEQUENTLY HUGGED DOWN AGAINST 67

Open: 66.00 Hi: 67.25 Lo: 64.00 Last: 64.87 Change: -.88 Vol: 7334

11/26/97   NEXTEL COMM INC CL A (NXTL)   25.62

INCORRECT PRICE PRINT

SELL OUT OF ACTUAL LOW OF THE DAY

BUY

HUGGING UP AGAINST PRIOR INTRADAY RESISTANCE AT 25 3/4

SLIGHT CONSOLIDATION MEANS RISKIER TRADE BUT BREAK OF PRIOR INTRADAY RESISTANCE AT 25 3/4 MAKES IT WORTH CONSIDERING

Open: 26.50 Hi: 26.56 Lo: 25.50 Last: 25.62 Change: -.50 Vol: 7303

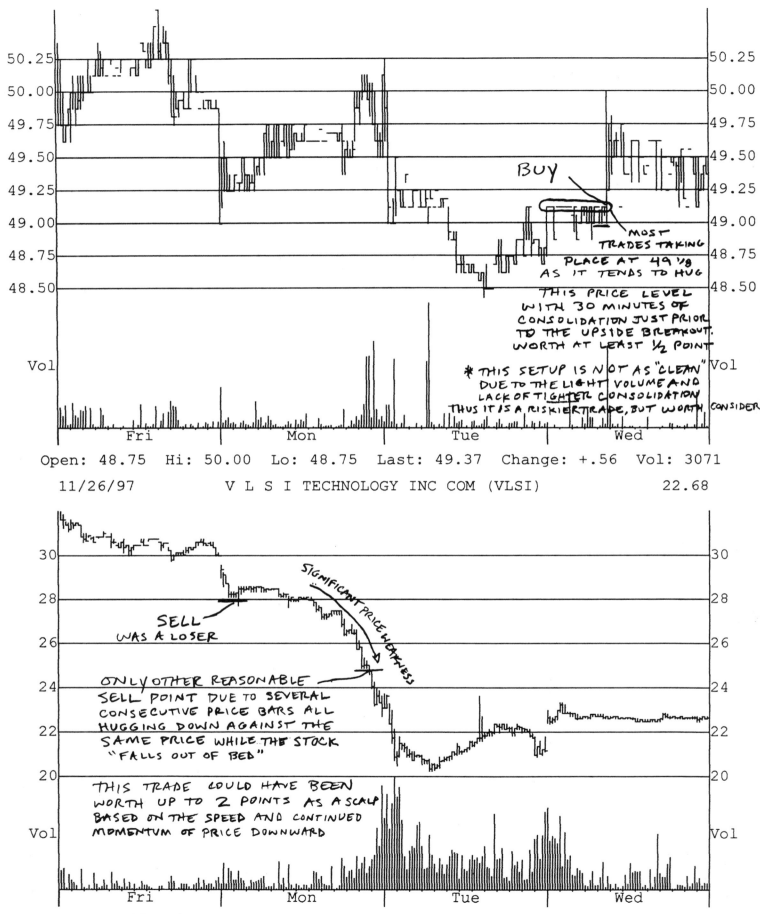

11/26/97   TEVA PHARM INDUSTRIES LTD A D R (TEVIY)   49.37

BUY

MOST
TRADES TAKING
PLACE AT 49 1/8
AS IT TENDS TO HUG
THIS PRICE LEVEL
WITH 30 MINUTES OF
CONSOLIDATION JUST PRIOR
TO THE UPSIDE BREAKOUT.
WORTH AT LEAST 1/2 POINT

* THIS SETUP IS NOT AS "CLEAN"
DUE TO THE LIGHT VOLUME AND
LACK OF TIGHTER CONSOLIDATION
THUS IT IS A RISKIER TRADE, BUT WORTH CONSIDER

Vol

Fri   Mon   Tue   Wed

Open: 48.75   Hi: 50.00   Lo: 48.75   Last: 49.37   Change: +.56   Vol: 3071

11/26/97   V L S I TECHNOLOGY INC COM (VLSI)   22.68

SIGNIFICANT PRICE WEAKNESS

SELL
WAS A LOSER

ONLY OTHER REASONABLE
SELL POINT DUE TO SEVERAL
CONSECUTIVE PRICE BARS ALL
HUGGING DOWN AGAINST THE
SAME PRICE WHILE THE STOCK
"FALLS OUT OF BED"

THIS TRADE COULD HAVE BEEN
WORTH UP TO 2 POINTS AS A SCALP
BASED ON THE SPEED AND CONTINUED
MOMENTUM OF PRICE DOWNWARD

Vol

Fri   Mon   Tue   Wed

Open: 22.50   Hi: 23.37   Lo: 22.37   Last: 22.68   Change: +1.43   Vol: 43554

DAY TRADERS COURSE

A real-time training course is available which offers both classroom style learning sessions as well as hands on guidance during "live" trading. This is best done with a group of several traders since the synergy will help foster the exchange of ideas. The one-on-one personal interaction brings alive the book's trading strategies in 10 plus hours of classroom training and 5 full days of market trading. You will understand and recognize the nuances of how to actually trade profitably. The goal is to raise your trading skills to a higher level. Additional materials and information are also provided.

Whether you trade from home or at a day trading firm, a week of on-site training is available to you. The only requirement is that you have access to NASDAQ level II quotes with price charting capabilities, and a week's worth of your time devoted to learning and sharing ideas.

Although I enjoy trading, I also enjoy teaching. If you are interested in serious training that is crafted to your needs, fax me at the phone number listed below for details and fees. Provide your name and phone number, and I will return your call as soon as possible (usually after market hours).

Barry Rudd   FAX   214-827-9530

Traders Press Inc.®
PO Box 6206
Greenville, SC 29606

Publishers of:

A Complete Guide to Trading Profits (Paris)
A Professional Look at S&P Day Trading (Trivette)
Ask Mr. EasyLanguage (Tennis)
Beginner's Guide to Computer Assisted Trading (Alexander)
Channels and Cycles: A Tribute to J.M. Hurst (Millard)
Chart Reading for Professional Traders (Jenkins)
Charting Commodity Market Price Behavior (Belveal)
Commodity Spreads: Analysis, Selection and Trading Techniques (Smith)
Comparison of Twelve Technical Trading Systems (Lukac, Brorsen, & Irwin)
Cyclic Analysis (J.M. Hurst)
Exceptional Trading: The Mind Game (Roosevelt)
Fibonacci Ratios With Pattern Recognition (Pesavento)
Geometry of Markets (Gilmore)
Geometry of Stock Market Profits (Jenkins)
Harmonic Vibrations (Pesavento)
How to Trade in Stocks (Livermore)
Hurst Cycles Course (J.M. Hurst)
Magic of Moving Averages (Lowry)
Market Rap: The Odyssey of a Still-Struggling Commodity Trader (Collins)
Pit Trading: Do You Have the Right Stuff? (Hoffman & Baccetti)
Planetary Harmonics of Speculative Markets (Pesavento)
Point & Figure Charting (Aby)
Point & Figure Charting: Commodity and Stock Trading Techniques (Zieg)
Profitable Grain Trading (Ainsworth)
Profitable Patterns for Stock Trading (Pesavento)
Short-Term Trading With Price Patterns (Harris)
Stock Market Trading Systems (Appel & Hitschler)
Stock Patterns for Day Trading (Rudd)
Stock Patterns for Day Trading 2 (Rudd)
Technically Speaking (Wilkinson)
Technical Trading Systems for Commodities and Stocks (Patel)
The Amazing Life of Jesse Livermore: World's Greatest Stock Trader (Smitten)
The Professional Commodity Trader (Kroll)
The Profit Magic of Stock Transaction Timing (Hurst)
The Taylor Trading Technique (Taylor)
The Traders (Kleinfeld)
The Trading Rule That Can Make You Rich* (Dobson)
Trading Secrets of the Inner Circle (Goodwin)
Trading S&P Futures and Options (Lloyd)
Understanding Bollinger Bands (Dobson)
Understanding Fibonacci Numbers (Dobson)
Viewpoints of a Commodity Trader (Longstreet)
Wall Street Ventures & Adventures Through Forty Years (Wyckoff)
Winning Market Systems (Appel)

Please contact Traders Press to receive our current catalog describing these
and many other books and gifts of interest to investors and traders.
800-927-8222 ~ 964-298-0222 ~ *Fax* 864-298-0221
***E-mail* Catalog@TradersPress.com *Website* http://www.TradersPress.com**